Meaning and Truth in Religion

Meaning and Truth in Religion

BY

WILLIAM A. CHRISTIAN

PRINCETON UNIVERSITY PRESS

PRINCETON, NEW JERSEY

1964

Printed in the United States of America
by Vail-Ballou Press, Inc., Binghamton, New York

ACKNOWLEDGMENTS

I am indebted to Robert Brumbaugh, Malcolm Diamond, Noel Fleming, Julian Hartt, George Lindbeck, H. H. Price, and Rulon Wells for reading the manuscript at one stage or another and making helpful comments (some spoken, some unspoken), to Yale University for a year's leave spent at Oxford, where the first draft was written, and to the publishers mentioned in footnotes for use of quotations. An article, "Truth-claims in Religion," which embodied some parts of Chapters I and II, was published in the *Journal of Religion* in 1962.

WILLIAM A. CHRISTIAN

Timothy Dwight College
Yale University
June 1963

Contents

Meaning and Truth in Religion

CHAPTER I

<><><><><><><><><><><><><><><><><><><><><><><><><><><><>

Introduction

<><><><><><><><><><><><><><><><><><><><><><><><><><><><>

1. *The character of this study*

Saying what we mean and meaning what we say are not the same thing, as the Hatter told Alice. Saying what we mean depends on knowing the possibilities and limits of discourse, and on knowing what in particular we want to say in the circumstances. So it depends on knowing—intuitively, at least—the logic of the discourse in which we are engaged, and also on a certain presence of mind.

Meaning what we say depends on holding our beliefs freely, without the inner compulsions which give rise to self-deception, and on being reflective about our beliefs, so we can know what on the whole we want to say. Holding beliefs freely depends on an openness to facts and a readiness to believe in accord with them. Being reflective about our beliefs depends on having some pattern of connections among them. Then what we say in some utterance will have the force of our unspoken beliefs behind it.

Philosophy can contribute to freedom of discourse and freedom of belief, at least indirectly, and this essay in the philosophy of religion aims to do so by studying the structure of religious inquiry and discourse. It draws on the literatures of various religions for examples, and it deals with various functions of religious utterances, including confessional expressions of experiences, injunctions to actions, and the conveyance of suggestions by narratives and figures of speech. But its principal object is to show how, along with these functions, another type of significance is possible, that is, how religious utterances can express genuine truth-claims, and to show how confessions, injunctions, and suggestions are related to these claims.

So the central question before us is, "How are religious truth-claims possible?" though many related questions about the meanings of religious utterances will arise also. I begin by explaining some of the limits of this question.

First, it refers to specifically religious truth-claims. Religious utterances taken generally can be distinguished from utterances of other types, though there will always be border-line cases. And typical religious utterances are clearly different from typical moral, or scientific, or esthetic, or speculative [1] utterances.

It is true that particular religious beliefs often involve claims of other types as well, and these other claims may be deeply important to a religious individual or to a religious community. Historical or moral or speculative claims may acquire religious import. But these different claims must be judged in accord with different principles of judgment. I do not mean to isolate religious claims from others but only to distinguish them. I shall indicate how other claims may occur in the course of religious arguments. And I shall argue that there are structural similarities among inquiries of different types.

Second, my argument is not designed to show that some religious assertions are true. It aims only at showing how religious truth-claims can be made and how these claims can be judged. I have not set out to answer religious questions but, instead, certain philosophical questions about religion. I have not asked those questions which are treated in natural theology, such as, "Does God exist?" And I do not claim to set forth the doctrines of a particular religion. I do not propose religious doctrines in either of these senses. Instead, I want to explain what it means to have a religious

[1] I have discussed some distinctions and relations between religious truth-claims and speculative truth-claims in "Some Uses of Reason," in Ivor Leclerc, ed., *The Relevance of Whitehead*, London, G. Allen and Unwin, 1961.

belief of any kind, and to show the conditions of justifying such beliefs.

What I have done leaves ample room for theology, and I hope to show how theological questions get their point, though I am not now asking them, and to show the functions of doctrinal schemes. For example, a theory of religious inquiry can give a certain perspective on doctrines about revelation and faith. Though this would not be a theological perspective, it would be a step toward understanding what theologians are doing.

In recent years the philosophy of religion has shown new signs of life. This is partly because we can distinguish its problems from theological problems better now than a generation ago. Both of these disciplines have gained in clarity and power from this development. The distinction does not need to become a divorce. For any subject we study may bring unexpected rewards; its very limitations may help us understand what lies beyond its boundaries.

Third, I shall not proceed by taking perceptual claims ("The postman is at the door") or scientific claims ("The speed of light is constant") as paradigm cases of truth-claims, though these are *good* cases of truth-claims. Those who do so will construe my argument as an argument for extending the meaning of "truth" beyond the limits of such cases. I do not propose it in this way. Instead, I propose to explain some senses in which "true" and "untrue" can be used in religious judgments, and to argue that these are good senses, i.e., that they are significant and that they are not misleading. So I would like the reader to begin without prejudice, though not of course without convictions. My own basic conviction is that there is a general logic of inquiry, which becomes specified in various ways when specific interests (for example, scientific, moral, or religious interests) prompt us to ask questions of various sorts.

Fourth, I shall not argue that all religious utterances do

make truth-claims, but only that some might do so. Indeed, many religious utterances do not purport to do so (for example, prayers, meditative utterances, confessions, and injunctions). Also, one finds explicit refusals to claim propositional truth, as in some varieties of mysticism and existentialism. My main object is to explain the conditions under which religious truth-claims, judgments, and arguments are *possible*.

Religion, like politics, science, and art, is a certain kind of human activity. Further, this is in principle a deeply personal kind of activity. Religious people are concerned with the attainment and enjoyment of some state of things (detachment, or enlightenment, or salvation, or the Kingdom of God, or harmony with Nature, or identity with Brahman, for example) in this world or in another world or in both. That is why religious thought is predominantly imaginative, intuitive, and personal.

Still, all human activities involve both concepts and interpersonal relations. So it is not strange that in religious literature disagreements appear, arguments are offered, conclusions are drawn, and beliefs are proposed. Further, the feelings and activities of religious people are intimately connected with beliefs which they hold to be true. It seems abundantly evident that the founders, teachers, prophets, and sages of the great religious traditions of the world have been seriously concerned with truth. For example:

"Formless, that self-luminous Being exists within and without, higher than the highest. . . . From him issue life, and mind, and senses—ether, air, water, fire, and the earth. . . . He is the innermost Self in all beings. . . . He who knows him hidden in the shrine of his heart cuts the knot of ignorance even in this life."

"Something there is, whose veiled creation was
Before the earth or sky began to be;
So silent, so aloof and so alone,

It changes not, nor fails, but touches all:
Conceive it as the mother of the world.
I do not know its name;
A name for it is 'Way'. . . ."

"Hear, O Israel: the Lord our God, the Lord is One."

"The time is fulfilled, and the kingdom of God is at
hand: repent ye and believe in the gospel."

"Moreover it could not be said: 'There is not Nirvana.'
Why is this? Because the practice of Dhamma is not
barren. For if Nirvana were not, there would be barrenness in regard to (spiritual) attainment. . . . But
due to the attainment of Nirvana, there is not this
barrenness. . . ."

"Your God is one God: there is no God but He, the
Compassionate, the Merciful."

The force of these passages depends on their claims, and
the assurance they express, that something or other is the
case. Their promises and admonitions have point because
something is the way it is. This holds also for those forms
of religion which fall outside the major traditions. For example:

"For, in so far as we are intelligent beings, we cannot
desire anything save that which is necessary, nor yield
absolute acquiescence to anything, save to that which
is true; wherefore, in so far as we have a right understanding of these things, the endeavor of the better
part of ourselves is in harmony with the order of nature as a whole."

"Thus in the conception of Humanity the three essential aspects of Positivism, its subjective principle,
its objective dogma, and its practical object, are united.
Towards Humanity, who is for us the only true Great
Being, we, the conscious elements of whom she is com-

posed, shall henceforth direct every aspect of our life, individual or collective. Our thoughts will be devoted to the knowledge of Humanity, our affections to her love, our actions to her service."

"My great religion is a belief in the blood, the flesh. . . . We can go wrong in our minds. But what our blood feels, and believes, and says, is always true."

Indeed, seriousness about truth is a pervasive, if variable, feature of religion, to which we ought to do justice.

Certainly religious utterances express feelings and are symptoms of attitudes. Also, they are used to declare feelings, attitudes, and policies. Again, they are used to evoke feelings and enjoin attitudes, policies, and actions. We ought to do justice to these important functions of religious utterances also, and they have had a great deal of attention from philosophers in recent years.[2] Our problem is to see whether, along with these expressive, declarative, evocative, and injunctive functions, religious utterances may have another function also, namely, to say something which is true or untrue. So I shall be arguing against the view that these utterances have no logical significance whatever but bear their meanings *only* in these other ways.

Religious utterances could make truth-claims only if principles of judgment are available. But the extent and the depth of religious conflicts, which, like moral and political conflicts, so often seem beyond the range of reasonable argument, should warn us that there is no simple and easy procedure for settling basic religious questions. (*a*) Clearly no quasi-mechanical decision procedures are available, such as we have in certain parts of logic and mathematics. (*b*) Further, I shall argue that no basic religious question can

[2] For example, John Wisdom, "Gods," in A. Flew, ed., *Essays on Logic and Language*, New York, Philosophical Library, 1951, and Paul F. Schmidt, *Religious Knowledge*, Glencoe, Ill., Free Press, 1961. See chapter VII below, especially section 6.

be settled absolutely by adducing some one purely public fact. (*c*) Further, I shall argue that there are no a priori norms of judgment for deciding basic religious questions, i.e., norms such that, if the question at issue is rightly understood, a certain answer and no other inevitably follows. If the possibility of a genuine truth-claim depended on such decision procedures as these, no basic religious truth-claims would be possible. My argument is that these limitations do not rule out the possibility of genuine truth-claims.

The course of the argument is as follows: This chapter and the next introduce the problem and some concepts we shall need later on. Chapters III and IV discuss some general theories of religion. This will be useful in three ways: it will keep the range and variety of religious beliefs in view; it relates the argument to some important historical figures—Kant, Schleiermacher, and Otto; and it is essential for showing how principles of religious judgment are possible.

Chapters V–VII develop a theory of religious inquiry, to explain the nature of religious questions, suppositions, suggestions, and judgments. This is important because deliberation and discourse are phases of a rhythmical process. In responsible deliberation we anticipate proposing our conclusions and supporting them with reasons. When we make proposals for belief we mean to contribute to responsible deliberation about some significant question. Philosophical understanding is impoverished if either phase is neglected.

Chapters VIII–XI examine various kinds of arguments by which religious beliefs can be objected to or supported, giving a number of specimen arguments. Chapter VIII brings out the shape of arguments about consistency and coherence, and of dialectical arguments. Chapter X discusses arguments about references, making use of a list of types of references developed (with extended examples and historical allusions) in Chapter IX. Chapter XI explains the kinds of arguments needed to support religious predications.

Finally, Chapter XII draws some conclusions about the possibility of truth in religion.

As this sketch suggests, I want to study not isolated linguistic expressions but the structure of meaning in religious discourse, and this both in breadth and in depth. I want to show both how an utterance is related to others on its own logical level, and how it is related to utterances on other levels and of other kinds, which it presupposes, or explicates, or elaborates, or conveys.

A problem like this should, ideally, be worked at from two opposite directions at once. We need to construct general theories of meaning and truth applying to *all* types of discourse, including moral discourse, scientific discourse, esthetic discourse, and religious discourse. At the same time we need to explore more thoroughly *each* of the particular domains of human experience and discourse.

The reason for this is as follows: Any general theory of meaning and truth must be generated from some suggestion, which yields a conceptual model. This model determines the shape of the theory. For example, some general theories take certain types of scientific statements as their paradigms. Now we cannot do without models in the construction of theories. But, if we are constructing a general theory, we have to extend the concepts derived from the model, so they will apply to other facts than those from which the model itself is derived. The problem is to extend the concepts in such a way that their use will not distort these other facts when the theory is applied to them.

So we also need studies which concentrate on some one domain of human activity and discourse and bring out its distinctive features. Such studies mean to show what moralists, or scientists, or religious people are doing when they think and speak. Beginning with some particular domain of human experience, they aim at a theory of meaning and truth in morality, or in science, or—as this essay does—in religion.[3] Incidentally, such studies prepare the way for more adequate general theories of meaning and truth.

This means that we must borrow from the phenomenology of religion,[4] though we must use what we borrow in our own way. In this respect the philosophy of religion [5] is like the philosophy of law, the philosophy of science, and certain other branches of philosophy. To philosophize in any of these ways we need to know the kinds of situations in which certain distinctive concepts arise, and how these concepts are used. Otherwise we shall not see the point of the concepts with which we are dealing.

Though we begin with the phenomena of religion, we do so with a philosophical aim in view—to study the logic of religious beliefs. To illustrate this point consider religious conversions. Statistics on conversions are important for—among others—sociologists and mission boards. The emotional patterns involved in conversions and their effects on behavior are important for—among others—psychologists and missionaries. But philosophers should be concerned with the logic of religious conversions, that is to say, with the logical significance of the acquisition and replacement of religious beliefs.

For example, take a case of conversion from one religious faith to another. If it occurs on a reflective level it must

[3] Ninian Smart, *Reasons and Faiths*, London, Routledge and Kegan Paul, 1958, is also a study of this sort, and an acute, richly developed, and illuminating one. It explores the structures of doctrinal schemes much more than I have done.

[4] See, for example, G. van der Leeuw, *Religion in Essence and in Manifestation, A Study in Phenomenology*, J. E. Turner, tr., London, G. Allen and Unwin, 1938. This deals with religion in sophisticated cultures as well as preliterate and uncritical cultures, though not so much as one might like.

[5] The problem of this study is by no means the only problem for philosophy of religion. See in the *Journal of Religion* "Three Kinds of Philosophy of Religion," 37:31–36 (1957), and "Philosophical Analysis and Philosophy of Religion," 39:77–87 (1959).

involve [6] replacement of some belief by another; some p takes the place of some q. This implies a judgment to the effect that p is true and q is not, or at least that p is more adequate to some set of requirements than q is. And it implies that both p and q are relevant to some one question and are incompatible answers to it.

So it becomes philosophically important to see what questions are being asked, implicitly or explicitly, in such cases and what sorts of proposals are being accepted or rejected.

2. *Religious discourse*

First I should explain what I shall mean by a *proposal*. I shall mean an utterance addressed to other human beings in which something is put forward for acceptance. So this rules out *prayers* (of praise, confession, thanksgiving, petition, and intercession), such as:

"An island you are to those swept along by the flood,
a shelter to the stricken,
A refuge to those terrified by becoming, the resource
of those who desire release."

"Our Father, who art in heaven,
Hallowed be thy name.
Thy kingdom come. Thy will be done
On earth as it is in heaven."

For these utterances are not addressed to other human beings. It also rules out *meditative utterances*, such as:

"The Lord is my shepherd."

"The Jewel in the Heart of the Lotus."

For these utterances are not addressed at all. They present something to be entertained and contemplated by those who utter them. But we need to consider utterances which are

---

[6] Of course a religious conversion is never just—or even mainly— a change of belief.

likely to occur in conversations, not those which naturally occur only in private or in liturgical or quasi-liturgical settings.

Proposals are also different from *confessions*, such as:

"I believe in God."

"I take refuge in the Buddha,
I take refuge in the Dharma,
I take refuge in the Sangha."

But these are different in another way. For while some confessions are prayers and some are meditations, others are addressed to other human beings, as when someone "bears testimony." Even so they are not proposals, at least not explicitly, though testimonial confessions are used to convey proposals. For example, if I say to someone that I believe in God, I may mean to suggest to him that he should believe in God also.[7] But I am not making an explicit proposal. Confessions are assertions but they are not in themselves proposals.

Proposals are of different kinds. Some are *injunctions* to act in certain ways, outwardly or inwardly, such as:

"Perform every action with your heart fixed on the Supreme Lord.
Renounce attachment to the fruits."

"Remember the Sabbath to keep it holy."

"Therefore, O Ananda, be ye lamps unto yourselves.
Rely on yourselves, and do not rely on external help."

Closely related to these are suggestions of patterns of conduct, paradigms conveyed by narratives and other devices, such as:

"Ye are the light of the world."

[7] He may understand this quite well and might respond by saying, "But how can you, in view of . . . ?" If this is a logical "can" it is a sign that he is replying to an implicit proposal for belief.

"A skillful soldier is not violent;
An able fighter does not rage;
A mighty conqueror does not give battle.
A great commander is an humble man."

"Him I call indeed a brahmana whose path the gods do
not know, nor spirits, nor men, whose passions are
extinct, and who is an arhat."

We are mainly concerned with *proposals for belief*.[8]
For, while injunctions, as well as confessions, may convey
truth-claims implicitly, this is not their primary function.
We are not tempted to say of injunctions that they are true
or that they are untrue. They call for another sort of response, as we shall see. But a proposal for belief is a claim
to truth and calls for judgment. Of course an utterance
which looks like a proposal for belief might turn out to be
a complex of confessions and injunctions. Our problem is
whether this must be the case. To put the question another
way, Do some religious proposals express propositions, in
some reasonably strong sense of that term?

A proposal for belief is different from an *informative
utterance*, that is, an utterance in which someone who is in
a position to know something tells someone else, who is not

---

[8] Sometimes we may need to distinguish among (*a*) a particular
form of words, as, for example, a particular sentence; (*b*) a particular utterance, as, for example, a particular use of a sentence on
some occasion; (*c*) what a particular utterance conveys, what is
said by means of the utterance; and (*d*) the kind of function (e.g.,
to confess or to enjoin) a particular utterance has in discourse. So,
for example, we could say that in some utterance a sentence is
being used (or that it would ordinarily be used) to convey a certain confession or to convey a certain injunction. Or we could say
that a certain sentence conveys a certain proposal for belief. In
this latter case we can speak of the proposition which this use of
the sentence would naturally express. I shall not always introduce
these distinctions; ordinarily I shall rely on the context to make
such points clear.

in a position to know it, what is the case. For example, A tells B, who has no watch, the time of day; or a Sanskrit scholar tells someone who does not know Sanskrit the meaning of a Sanskrit word; or a research student tells his director the observed outcome of his experiment.

The setting of a proposal for belief is different from the setting of an informative utterance. The questions which elicit informative utterances are not questions the informer is inquiring about; they are not real questions for the informer, though he may have reached his answer by inquiry. Also, the questioner is asking for information. B is not asking A for his opinion on the time of day, and the research director is not asking the student for his conclusions about the experiment.

The questions which elicit proposals for belief, on the other hand, are real questions for both parties. Both M and N are engaged in a common inquiry, aimed at answering a common question. Thus neither is in a position of knowing the answer. But, since they are asking a common question, which is a real question for both, they have some common supposition. So, while requests for information may be "spot questions," more or less isolated from any sustained common inquiry, the questions which elicit proposals for belief belong to the structures of sustained inquiries. Theories of various sorts—moral theories, scientific theories, speculative theories, religious theories—are proposed as answers to such questions.

If I ask a Hindu scholar whether Ramanuja taught that knowledge of the self involves apprehension of God, in some circumstances his answer might function as an informative utterance. But if I ask him, in the course of a religious discussion, whether knowledge of the self involves apprehension of God, his answer would be at best a proposal for belief. From the limitations on settling basic religious questions mentioned above it would follow that answers to such questions cannot be informative utterances. The problem is, Can some such answers be genuine proposals for belief and *thus* make truth-claims?

I shall next introduce some prima-facie proposals for belief by considering the possibility of religious disagreements.

~~~~~~

CHAPTER II

Disagreements and Truth-Claims

~~~~~~

1. *Religious disagreements*

Ordinarily we suppose that proponents of religious systems like Hinduism and Judaism disagree with each other. We recognize that many differences between these systems are differences of style, like the difference between expressionist and representational painting. Religious systems exhibit different styles of life. Hence conflicts of injunctions may occur. But these conflicts do not amount to disagreements, unless we extend the term to cover "disagreements in attitude."

Further, we recognize that sometimes different religions are saying the same thing, or nearly the same thing, in different languages or by different usages in the same language. A mountain is being viewed from different perspectives. Nevertheless we suppose that, along with these other differences among religions, some real disagreements occur.

There are two ways such disagreements might occur, corresponding to two sorts of religious proposals, which I shall call doctrinal proposals and basic proposals. Beginning with proposals of doctrines, let us take for an example:
A. Jesus is the Messiah.
Other examples of doctrinal proposals would be:
Israel is the Chosen People.—Allah is merciful.—Atman is Brahman.—All the buddhas are one.

Now it might be argued that, when Jews say Jesus is not the Messiah and Christians say Jesus is the Messiah, this is not a full-fledged disagreement. Because, we might say, even though the same sentence is being used by both, they do not mean the same thing by it. Jews mean by "the

Messiah" a nondivine being who will restore Israel as an earthly community and usher in the consummation of history. Christians mean a promised savior of mankind from sin. Two different Messiah concepts are being expressed; hence two different propositions are being asserted.

If we think along this line about doctrinal disagreements, we might come to Schleiermacher's conclusion that Christian dogmatics is only for Christians. And, going beyond Schleiermacher's conclusion, we might argue more generally for the logical isolation of doctrinal systems from one another. We might say that argument about some doctrine can go on significantly only within the community whose faith the doctrine expresses. Within the community there are common concepts, so that rules of relevance in doctrinal arguments are possible. Also, the community has norms of judgment to appeal to, for instance, "What does the Bible say?" But, we might argue, no two doctrinal systems have enough common concepts to make significant disagreements between them possible. No common rules of relevance, much less common norms of judgment, can be formulated. How could a Christian and a Taoist significantly disagree about whether the Holy Spirit proceeds from the Father and from the Son, or only from the Father?

Indeed, it would seem that on this view there would be no doctrinal proposition about which Christians and non-Christians, for example, could really disagree. In cases of apparent disagreement, like the apparent disagreement between Jews and Christians about A, it would turn out that the parties to the apparent disagreement are not really considering the same proposition.

Some historical considerations make this view of doctrinal schemes implausible. Historically, some religions have come into existence out of others. For example, Buddhism came out of Hinduism, and Christianity came out of Judaism. And the conflicts which attended the emergence of these new religions are difficult to explain if no doctrinal disagreements were involved. Again, in the course of history various religions have come into conflict as the result of cultural invasions, for example, Hinduism and Islam, Stoicism and Christianity, Shinto and Buddhism. Again, it is difficult to do justice to these encounters without supposing that some doctrinal disagreements, as well as other points of conflict, existed in these cases.

So let us reconsider the apparent disagreement about A. We might say that, though Jews and Christians have different concepts of the Messiah, we can reformulate the proposal so that significant disagreement is possible, as follows: B. Jesus is the one whom God promised to send to redeem Israel.

We could grant that Jews and Christians have different concepts of Israel, and perhaps even different concepts of God. But these concepts might overlap enough to allow B to be significant for both. Then we could say that Jews and Christians consider the same proposition but judge it differently. Jews judge it is untrue; Christians judge it is true. Thus there could be a real disagreement, not merely an apparent one.

May we go farther? Might there have been a genuine disagreement about B not only between, say, Paul the Apostle and Rabbi Gamaliel, but also between Paul and a Stoic philosopher, for example, Seneca? Now we can conceive that, if Seneca were confronted with B, he would be perplexed, because he thinks God does not act in history as this seems to suppose. God does not "promise" anything in this way, he would think, and he does not "send" anyone in this way. So, Seneca would think, the proposal as it stands does not really make good sense. So a negation of it would not make good sense either.

In this case Seneca is denying one of the presuppositions of B if (but only if) there is some overlapping between his concept of God and Paul's concept of God. And this might be the case. Then we could say that for Paul—and Gamaliel

—*the being who rules the world* acts in history and that for Seneca this being does not do so (at least not in the same way). So a disagreement about B would derive from a disagreement about:

C. The being who rules the world acts in history.

Here we have extended the range of possible disagreements, and we have done it by finding a common reference ("the being who rules the world"), and constructing a proposition implied by the one with which we began. Beginning with an apparent disagreement, we locate a real one. In the two concepts, Paul's conception of God and Seneca's conception of God, we find a common reference. So Seneca might even be said to disagree with Paul about A, in an indirect way. "If that is what you mean by the Messiah (someone promised and sent by the being who rules the world)," he might say, "I do not believe that is true."

Might we go still farther in this manner? Might there be a real disagreement about A in some such indirect way between a Christian and a Neoplatonist like Plotinus? Now the Neoplatonist, confronted with C, might be perplexed in the way the Stoic was perplexed about B. And he might express his perplexity by saying: "But the source of all being (to which I suppose you are referring) does not rule the world in any way at all, much less by acting in history in the way you say. So what you are saying does not seem to make good sense."

Again, we might look for overlapping concepts to use in constructing a proposition about which real disagreement would be possible. And we might construct the proposition:

D. The source of all being rules the world.

About this there might be real disagreement. The Christian (and the Jew and the Stoic) might say it is true; the Neoplatonist might say it is untrue. Again we have found a common reference. And this reference gives us a logical subject of which some predicate could be said to be true or untrue.

In this manner we might go a long way. We might continue to extend the range of religious disagreements by looking for common references and then formulating predicates which bring out points of direct disagreement. The aim is to find something which both parties to the apparent disagreement can say something about, i.e., some common logical subject, and then find some predicate which one party means to affirm of this subject and the other party means to deny of it. This would be a general rule for formulating doctrinal disagreements.

There is another way in which we can extend the range of religious disagreements. We can look for some common predicate, some predicate both parties mean to assign to some subject or other, and for different logical subjects to which this predicate might be assigned by the two parties.

These would be disagreements of a different logical sort from doctrinal disagreements. Doctrinal disagreements are of the form:

$$Fm \mathbin{/} Gm$$

For example:
Jesus is the Messiah. / Jesus is (only) a teacher.

These other disagreements would be of the form:

$$Fm \mathbin{/} Fn$$

For example:
God is the ground of being. / Nature is the ground of being.

To distinguish these disagreements from those we have been considering, let us call them basic religious disagreements. And let us say that, as doctrinal disagreements are about doctrinal proposals, basic religious disagreements are about basic religious proposals. So we have two sorts of religious proposals in which truth-claims might be made.

2. Basic proposals and basic disagreements

In the rest of this study we shall be mainly, though not exclusively, concerned with proposals of this latter type. Though they have been neglected by many philosophers, it is a great mistake to neglect them if we want to understand the logical structure of religious discourse.

As examples of predicates which would be useful in formulating basic religious proposals we can take the following: "the ground of being"—"the supreme goal of life"—"that on which we unconditionally depend"—"more important than anything else"—"ultimate"—"holy." A number of similar predicates can be found in religious literature, and others could be constructed.

The subject terms of basic religious proposals express the central concepts of various doctrinal schemes, as, for example, "the gods"—"Nirvana"—"Brahman"—"the One"—"God"—"Nature"—"the Absolute"—"Humanity." Many similar concepts can be found in religious literature, and others could be constructed. Though the concept expressed by the subject term of a basic proposal belongs to some doctrinal scheme, the concept expressed by the predicate term may or may not belong to the scheme. Doctrinal schemes do not always include explicit statements of basic proposals, though sometimes they do. When they do not, basic predicates can be borrowed from other schemes, or they can be constructed, for the purpose of expressing the truth-claim of the scheme as a whole.

The distinctive feature of basic proposals lies in their predicates. It is true that their subject terms must express central concepts of doctrinal schemes. And this rules out many of the subject terms in a doctrinal scheme. For example, "Moses" could not be the subject term of a basic proposal for Judaism; "God," not "Moses," expresses the central concept of Judaism. Similarly, "Nirvana," not "the Sangha," expresses the central concept of Theravada Buddhism.[1] But this is not a sufficient criterion for basic pro-

---

[1] Determining the central concept of a scheme is a problem for phenomenological investigation and logical analysis. In some schemes this is not easy. If we could not find any central concept, then we could not formulate a basic proposal for that scheme.

posals, because many doctrinal proposals also express central concepts by their subject terms; for example, "God is merciful" and "Nirvana is the extinction of desire."

The predicate of a basic proposal expresses a concept which is basic to the inquiry to which the doctrinal scheme is relevant. As we shall see, there are various ways of formulating basic questions and suppositions in religious inquiry. (Or, we could say, there are various inquiries we would call religious, with various basic concepts.) Hence various basic predicates are possible.[2] So, if F stands for some basic predicate, a basic question would have the form, "Of what is F true?"; a basic proposal would have the form, "F is true of m"; and a doctrinal scheme would elaborate this answer by explaining the nature of m and its relations to other things. Thus the marks of a basic proposal are (a) that its subject term expresses the central concept of some *scheme* and (b) that its predicate expresses the basic concept of some *inquiry*.

The relation between basic proposals and doctrinal proposals is as follows: (a) A doctrinal proposal presupposes some basic proposal in the following way: the basic proposal gives the point and the importance of the doctrine. For example: "What is the point of saying that the self is annihilated in Nirvana?" "The point is to explain something about the supreme goal of life, for Nirvana is the supreme goal of life." Thus the meaning of a doctrine is partially dependent on the meaning of a basic proposal in a certain way. It depends on a basic proposal for explanation of its context in experience and discourse.

The following imaginary conversations illustrate the way

[2] It follows that there are a number of "logical strands" in religious discourse, which may be woven together in various ways. See Ninian Smart, *Reasons and Faiths*, 14-16, 197-198. Smart identifies and discusses three such strands—a numinous strand, a mystical strand, and an incarnation strand. But he seems to allow that other strands may be identified, for example, a pantheistic strand as in Stoicism (57).

a doctrinal proposal depends for its meaning upon, and thus presupposes, a basic proposal:

M: "Allah is merciful."
N: "Yes. My father is merciful too."
M: "You misunderstand. The fact that Allah is merciful is quite another thing than the fact that your father is merciful. For Allah is the Lord of all."

M: "The self is annihilated in Nirvana."
N: "Yes. It is a pity that we all die and come to nought."
M: "You fail to see the point of what I am saying. Nirvana is the supreme goal of life."

M: "Jesus is the Messiah."
N: "What do you mean by the Messiah?"
M: "I mean the one God sent to redeem Israel."
N: "But Cyrus is the one who redeemed Israel. He let the exiles go back to Jerusalem and rebuild the temple."
M: "You misunderstand 'redeemed.' This means to reconcile God's sinful people to him."
N: "Why is this needed? Why not reconcile them to one another?"
M: "Because God is the ground of being, and they must be reconciled to him before they can be reconciled to one another."

(b) Conversely, the meaning of a basic proposal is partially dependent on some doctrinal scheme, but in another way. For example, "What do you mean by Nature, when you say that Nature is that on which we unconditionally depend?" and "How is it that we unconditionally depend on Nature?" For an answer we might be directed to the scheme which is stated in Spinoza's *Ethics*. A doctrinal scheme elaborates the meaning of the subject term of a basic proposal. It explains what the subject is and how it is related to other things, including human beings and their experiences.

In these ways basic proposals and doctrinal proposals are interdependent, though their functions are distinguishable. Without some basic proposal we would not be able to explain the point (and, in *this* sense, the significance) of a doctrine. Without some doctrine or other we would not be able to explain the content of the concept expressed by the subject term of a basic proposal (and, in *this* sense, the significance of the basic proposal).

Formulation of basic disagreements is important because we can bring out in this way significant disagreements between those religions which have little or no obvious point of contact in their doctrines. Sometimes it is difficult to find a common logical subject to which doctrines in different religions seem to refer.

For example, in the course of the transition above from A to D, it becomes somewhat less convincing to treat "the source of all being" as a reference to a logical subject common to Christians and Neoplatonists than to treat "Jesus" as a reference common to Jews and Christians. In this particular historical context, "the source of all being" begins to look more like a predicate expression than a reference to a logical subject. So we begin to see, beyond any doctrinal disagreement which could be formulated in the way explained above, a more fundamental disagreement, namely, about what it is that is "the source of all being." This is a basic religious disagreement. Christians said that God (as explained in the creeds of the church) is the source of all being; Neoplatonists said that the One is the source of all being.

The limited range of doctrinal disagreements becomes even clearer if we take two religions which have less of a common heritage than Christianity and Neoplatonism do, for example, Theravada Buddhism and Islam. If we take Nirvana and Allah as their central concepts, it is unpromising to look for a common reference in these concepts and thus to formulate a doctrinal disagreement. But we might find some predicate which, we could say, Theravada Buddhists mean to assign to Nirvana and Moslems mean to assign to Allah. In this way we might formulate a basic disagreement.

This discussion of religious disagreements is useful in two ways. First, it has introduced two kinds of possible proposals for belief and, second, it bears directly on the conditions of significant truth-claims to be discussed next. For if genuine disagreements are not possible, then significant truth-claims are not possible.

3. *Truth-claims*

Deciding whether some religious proposal makes a truth-claim is different from deciding whether it is true. In the former case we are deciding only whether a judgment is *in order*. In making judgments we decide whether truth-claims are valid or not, whether a proposition is true or untrue. So we are asking here only for conditions in which we might properly take some proposal as a candidate for being true. I suggest four such conditions:

a. The proposal must be capable of self-consistent formulation.
b. The proposal must be liable to significant disagreement.
c. The proposal must permit a reference to its logical subject.
d. The proposal must permit some support for the assignment of its predicate to its subject.

I shall state the first condition very briefly, leaving the question of paradoxes for later discussion, and spend more time on the other three conditions.

a. Suppose we are trying to formulate some proposal and suppose that, each time we try to express it, it comes out in a pair of contradictory statements. Then what we have offered so far is at best only a suggestion. (At worst we are simply confused.) Though suggestions are necessary in religious discourse, as we shall see, we have not yet succeeded in saying something which might be judged to be true or untrue. We might think we have some proposition in mind, but we would grant that we have not yet made it explicit. So it seems that we cannot make a significant truth-claim unless the proposal is capable of self-consistent formulation.

b. The reason for the second condition is as follows: If something cannot be negated consistently, then it has no significant consequences. Therefore, it seems, nothing can count for or against its being true. And if this is the case, then it seems that no significant truth-claim is being made.

For example, suppose "God is the ground of being" is construed in such a way that: (1) it makes no sense (since it would involve a self-contradiction) to say that God is not the *ground of being* (adding perhaps that God is an illusion and therefore not the ground of being), *and* (2) it makes no sense to say it is not *God* that is the ground of being (adding perhaps that it is Nature or the Absolute that is the ground of being). Then the proposal, construed in this way, would exclude the possibility of any consistent alternative.

In this case it seems that "God is the ground of being" is being construed as a tautology. It would still be possible to claim it is logically true. But we want to know whether religious proposals make claims to truth in a stronger sense. This is what I have meant by a significant truth-claim—a claim to other-than-logical truth. So, to count as a truth-claim of this latter sort, the proposal would have to be construed in such a way that it would make sense to insert before it the words, "It is not the case that . . ." This negation might then be developed in either of the two ways mentioned above. However it is developed, the proposal would mean that this negation is untrue.

Let us take another example. Suppose "Nirvana is the supreme goal of life" were construed in such a way that: (1) it is not logically possible to say that Nirvana is not the supreme goal of life (adding perhaps that it is irrelevant to moral values), *and* (2) it is not logically possible to say that it is not Nirvana (but, say, the vision of God) that is the supreme goal of life.

Then the proposal would have no consistent alternative. An apparent disagreement with it would be an infallible sign that it has not been understood. Further, it would have no significant logical consequences. This can be shown by considering the following sentences:

A. Nirvana is the supreme goal of life.
B. Existence is unhappiness.
C. Existence is not unhappiness.
D. Nirvana is not the supreme goal of life.

Now suppose that A is so construed that it *does* have a significant logical consequence. Suppose that B follows from it (i.e., that if A is true then B is also true). And suppose that C is logically possible, so B is a genuine assertion and not itself a tautology. Then D is logically possible, since if C is true then D is true. Thus if A has some significant consequence, then it has some consistent alternative. It is not being construed as a tautology.

But if a proposal has no significant consequences, because it is construed as a tautology, then we would have no way of telling what *might* count for or against its being true. Then it would become very doubtful, to say the least, whether any significant truth-claim is being made.

I conceive this second requirement for truth-claims as a very weak one. Its weakness can be illustrated by reference to Anselm's ontological argument. If the argument is a significant argument (i.e., if it would establish something which was not previously established), then a negation of its conclusion must be logically possible in the sense of "logically possible" that I have in mind.

And if I understand Anselm correctly, this is the case. He did not really think he was wrestling with a shadow. He thought he had a real opponent, against whom an argument was needed (though at the end of chapter iii of the *Proslogium* he seems tempted to think of the fool not in the Biblical sense of "fool" but as a stupid person). He did not suppose that "There is no God" is senseless. If it were senseless, then an argument against it would have been out of order.

So, to make a significant truth-claim, one condition that his conclusion ("God exists both in the understanding and in reality") must satisfy is that a negation of it (e.g., "God exists only in the understanding") should be logically possible. I take it that Anselm grants this possibility.[3] He admits a sense in which it can be conceived that God does not exist, and he explains this sense as follows: "In one sense, an object is conceived, when the word signifying it is conceived."[4] This means, I suppose, having *some* conception of the object, if the word is *taken as* signifying the object, though not perhaps a complete and adequate conception of the object. (For if the word were *not* taken as signifying the object—as if, for example, someone should utter a word from a foreign language without knowing in the least what it meant—then an argument would not be in order. What would be in order in that case would be instruction in the use of the word.) We may well ask, "When is a conception

---

[3] If Anselm's argument were aimed at an intelligent atheist, its first premise would have to be something like "We conceive a being than which nothing greater can be conceived" instead of "We believe that thou art a being. . . ." And, for his conclusion to make a significant truth-claim, a negation of this reformulated first premise would have to be logically possible. Would Anselm have granted this also?

[4] *Proslogium* iv (Deane, tr.).

(relatively) complete and adequate?" But this is different from asking whether or not a statement makes *some* sense.

So this requirement for truth-claims is only that it must be possible to negate the proposal in question without being self-inconsistent. Arguments that might count against the negation, including dialectical arguments like Anselm's, would still be in order.

c. The third condition of making a significant truth-claim is that it must be possible to make a reference to the logical subject [5] of the proposal. The term used for the logical subject must mean something and it must mean something in a certain way. It must mean something not only in the sense that the proposer knows what he is talking about but also in the sense that others might (a logical "might") be able to learn what he is talking about. Making a reference consists in putting others in mind of what is being talked about. So this condition is that others might be led to understand what the proposer is talking about. Some answer to the question, "What is it to which you are referring?" must be possible. Otherwise, it seems, a significant truth-claim is not being made.

Suppose, for example, it is proposed that "JHWH is the lord of life." Then it would be in order to ask, "What do you mean by JHWH?" meaning, "What is it to which you are referring?" The proposer might well respond by saying, "JHWH is the one who led Israel out of Egypt." Similarly, for other proposals references might be made as follows: "Zeus is the hurler of thunderbolts"—"Nature is the whole of which all other things are parts"—"God is the first cause of all particular effects"—"Nirvana is the state in which no craving remains."

This condition requires of a proposal of the form "*m* is

---

[5] The logical subject of a religious proposal does not have to be a single individual. "The gods" would be a proper subject term in a polytheistic proposal. This point is of more than antiquarian interest.

F" that there should be additional information about *m*, beyond saying it is *F*. Further, this additional information must be of a certain kind. For example, in answer to the question about JHWH it would not be relevant to say, "JHWH is powerful." This would not tell the questioner what he wants to know. A reference is being asked for. So the proposer must (1) adduce some fact or other as a starting point for his reference; and (2) he must, by employing some interpretative category, connect this fact with the logical subject of his proposal.

Thus, in the examples given above, the Exodus from Egypt, thunderbolts, particular things and states (effects) in general, and cravings are the facts used as starting points. To be used in this way, a fact must be independent of the proposal. It must be logically possible to accept the fact without accepting the proposal. Then in each case the proposer aims to lead the proposee from this factual starting point to the logical subject of the proposal, which is the goal of the reference. He does this by making use of some mediating category or other, for example, "the hurler of," "whole," "cause," or the notion of a limiting state.

Why is it that the possibility of making a reference is a condition of making a significant truth-claim? This can be seen by considering some cases in which it is not possible to make a reference.

Suppose someone who, we might say, does not know what he is talking about. Suppose he has something in mind (or feels he has something in mind) that he means to designate by the subject term of his proposal. But what he has in mind is so extremely unclear that he could not know how to begin or proceed in making a reference to it. Then he would not be in a position to make a truth-claim.

Or suppose the proposer has something in mind with reasonable clearness. Still it might happen that no facts are available as starting points for references to it. This might be so for a fantasy which, we would say, is quite out of touch with reality. In such a case the object mentioned is useful only as a symptom of a state of mind. That, we say, is all we can make of it.

It is different with the imaginary objects mentioned in fairy tales, myths, and other literary works. Bluebeard, the Augean stables, and Falstaff are more important than purely autistic fantasies. There is truth, we say, in these fictions. But, though they are vehicles of poetic truth, it is neither appropriate nor logically possible to make a reference to one of them, except in a peculiar sense which we need not explore. They are not meant to be referred to.

I suppose that the logical subjects of basic religious proposals are meant to be referred to. They are not proposed as things are proposed in fairy tales, myths, and poetry. It is true indeed that myths often bear a religious meaning and that in religious literature symbols abound. The difference is that the myths and symbols, when used in serious religious discourse, are meant to point to something. So the important question is whether in religious discourse truth-claims of another sort than claims to poetic truth are possible, truth-claims of which one necessary condition is the possibility of making references.

Let us take an extreme case. Suppose the subject term of a proposal has no connotation for the proposee. Suppose he has never heard of Ahura Mazda, but the expression sounds to him like a proper name. So he says, "Will you please tell me what you are referring to when you speak of Ahura Mazda?" Clearly it will not do to give him another proper name (e.g., Ormazd) which is equally without sense for him. This would not help. What is needed is either some synonym which would have both a sense and a reference (which would amount to giving an implicit reference) or some description which contains an explicit reference, for example, "the source of light and goodness."

Now suppose that in this case the proposer literally has nothing to say. (Which is not at all the same thing as saying nothing. There can be meaningful silences.) Suppose the subject term cannot be explained by any reference, implicit or explicit. Then the term is only a name. (Or, we might say, it is a word that only sounds like a name. We are misled by its position in the sentence.) Then would it seem that a significant truth-claim is being made?

d. The fourth condition of making a significant truth-claim is that it must be possible to give some support to the predication made in the proposal. It must be possible to give some reason for saying that *m* is *F*. And giving a reason means bringing up some fact or other according to some principle of judgment. So we need to consider how there can be principles of judgment for basic religious proposals.[6]

Since these principles would have to be formulated "in the frame of" some particular predicate, let us consider proposals of the form, "*m* is holy." And let us construe "holy" after the manner of Rudolf Otto [7] as a complex category having both rational and nonrational elements. Whatever is holy is numinous; it is *mysterium tremendum et fascinans*. This is the nonrational element in the category of the holy. But in an experience of something holy the numinous is schematized by rational concepts. That is, when we say of something holy that it is powerful, we are using the concept of power as a schema for apprehending the numinous object to which we are referring. We are not using the concept in the way we apply it to "natural" objects. We are using it as an open pattern, so to speak, through which the numinous character of the object can shine.

[6] It is too much to ask that, in religious inquiry, any set of principles of judgment should be *complete.* I suppose that this would be the case only for questions for which there is a calculus. In other cases "good judgment" is needed, whether in religion or in morality or in science.

[7] *The Idea of the Holy (Das Heilige,* 1917), J. W. Harvey, tr., London, Oxford University Press, 1950. But Otto does not *use* this concept in the way I shall use it. See, in the next chapter, section 7.

Now suppose that some proposal of the form, "*m* is holy" (reading, for *m*, Allah or Nature or Mankind or the One or the sun, for example) has met the first three conditions we have discussed. Suppose it can be explicated with reasonable consistency, that it is liable to disagreement in the way explained, and that a reference to *m* is possible. Then it is being claimed that, for *any n*, *m* is holier than *n*. So, for some *n*, we need principles to guide us in deciding whether or not *m* is holier than *n*.

Then we can say that *m* is holier than *n*: if (1) *m* is more numinous than *n; and* if (2) *m* is more susceptible of rational schematization than *n*. Thus *n* might fail to be as holy as *m* in either of two ways, or in both. (1) It might be less numinous than *m*. The feelings appropriate to it are less sharply in contrast with the feelings appropriate to other objects. It is deficient in "otherness," in being other than "natural" things (i.e., the rest of the universe relative to it). This might count against *n*, for example, if *n* is a mountain, an emperor, or, in the modern world, the sun. (2) It might be less susceptible of rational schematization. This might count against Caliban's god (in Browning's poem), for example, or against the "momentary gods" who appear in primitive religion, and more generally against anything which lacks consistency of character or endurance in being.

Now if something *m* is holier than any *n* whatever, then *m* is holy in an eminent sense also. It is not only "holiest," in a sense analogous to "highest" as in "the highest mountain"; it is holy in a further sense of "holy," in which it would be self-inconsistent to say that both *m* and *n* are holy. It is holy in a uniquely applying sense of "holy." This is made explicit in a line of a well-known hymn: "Only Thou art holy."

The reason for this lies in the meaning of "numinous," which is itself built into the meaning of "holy." If something is numinous it stands in contrast with all other things. If something *m* is more numinous than something *n*, then *m* stands in sharper contrast with all other things (including *n*) than *n* does (when *m* is included among the other things). So, if *m* is more numinous than any *n* whatever, this would mean that the contrast between *m* and all else is the sharpest possible contrast. Now we could not do justice to this consequence by saying only that *m* is holier than anything else. This would suggest only a relative contrast between *m* and other things. This would be like saying, "Everest is the highest mountain." We need a way of indicating a maximal contrast, not just a relative contrast, between *m* and all else, and this can be done by using "holy" in a uniquely applying sense also. So, if anything is holier than everything else, it is holy in this eminent sense.

Taking "holy" in this sense, it would be logically proper to apply it to any one of a number of logical subjects. But it would not be proper to apply it to a multiplicity of logical subjects. It can be true of only one logical subject. Either *m* or *n* may be said to be holy in this sense, but not both. So this is a different sense of "holy" from that in which we say that a mountain *and* a book *and* a saint are holy.

The principles I have formulated are in the frame of a particular predicate. They are not designed for use in judging any and every religious proposal. For proposals using other predicates, other rules of judgment would have to be formulated. It may turn out that all predicates used in basic religious proposals have certain functions in common. But we do not need to reduce all basic predicates to some one. Just as various general theories of religion are possible and useful, so various predicates derived from these general theories are possible and useful.

It may be easier to formulate rules of judgment in the frame of one predicate than in the frame of another. One set of rules may give more guidance to judgments than another set does. In this way some predicates may give more significance to truth-claims than others do.

My main point can be put as follows: Suppose that some

basic religious proposal of the form, "*m* is *F*" should satisfy the first three conditions above. Then it would seem fair to ask, "Is there any reason at all for thinking that *m* is *F?*" And if no reason at all is available (whether or not the proposer himself can think of one), then it does not seem that a significant truth-claim is being made.

Finally, I return briefly to the point with which I began. Deciding whether religious proposals make truth-claims is different from making religious judgments and arguing for them. Suppose we take some proposal as making a truth-claim, and suppose we want to decide whether to accept, or reject, or suspend judgment on this claim. Then, along with many other considerations, we would need to see whether (1) an adequate reference (i.e., one whose factual starting point is firm enough and whose mediating categories are sufficiently perspicuous) to its logical subject and (2) adequate support for the predication are available. Later we must consider how such decisions might be made. So far I have been asking only, "Under what conditions would it be appropriate to take some religious proposal as making a significant truth-claim?"

CHAPTER III

Some Theories of Religion

I. *Introduction*

Since principles of judgment for basic proposals have to be formulated in the frames of basic predicates, we need to see how these predicates are derived. They are meant to be applied to logical subjects which have central positions in religious systems.[1] And they must be capable of being applied to (though not true of) more than one such logical subject, if basic disagreements, of the form Fm/Fn, are possible. So we ought to see how general theories of religion can be constructed. That is the object of this chapter and the next. For a general theory of religion is one which applies equally well to more than one form of religion, and from general theories of an appropriate sort we can derive basic predicates.

General theories of religion are ways of marking out the domain of religious activity in human life. Then contrasts with the domains of scientific activity, moral activity, and other domains would be possible. And this would help to clear up confusions between propositions of different types, where predicates get out of place.

General theories must be adequate to such systems as Hinduism, Judaism, Buddhism, Christianity, and Islam, but they should do something more as well. They should yield some criteria for recognizing novel forms of religion. Suppose the domain of religion were defined simply by pointing to these systems. Then we would have no way of recognizing novel forms of religion, although, from the history of

---

[1] A number of types of logical subjects of basic proposals, and some modes of referring to them, will be discussed in chapters ix and x.

religion, we have good reason to expect some to emerge. One reason for inventing general concepts is to domesticate, so to speak, the novel and the strange. Putting the point another way, the novel and the strange in our experience force us to revise our categories and add new ones to our stock, to do justice to the connectedness of things as well as to their individual differences. Only so can thought survive in a world that is productive of novelty.

2. *Worship and awe*

Since worship is an activity we commonly take as distinctive of religion, we might use this term to formulate a basic religious predicate. We could say that in a religious judgment something is being judged to be worshipful. This would mean that it is worthy of worship; it has a rightful claim on human beings for their worship. This would not be a wrong move, though it would leave a good deal to be explained.

Suppose we explain "worship" by referring to some quality of feeling in the worshipper, for example, awe, which is often said to be distinctive of religious experience. And suppose we could distinguish between awe and such feelings as profound fear and a sense of the sublime. This would still leave something to be done. For our aim is not to characterize religious experience but to distinguish the sort of thing people are concerned *with* when they are religious. We need to say what distinctive attributes or functions are ascribed to objects of religious feelings.

From the quality "awe" we can derive the attribute "awe-inspiring" to use in religious judgments, much as we derive "worshipful" from the act of worship. And if we are told something is awe-inspiring we know more about it, in a certain way, than if we are told only that it is worshipful. We are being given a reason why the object has a rightful claim to be worshipped. The implicit premise would be: "Worship is the right response to what inspires us with awe." This takes us a step farther than saying it is worshipful, by telling us something the object does. *"m* is awe-inspiring" tells of a causal relationship. We say that *m* elicits awe or that it fills us with awe, makes us awe-struck.

If we should want to use "awe-inspiring" as a basic predicate, we would have to see what principles of judgment it would yield. Perhaps we could formulate some such principles, relying on distinctions between awe and other sentiments. But these principles might be somewhat meager for our purpose, namely, to give some sense to decisions between *"m* is awe-inspiring" and *"n* is awe-inspiring." We might need more of a framework for arguments than they would give us.

3. *Religion as worship of God*

Now consider a theory which is problematical in another way. Sometimes it is said that religion is worship of God, meaning that all (and only) those who worship God are religious.[2]

For some purposes it is right to say this. For example: (*a*) This is a commonly accepted interpretation of religion in our own culture. So it ought to be mentioned in a dictionary. (*b*) Within any particular religious community where "God" is the central concept and where "religion" is a favorable and not a pejorative term,[3] this is not misleading. It will be understood that "true religion" or "pure religion" is meant.

Our own purpose is a different one. We need predicates which would be usable in religious judgments more gener-

[2] Or that religion is "a sense of the divine." I shall not deal with this weaker expression separately. For either it is equivalent to what Rudolf Otto would mean by "a sense of the holy," which I discuss later, or it is a milder version of "worship of God."

[3] Thus excluding cases like Jehovah's Witnesses, who reject "religion" because it is a part of that human culture which rebels against God and is therefore doomed to destruction. Note also some of Karl Barth's earlier utterances.

ally, not just within some one religious community, and not just in our own culture. This will become clearer as we consider some problems about construing religion as worship of God.

a. If we speak of religion as worship of God, in answer to a question like "What is religion?", we risk obscuring theological differences. In our own culture the term "God" has been used to express a number of meanings, to say nothing of equivalent terms in other cultures. Consider, for example, II Isaiah, Aristotle, Cleanthes, the Fourth Gospel, Plotinus, Spinoza, Leibniz, and various contemporary conceptions of God. In view of this diversity we have a choice between two courses. We may stretch the concept of God, or we may restrict it.

(1) We may try to devise a formula to cover all these instances, stretching the concept to cover all the historically important senses of the term. Suppose we begin by substituting for "God" some expression of the form, "a being who (*a*) created the world, (*b*) . . . . , (*c*) . . . . ," with a view to getting an adequately general concept. Then we remember that Plotinus insisted that God is *beyond* being, and that Spinoza denied that God is the creator of the world. So we would have to substitute some other expression for "a being" and some other expression for "created the world," to cover their views. It would be difficult though perhaps not impossible to construct a formula of this sort.[4]

---

[4] It might seem that this is what Paul Tillich is doing in the following passage: "If God is understood as that which concerns man ultimately, early Buddhism has a concept of God just as certainly as does Vedanta Hinduism. And if God is understood as that which concerns man ultimately, moral or logical concepts of God are seen to be valid in so far as they express an ultimate concern. Otherwise they are philosophical possibilities but not the God of religion." *Systematic Theology,* I, 220, Chicago, University of Chicago Press, 1951.

Or perhaps he is speaking theologically, and saying that there

(2) Instead of stretching the concept of God in this way, we may restrict the connotation of the term to some one historically important sense, for example, the conception of a creator. So if someone should bring up the case of Spinoza we would have to say that Spinoza was not religious.

How could we justify restrictions of this kind? (*a*) We might argue that the sense of the term we select is the only one that allows a coherent theoretical development of a conception of God. Or (*b*) we might argue that the sense we select has been more important, historically speaking, than any other.

But neither of these is a good argument for a general theory of religion (though either might be used to support some religious *proposal*). Against the first, a general theory needs to allow for the possibility that someone may be religious and yet have concepts which cannot be theoretically developed. Against the second, a general theory should be applicable to historically unimportant cases as well as to important ones. Sometimes we revise our judgments about what is historically important. So it should be possible to say that something is both a form of religion and, historically speaking, relatively unimportant.

is something—God—which is the *true* object of all ultimate concerns. So when a Buddhist speaks of Nirvana he is *really* referring to God. I am using the expression "have a concept of God" in a phenomenological, not a theological, way. Whether or not we agree with Tillich theologically, we need some way of making the phenomenological point that Theravada Buddhism is atheistic.

A third interpretation of Tillich's remark is conceivable. Perhaps he is using "God" as a predicate expression. Then the first clause in the passage would function not as a reference to a logical subject but, instead, as a statement of an equivalence between two predicate expressions. Compare Gandhi's remark, "Rather than say that God is Truth I should say that Truth is God" (*My Religion*, 40, Ahmedabad, 1955). But I am discussing those theories which use "God" as a subject term and in a referring way. Gandhi is saying that instead of taking "God" as a subject term he would take "Truth" as a subject term.

b. A more weighty objection is that this theory rules out too much. It is highly implausible to interpret primitive Jainism and Theravada Buddhism, for example, as teaching worship of God. In addition there are problematical cases like Confucianism, Taoism, and the mystery cults of the ancient Mediterranean world. In the unproblematical cases it would be clearly a mistake, and in the problematical cases it would be at least misleading, to say that they teach and practice the worship of God.

Yet there are strong reasons for calling these institutions and movements, and the people who participate in them, religious. It would be wrong to say that the *Tao Tê Ching* is not religious literature. "I am a Theravada Buddhist" is certainly a proper answer to the question "What is your religion?" though Theravada Buddhists do not believe in God. It is in accord with both common and learned usage to speak of people who are religious but do not believe in God.

c. It is true that most religious people in our culture worship God, that very often when religion is mentioned worship of God is a part of what is meant, and that most people who believe in God are religious. But this group of facts does not resolve our problem. Let us get more clearly in mind just what we need from theories of religion. For some good theories are not suited to our purpose, though useful for other purposes. This will bring us to the main objection, for this purpose, to saying that religion is worship of God.

We need theories which will yield predicates for formulating basic religious questions and proposals. These predicates would apply to objects of religious sentiments. But, while they would express attributes or functions of such objects, they should not designate any one such object. That is why theories which make belief in God essential to being religious will not serve our purpose.

The crucial consideration is that at the beginning of an

inquiry the question needs to be so stated that no relevant answer will be *ruled out*. The reason is simple. No good question answers itself. We may be sure we know the right answer. But if the question is put in such a way that this is the only relevant answer, then the question is not a good question. And without good questions there is no inquiry. So we should not define our question in terms of some specific answer to it. In explicating some basic religious predicate, such as "worshipful," we must say not of what subject it is true but what is its sense.

4. *Kant on religion*

We can learn something from looking at the historical background of our problem. We ought to begin with Kant's treatment of religion, for while he did not pose this problem for himself—at least not clearly—he led his successors to pose it.

Kant's main contribution to the study of religion is the theory of religion and morality set forth in the second critique, in *Religion Within the Limits of Reason Alone*,[5] and elsewhere. In these discussions he does not give a general theory of religion; instead, he makes a religious proposal. He does not seem to have posed for himself—certainly not clearly—the problem of formulating a general theory of religion.

Kant is interested in a particular kind of religion, namely, "pure religious faith," which may be put most succinctly as "the recognition of our duties as divine commands." This he *recommends* on the grounds of its universality, its simplicity, and its conduciveness to morality.

Kant is well aware that there are, ordinarily speaking, other kinds of religion than pure religious faith. He is familiar with traditional Christianity, and he mentions primitive, classical, and Oriental forms of religion. But he is not content to think of pure religious faith as one religion

[5] Greene and Hudson, tr., New York, Harper, 1960.

among many. He goes so far as to say that pure religious faith is really the only (true) religion, though there are many "faiths" (by which he means cults) based on various versions of divine statutory laws (*Religion*, 98). These cults with their varying forms of religious expression are "vehicles" (97) of pure religious faith.

This move on Kant's part resembles the kind of apologetic sometimes offered for Vedanta Hinduism. For example, "The Vedānta is not a religion, but religion itself in its most universal and deepest significance." [6] In both cases this move is a confusing one. John Dewey's distinction between religions and "the religious quality" in experience [7] is confusing in a similar way.

In all these cases, as a matter of fact, proposals are being made and argued for, and counterproposals are therefore logically possible. But saying that pure religious faith is the only religion, or that Vedanta is religion itself, or that a certain quality of experience is *the* religious quality, might lead an unwary reader to think that no religious counterproposals are logically possible. Taken literally those remarks *look* like general theories of religion, but they are being *used* to make particular religious proposals. Something is out of key. One reason for the confusion is that the writer has no adequate general theory at hand as a setting for his proposal.

Kant does indeed have an assumption which functions in place of a general theory of religion. He assumes that belief in God is essential to religion. For example, when he says that, though morality does not need religion for its own sake, yet it "leads ineluctably to religion" (*Religion*, 5), he means that pure practical reason requires us to postulate the existence of God. He does not explicitly offer this as a

---

[6] S. Radhakrishnan, *The Hindu View of Life*, 23, New York, Macmillan, 1927.

[7] See *A Common Faith*, chapter 1, New Haven, Yale University Press, 1934.

general theory of religion. Instead, he accepts implicitly a restriction which is common in our culture.

Kant accepts this restriction as a matter of course because he does not seriously and persistently ask, "When do concepts and judgments have religious significance?" as he *does* ask, "When do concepts and judgments have moral significance?" So his theory is not very useful as an instrument of analysis in the study of religion. Instead, it is an answer to the question, "What sort of religion should I have?" Kant tells us about the only sort of religion he thinks worth having.

My second point about Kant can be put very briefly. Though Kant did not pose our own problem for himself, his critical method in philosophy led some of his successors to pose it. He did not write a critique of religious judgment. But this task might easily suggest itself to later philosophers who learned his method. No doubt it has not yet been carried through with the acuteness and rigor that Kant might have brought to it. But since his time a number of philosophers have addressed themselves to the problem. One of the most important of these was Friedrich Schleiermacher.

5. Schleiermacher

The development of modern science has made it necessary for philosophers to explain how nonscientific concepts and judgments are like, and how they are different from, scientific concepts and judgments. Kant was among the first to meet this need by constructing a general theory of how our concepts and judgments get their significance. One way of putting the lesson Kant helped us learn is as follows: We must consider the sort of interest in which an inquiry originates and gets its direction, in order to understand the functions of concepts and judgments in that inquiry.

Kant showed how moral reflection is different from science, both in its spring and in its concepts and judgments. Morality is not generated by science, and its concepts are not deducible from scientific concepts. And Kant developed a theory about the way in which moral concepts get their meaning. But he did not show how, in *general*, religious concepts get their significance.

Schleiermacher, who had learned much from Kant, went a step farther. He set out to show how religion differs not only from science and metaphysics but also from morality. He meant to show how religion has "a province of its own." [8] Let us see how Schleiermacher's treatment of religion differed from Kant's.

Though Kant did not develop a general theory of religion in an explicit and critical way, he did assume that belief in God is essential to religion. What is more, he assumed that a particular conception of God is essential to religion. Under the influence of Spinoza and Schelling, Schleiermacher vigorously attacked the traditional conception of God as a transcendent individual, which Kant had taken for granted. He said that this conception, like the popular conception of immortality, was naïve and irrational. What is more to the point, above and beyond his objections to this particular conception of God, he thought it absurd to suppose that being religious depended on having some particular conception of God or other. The existence of a religious consciousness, he said, does not depend on any prior knowledge of God. In these ways he criticized the assumption which, for Kant, had taken the place of a general theory of religion.

Also, he objected to Kant's theory of religion and morality. Kant had said that pure practical reason requires us to postulate the existence of God, and therewith the adjustment of happiness to virtue in a future life, in order to make sense of the moral life in a nonmoral world. The spring of religion lies in the moral life. This spring determines the

[8] Friedrich Schleiermacher, *On Religion: Speeches to its Cultured Despisers*, 21, New York, Harper, 1958. John Oman, tr., with an introduction by Rudolf Otto.

central concepts and judgments in rational religion. Pure religious faith is moral faith.

Schleiermacher thought this confused morality and religion, with unfortunate consequences for both. For, on one hand, "every external incitement is alien to morality" (*On Religion*, 99). And, on the other hand, "piety cannot be an instinct craving for a mess of metaphysical and ethical crumbs" (31).

Without tracing the development of Schleiermacher's theory of religion after the *Reden* (*On Religion*) of 1799, let us consider his discussion in the early sections of *The Christian Faith* of 1830 (2nd ed.),[9] where he is giving a philosophical introduction to theology. There he defines piety (*Frömmigkeit*) as "the feeling of absolute dependence" (*das schlechthinige Abhängigkeitsgefühl*).

"Absolute dependence" is a mode of self-consciousness. It is one way in which we are conscious of ourselves. In our ordinary experience we are conscious of ourselves as creating or modifying the objects with which we are concerned. But there are no moments in experience when we are, as it were, absolute creators. We do not have any feeling of absolute freedom. In all our experience there is some element of givenness to be reckoned with, so that our freedom is never unlimited. Ordinarily, however, we do add some determinations—sometimes more, sometimes less—to the things we experience. So, in our ordinary experience of the world, feelings of freedom and feelings of dependence are mingled. Ordinarily we are conscious of ourselves as being determined by and at the same time determining, to some extent or other, the world we experience.

Though we cannot have a feeling of absolute freedom, since we are finite beings, we do have a feeling of absolute or—better—unmixed (*schlechthinig*) dependence. We are

[9] Translation edited by Mackintosh and Stewart, Edinburgh, T. and T. Clark, 1928.

conscious of ourselves as standing in relation to something which we do not determine at all. And this is the religious self-consciousness.

By saying that this is a feeling Schleiermacher meant to distinguish it from knowing as well as from acting. He wanted to distinguish this mode of self-consciousness from particular conceptions of "that on which we absolutely depend." Such conceptions vary widely, since they are suggested by various sensible experiences in different historical environments, and since they are developed theoretically in metaphysical and theological systems of various types. This is what he means, I take it, when he urges that the religious self-consciousness does not depend on any prior knowledge of God.

But by "feeling" he did not mean an emotional quality, either. Having this feeling is not in the same class with having a feeling of pleasure or of anger. It is rather a mode of self-consciousness. We are conscious of ourselves as having some status or other, as standing in some relation or other, though the feeling itelf does not give us a theory about that in relation to which we stand. There are, indeed, religious emotions which attend this mode of self-consciousness. But having this sort of self-consciousness and having emotional feelings are not the same sort of thing.

Now we need to ask what sort of theory this formulation expresses. In particular we need to ask whether this gives us a good general theory of religion of the sort we need. The main problem is whether, as Schleiermacher explains and develops his theory, the religious self-consciousness does in fact come to be tied to a particular conception of its object or not, and, if so, what the consequences of this are.

This problem arises when Schleiermacher begins to use the expression "God-consciousness" as equivalent to "the feeling of absolute dependence." It is true that he introduces the term "God" as a functional term. The following passage makes this fairly clear:

"As regards the identification of absolute dependence with 'relation to God' in our proposition: this is to be understood in the sense that the *Whence* of our receptive and active existence, as implied in this self-consciousness, is to be designated by the word 'God,' and that this is for us the really original signification of that word" (*The Christian Faith*, 16).

This sounds as though we are not to read into the term "God" any meanings it may have acquired in other contexts than this—for example, the conception that God is absolutely supernatural or absolutely complete—unless it can be shown that whatever we are absolutely dependent on must have these attributes. It sounds as though the referential function of "God" is meant to be equivalent to that of "that existence outside of us to which the consciousness of absolute dependence refers" (35). This would leave open a wide range of possible conceptions of that on which we absolutely depend.

This impression is strengthened by Schleiermacher's treatment of variations in religion and in particular the varieties of religious conceptions. Since his main concern, in this introduction to Christian dogmatics, is to bring out the distinctiveness of Christianity, it is natural for him to concentrate on monotheistic religions. But he recognizes other varieties, including idol worship and polytheism, and says, "We must never deny the homogeneity of all these products of the human spirit" (38). He finds pantheism "compatible with piety" if it "is taken as expressing some variety or form of Theism" and is not "simply and solely a disguise for a materialistic negation of Theism" (39).

This last remark, however, might make us suspect that Schleiermacher's theory has—built into it, so to speak—a bent toward a particular religious conception. This suspicion is reinforced when he says that in idol worship the self-consciousness is "confused," "since in it the higher and the lower are so little distinguished that even the feeling of absolute dependence is reflected as arising from a particular object to be apprehended by the senses" (35). Also, he says that in polytheism "the feeling of absolute dependence cannot appear in its complete unity and indifference to all that the sensible self-consciousness may contain . . ." (35). For these reasons idol worship and polytheism are "subordinate forms, from which men are destined to pass" (34) to the more highly developed (i.e., monotheistic) forms of religion. After carrying his argument farther by steps we need not consider here, he concludes that Christianity is the most perfect of the highly developed forms of religion. From this it seems clear that his theory of religion tells us not only what sort of thing is to count as religion but also what forms of religion are better than others.

The question this poses is not whether these judgments—that monotheism is better than polytheism and that Christianity is better than Islam—are good judgments. We may or may not agree with them. The question is rather, Where does Schleiermacher find his grounds for making them? Does he deduce his norms of judgment from the theory of religion alone? *In* knowing what is meant by the "feeling of absolute dependence" do we also get a rule for telling whether one form of religion is better (more developed, more perfect) than another? It does look as though Schleiermacher thought this was the case. But I am less interested in arguing for this interpretation of Schleiermacher than in showing what would follow if this is what he means.

If this is true of Schleiermacher's theory of religion, then it is not the kind of theory we need. We need a theory which would yield a formulation of a religious predicate without designating a logical subject to which, rather than to others, the predicate truly applies. We need a theory to tell us what a relevant answer to a basic religious question would be, without telling us what the right answer is.

Why is this so? To make the reason clear let us distinguish "rules of relevance" from "norms of judgment." Rules of relevance tell us *what* to take account of in deciding the question at issue, what facts are relevant and what are not. For example, for "Is M honest?" a rule of relevance might be, "Give particular attention to M's moral dispositions and conduct." A more specific rule would be, "See whether he, habitually, does not deceive himself or others in what he says and does."

Norms of judgment guide us in weighing the relevant considerations. They tell us *how* to take account of the various relevant facts. For example, "Trust your own impressions of M more than N's opinion of M," or the contrary. They are principles in that they might guide others as well as ourselves toward settling questions in some nonarbitrary way. For another example, suppose the argument in Plato's *Euthyphro* took a different course than it does and, instead of being concerned with what actions are pious, was concerned with the proposal, "The gods are holy." Then it might be further proposed as a norm of judgment that "nothing is holy if it includes quarrels and enmity."

Now if a theory of religion yields a predicate for proposals for belief, it will yield some rules of relevance, but a theory can yield rules of relevance without giving norms of judgment. This means that theories of the latter sort are logically prior to those which prescribe norms of judgment. Certainly we need norms of judgment in religious inquiry. But first we need rules of relevance, and we will not find them if they are confused with norms of judgment. We should not confuse questions about meaning ("What is the sense of this predicate?") with questions about truth ("Of what is it true?"). But such confusion is unavoidable if we begin with a theory which gives principles of both kinds without discriminating between them.

Schleiermacher would have avoided this confusion if he had been more faithful to his own principles. Instead of objecting, on religious and speculative grounds, only to the particular conception of God to which Kant had tied religion, he should have objected more consistently, on logical grounds, to binding the religious consciousness a priori to any designation of that on which we are unconditionally dependent. His own lesson should be applied to himself. Though he denies that "this feeling of dependence is itself conditioned by some previous knowledge about God" (17), it is not clear that in working out his theory he made this claim good.

6. *A variation on Schleiermacher*

It would follow that to make use of Schleiermacher's theory of religion we would have to abstract his rules of relevance from the framework of his own norms of judgment in which it is embedded. We could construct a variation on his theory, which would not commit us to some particular religious view, for example, a Christian Spinozism.

We could speak of maximal dependence instead of absolute dependence, not ruling out absolute (unmixed) dependence but including it as a limiting case of maximal dependence, in the following way: Someone M may be relatively more dependent on something m than on something n, but M is maximally dependent on m only if he is more dependent on m than on all other things taken together. This would do some justice to what we would ordinarily mean by "religious dependence." For if, for any n, M is only relatively more dependent on m than on n, we would not ordinarily call this a religious relationship.

Then the basic question would be, On what am I maximally dependent? *Rules of relevance* for answering this question might include:

a. Consider things you depend on. For this preliminary rule to be useful some explication of "depend" would be needed. We might follow Schleiermacher's lead and construe it in such a way that the essential feature of something depended on is that it gives form and direction to our activity.[10] Then the opposite of "M is dependent on X" would be "M acts on X," meaning either [11] that X is the object of M's activity or that M's activity has some effect on X.

This rule would not exclude from relevance things which are both depended on and acted on. But it would rule out from relevance to the question anything on which we are in no way dependent, that is, anything which in no way gives form and direction to our activity, if there should be anything of this sort.

b. Consider especially those things which are depended on in important ways, things which, in Santayana's phrase, are "sources of our being." These would be things such that, if they did not exist and maintain their being, this would be a serious threat to our own being. Suggestions might arise in various ways. One's family, one's country, and various social institutions might come to mind, e.g., for a doctor, the complex network of institutions involved in the medical profession. Also, various entities referred to in religious and philosophical literature might be considered, for example, Nature, the Whole, one's Real Self, Atman, the Absolute, the Form of Good, God, Nirvana, and others.

It might be conceived that we are absolutely dependent on some one of these, perhaps in the sense that our activity has no effect on it at all. But this would not rule out things on which our activity might have some effect in some way, for example, as a part has some effect on a whole.

This rule supposes that we have some conception or other of ourselves. But it does not of itself prescribe any particular conception of ourselves. This would be a rule of a different sort, as we shall see.

These and other rules of relevance would focus the issue to be judged. Incidentally, they would help to bring out some of the common suppositions of the various proposals which might be offered as answers to the question.

[10] See *The Christian Faith*, 13.
[11] Since I am only suggesting *possible* constructions.

Then we would be in a position to give some *procedure for judgment*. A preliminary issue for judgment would be whether, in respect to some two (*m* and *n*) of these candidates, so to speak, we are more dependent on *m* than on *n*. But this would be only a way of eliminating some candidates. For being maximally dependent is different from being relatively more dependent. The final issue for judgment would be, On which of these things are we more dependent than on all other things taken together? [12]

Then further principles of judgment would be in order. These would be *norms of judgment*. For example, it seems clear that one's judgment on the question would depend in part on the way one looks at oneself. So it might be offered as a norm of judgment that anyone who is deciding the question should think of himself in some particular systematic way. Various systematic theories of the self are possible (Platonic, Kantian, Freudian, Jungian, existentialist, et cetera). So, for example, the following might be offered as a norm of judgment for deciding the question: Consider yourself a union of a body and a soul. Or, instead of offering some systematic theory of the self, rules might be offered which are merely cautionary, as, for example: Do not identify yourself completely with any social role. ("I am not *just* a doctor.") Similarly, other norms might be offered for guidance in judging the question. Insofar as these norms express or depend on significant truth-claims, they are liable to disagreement, as explained in Chapter II, and

[12] There is a difference between the formal structure of this issue for judgment and the formal structure of the issue for judgment about what is "holy," as indicated in chapter II. In each case there is a decisive contrast (one might even say an absolute contrast) between something *m* and all other things. This decisiveness is *built into* the predicate "holy" since this includes the notion of "otherness." What is holy is by definition marked off sharply from all other (i.e., "natural") things. Here this decisiveness has to be added explicitly, by means of this distinction between maximal and relative dependence.

would need to be argued for. And in any reasonably complete argument for some proposal it is likely that a great many such norms would occur.

My object in constructing this variation on Schleiermacher is not to interpret Schleiermacher, except in a negative way, i.e., by showing a way in which he does *not* develop his theory of religion. Nor do I mean to rule out or even to slight his own religious proposal. Starting with the way the question is put in this variation, it would still be legitimate to argue as he does. For example:

"We must assume an immediate tendency toward the Infinite. The antithesis between conscious being as a genus and the being given to consciousness must be abolished in self-consciousness; hence it must be affected by an other. But clearly not by one on which it can react; hence the feeling of absolute dependence." [13]

Again, he argues that in religious self-consciousness all opposition between oneself and other finite beings is done away with, and he says:

"This sympathy can occur only in so far as in each finite being there is a relation to something outside the totality. If it is to be possible, that Being must lie outside the realm of reciprocal interaction." [14]

Nor have I offered any criticisms of such arguments. I have meant only to formulate a question to which Schleiermacher's proposal and various counterproposals might be construed as answers. For if there is such a Being as he suggests, and if we are dependent on this Being in the way he says, then we are maximally dependent on it. But this variant formulation of the basic question would permit arguments

[13] Richard B. Brandt, *The Philosophy of Schleiermacher*, 274 (New York, Harper, 1941), translating from Schleiermacher's *Psychologie*, 522.
[14] *Ibid.*, translating from *Psychologie*, 546–547.

for other proposals also. Then each argument would have to stand on its own feet.

By loosening in this way the attachment of Schleiermacher's theory of religion to a particular world view and to a particular religious proposal, we could make some of his insights more useful for understanding the logic of religious discourse. Usually, however, it is more fruitful to construct a new theory, or let a new one grow out of the old, than to remodel the old theory.

7. *Rudolf Otto and others*

The most important theory of religion which has grown out of Schleiermacher's is that of Rudolf Otto in *The Idea of the Holy*, which we made use of in Chapter II. Like Schleiermacher he was deeply indebted to Kant, and he inherited from Schleiermacher a strong interest in religion as a distinctive mode of human experience. But he was interested in a far wider range of phenomena than either, and had far better information about primitive and Oriental religion.

As we have seen, Otto interprets religious experience as in essence a response to something which is both numinous (*mysterium tremendum et fascinans*) and schematizable by rational concepts. Such a reality is "holy." So "the holy" is the distinctive category of religion, as "oughtness" is the distinctive category of morality. In his development and explanation of this theory Otto gives many examples drawn from the history of religions. And his exposition is careful and systematic, so that his argument has considerable force. I call attention to three interesting points about the outcome of his argument.

a. His theory goes farther than theories which say, "Religion is worship" or "Religion is concern with the awe-inspiring." It yields a more direct characterization of objects of religious experience than they do. "*m* is holy" tells us about *m* more directly than "*m* is worshipful" or even "*m* is awe-inspiring." It tells us what there is about *m* that makes *m* worthy of worship or awe-inspiring.

b. Otto's theory has a wider range of application than theories which say, "Religion is worship of God." At least Otto means it [15] to apply to primitive forms of religion, to Taoism, and to varieties of Hinduism and Buddhism which we would properly hesitate to call theistic, though it may not, as a matter of fact, apply to all of these as well as we might wish.

On both these counts—in respect of the directness of its application to objects and in respect of its range of application—Otto's theory seems to promise a more useful predicate for the explicit formulation of basic religious proposals than some other theories do.

c. Otto carries on his phenomenological analysis in the framework of a certain normative theory of religious knowledge, somewhat as Schleiermacher did. When Otto says that the holy is an "*a priori* category" (112), he is not saying it is a concept constructed for the purpose of characterization and analysis. He thinks that our experiences of the holy point to a "hidden substantive source" (114) of knowledge in the depth of the soul, so that in having these experiences we are transcending phenomena and are in touch with noumenal reality. Incidentally, this gives him a standard, as did Schleiermacher's theory, by which he judges Christianity to be the supreme religion. So we are led to ask whether, instead of (or perhaps along with) constructing a general theory of religion, Otto is making a proposal—perhaps: "It is the ground of the soul (*fundus animae*) that is holy."

We do not need to use Otto's analysis in this way, however. We might distinguish between his general theory of religion and his theory of religious knowledge. We might make use of "holy" as a predicate, as suggested in Chapter II, without being committed to Otto's theory of the a priori.

[15] See chapters 15-16 and pp. 30, 39, 67, 195, 201.

Then the basic religious question would become, "What is holy?" Particular answers that might be proposed, and accepted or rejected in religious judgments, would be, for example, "God is holy," [16] "Nature is holy," "Nirvana is holy," and so on. It should be emphasized that Otto himself does not use the category in this way.

A similar theory is that of Gerardus van der Leeuw in *Religion in Essence and Manifestation* (*Phänomenologie der Religion*, 1933),[17] who treats religion as response to etxraordinary Power. Van der Leeuw stands at a later point on the historical line that runs through Kant, Schleiermacher, and Otto. His theory is less developed in its conceptual structure than Otto's, but it is applied much more widely and more systematically to varieties of religious experience.

Another general theory of religion which belongs in this same line of historical development is that of Paul Tillich, for whom religion is unconditional or ultimate concern.[18] His theory would yield such basic questions as "What is the ultimate?" and "What is the ground of being?"

In the next chapter I shall develop another general theory of religion to set alongside these. But first I shall sum up and explain some conclusions about the bearing of general theories of religion on religious inquiry.

8. *Conclusions*

a. Anyone who finds himself engaged in serious religious inquiry has *some* conception of the nature of the interest which prompts him to inquire and thus some conception of that about which he is inquiring. He has some notion of the

---

[16] If this is used to express a basic religious proposal it would have a different force than if it were used, as in treatises in systematic theology, to express a Christian *doctrine*, or a Jewish doctrine.

[17] Turner, tr., London, G. Allen and Unwin, 1938.

[18] See *Systematic Theology*, I, 8–15, 211–235.

scope of religious inquiry. His conception may be more or less clear.

b. Getting a clear conception of religious inquiry includes formulating a predicate for basic religious questions and proposals. Examples of expressions which can be used in this way are: "worshipful," "awe-inspiring," "that on which we depend absolutely," "holy," "ultimate," "ground of being."

c. A predicate for this use must be so formulated that its application is not restricted, a priori, to some one logical subject only. It must be applicable to more than one logical subject (though not *true* of more than one). A proposal designates some logical subject and assigns this predicate to it. Room must be left for the logical possibility of bad, false, mistaken, erroneous judgments (which are genuinely religious judgments but assign the predicate to wrong logical subjects), in order to give significance to good judgments. In this way we need to give some generality to the scope of religious inquiry. We need to characterize that class of objects, any one of which might be taken as the religious object without *absurdity*.

d. A predicate of this sort can be derived from a general theory of religion, which philosophy must borrow from the phenomenology of religion. A general theory is one that fits a number of cases well.[19] An ideally perfect general theory would be *equally* applicable to all the cases to which it is applied, and it would enable us to decide all doubtful cases. We can only approximate this ideal. No matter how we draw lines between religion and other interests, like magic, political loyalty, philosophy, moral responsibility, and esthetic enjoyment, there will be some doubtful cases. But for a given purpose some theories will be better than others.

e. Now we can restate and sum up some conditions a

[19] If only an *ad hoc* theory. It must apply to at least two contrasting proposals.

general theory of religion should satisfy, to yield such a predicate. Many theories might be useful for other purposes. No one can lay down rules for a theory to end all theories and serve all possible purposes. We can give some rules for theories which would serve *this* purpose.

(1) A general theory that is good for this purpose will yield a predicate which applies directly to the religious object, not to the religious person as an experiencing subject.[20] This counts against such theories as "Religion is morality touched with emotion" and "Religion is worship" (without saying anything about what is worshipped) and "Religion is concern with the awe-inspiring," though it counts more against the first than the second and more against the second than the third.

(2) It will not designate a logical subject of basic religious proposals. This counts against "Religion is worship of God," "Religion is obedience to Allah," and "Religion is union with Brahman," if "God" and "Allah" and "Brahman" are being used in a referring way as they are, in fact, ordinarily used.

(3) It will have a reasonably wide range of application, so that no relevant logical subjects are excluded from consideration a priori. The systematic and diagnostic value of any theory depends on adequate generality.

(4) It must permit us to give reasonable interpretations of both ordinary and learned usage, though, if it is to have much systematic and analytical value, it will not conform exactly to all current uses of "religion." Some of these uses indeed conflict with one another.

f. More than one general theory of religion might satisfy these conditions reasonably well. There is no good reason

---

[20] *Any* utterance in its immediate circumstances will *reveal* something about the speaker, some more and some less, depending on the circumstances. So "Jones is honest" will reveal something about the speaker, and so will "The table is brown." But, in the utterance, "honest" applies to Jones, and "brown" applies to the table.

to prescribe a single theory of religion for use in the formulation of explicit religious proposals. In the next chapter I develop another useful theory. But the theory of meaning in religion I am proposing does not depend on this theory of religion, and I shall not confine myself to it. At many points other theories will serve just as well and some may serve even better.

CHAPTER IV

✧✧✧✧✧✧✧✧✧✧✧✧✧✧✧✧✧✧✧✧✧✧✧✧

Another Theory of Religion

✧✧✧✧✧✧✧✧✧✧✧✧✧✧✧✧✧✧✧✧✧✧✧✧

1. *Religious interests*

In this chapter I develop a theory of religion[1] which can be used to throw light on religious predicates and principles of judgment from a different angle. The theory develops from a concept of religious interests.

The formula I shall expand and discuss is: a religious interest is an interest in something more important than anything else in the universe. Something m is more important than something n (for someone M) if (for M) m ranks above n in such a way that it has more weight than n when decisions are made. Then n is being subordinated to m in some way or other, for example, as less potent to more potent, or as less perfect to more perfect, or as part to whole, or as means to end, or as effect to cause, or in some other way. So a religious interest is an interest in something m to which all the other entities in the universe are in principle subordinated.

So, if M is religious, then for M there is something m such that, for any n, m is more important than n. We will permit as possible values of n whatever entities belong to M's universe. And we will mean by "M's universe" the total multiplicity of entities M can think of. Further, we will permit, as a possible value of n, an entity which includes in some way all other entities except m. So we can say both that, for M, m is more important than anything else, and that m is more important than everything else. M takes m as that which is most important[2] in the universe.

---

[1] See "A Definition of Religion," in *The Review of Religion*, 5:412–429 (1941).

[2] "Most important" fails to carry the full force of "more impor-

Then, on this theory, someone is religious if in his universe there in something to which (in principle) all other things are subordinated. Being religious means having an interest of this kind. A belief is a religious belief if it is about something taken in this way. A feeling is a religious feeling if it is a response to something taken in this way. An overt action is a religious action if it is expressive or symptomatic of taking something in this way.[3] Internal actions (decisions, resolutions, commitments) may initiate or reinforce or weaken or terminate interests. So, in addition to taking something as most important in the dispositional sense of "taking," there may be particular acts (overt or internal) in which something is taken as most important. These particular acts may not only express or be symptomatic of M's religious disposition; they may affect it.

A religious community would be a group with common symbols for what is most important and established patterns of action (rituals) in which these symbols are used. But we need not assume that all religious persons belong to religious communities, though most of them do.

An interest of this kind differs from a practical interest and it also differs from an esthetic interest.[4] A practical interest is an interest in the reconstruction of some object or objects of experience. For the purely practical man, who is

tant than everything else in the universe." I shall often use the former for brevity, but it will be misleading unless the reader mentally substitutes for it the longer expression.

[3] Though the intention of the act need not be to express the taking but only to do what the taking requires. If we needed to take account of hypocritical actions, as when the villain purports to be pious to win the hand of the innocent girl, we could say that in these actions the agent purports to take something in this way which he does not in fact take in this way.

[4] The following account of practical and esthetic interests resembles that given by John Macmurray in *The Structure of Religious Experience*, New Haven, Yale University Press, 1936. But my account of religion is of a different sort. He is clearly making a religious proposal and I do not mean to do so.

of course an abstraction, nothing is ever as it should be. Nature is a field of action and its forces are materials for use, whether by the gestures and incantations of a shaman or by the methods of scientific technology. A practical interest functions as a using.

An esthetic interest consists in enjoyment of an object which makes no other claim. The esthetic object as such does not ask the subject of the interest to reconstruct his ends and purposes. It is simply there to be enjoyed as it is and for what it is. The interest involves neither reconstruction of the object nor self-reconstruction of the subject.

In contrast with practical interests, a religious interest does not lead to reconstruction of its object. In contrast with esthetic interests, a religious interest involves a reorientation and a reconstruction of the self. That is to say, all other objects of interests are subordinated (in principle) to the religious object.

A religious interest is more like loyalty to a friend or to one's country, but it differs from a loyalty by having an unlimited scope. Also, a religious interest need not have the emotional tone that "loyalty" connotes. For example, a Buddhist's interest in Nirvana may lack the moral tone of loyalty. So Royce's "loyalty to loyalty" is only one of a number of varieties of religious experience.

Some citations from religious literature may give some concreteness to this abstract exposition.

From a Buddhist psalm:

> "Buddha the Wake, the son of man,/ Self-tamed, by inward vision rapt . . ./ To whom men honour pay as one/ Who hath transcended all we know;/ To whom gods also honour yield:/ . . . So is the Buddha in this world,/ Born in the world and dwelling there,/ But by the world nowise defiled,/ E'en as the lily by the lake."

From the *Tao Té Ching:*

> "Man conforms to the earth;
> The earth conforms to the sky;

The sky conforms to the Way;
The Way conforms to its own nature."

From Augustine in *On Christian Doctrine:*

". . . when the one supreme God of gods is thought of
. . . [men] endeavor to reach the conception of a nature, than which nothing more excellent or more
exalted exists. . . . And so all concur in believing that
God is that which excels in dignity all other objects."

From Gerrard Winstanley in "Truth Lifting up his Head
above Scandals":

"Ques.: But may not a man call him God, till hee have
this experience?
"Ans.: No: For if he doe, he lyes, and there is no truth
in him; for whatsoever rules as King in his flesh, that is
his God."

From J. C. Flugel in *Man, Morals and Society:*

"The religious emotions must be largely or entirely
secularized and be put in the service of humanity. The
religion of humanity is surely the religion of the nearer
future."

I offer these not as adequate support for the theory I am
sketching, but only to show it has some applications. An
argument for its adequacy would have to deal with more
difficult cases like those treated later.

2. *A predicate for religious judgments, and some variables in religion*

The predicate for explicit religious judgments this theory
yields is "more important than everything else in the universe" or, more briefly, "most important." Two points
about this predicate need to be noticed at once.

a. It does not apply to M's feelings nor indeed, speaking
more generally, to M's experience, as if we said, "Religion
is awe." It applies to the object of his interest, to what he

is interested *in*. It does not tell us about some quality of M's response, as "awe" does; it tells us about something *to* which M responds.

So this leaves room for a variety of emotional qualities with which a religious interest might be clothed, varying with different temperaments and cultures. Fear, awe, creature-feeling, serenity, bliss, love, detachment—these are some of a multitude of qualities religious experience might include. There might indeed be some emotional quality that is constant in all religious experience. The theory neither denies this nor supposes this; it leaves the question open.

The emotional intensity as well as quality of a religious interest may vary. It may be faint or intense. Sometimes when we say that M is more religious than N, we mean that M's interest is more intense than N's. At other times we mean that M's religion affects his other interests and his behavior more than N's does. So the effectiveness of a religious interest is another variable.

b. In applying to objects of interests, instead of to the subject, this predicate is like "holy." But notice how "more important" is different from "holy." "*m* is holy" characterizes *m*, and in this way is like "*m* is good" and "*m* is powerful," though unlike them in what it attributes to *m*. In contrast, "*m* is most important" assigns a function, not a character or an attribute, to *m*. Thus the similarity between the objects of M's and N's religious interests is a similarity not in attributes but in functions. For M, God is more important than everything else; for N, Nirvana is more important than everything else.

This leaves room for a variety of attributes of religious objects. The terms "powerful," "holy," "good," "supernatural," "inscrutable," "actual," and "ideal" express some of many such attributes. The theory neither asserts nor denies that all religious objects have some common attribute. Like the question about a common emotional quality, this question is left open also. And this leaves us ready, in our study of human history and psychology, to classify as a religious object (i.e., the object of a religious interest) an entity of any character whatever, so long as it has this function.

This feature of the predicate has an advantage for a theory of religious inquiry. It gives us a formulation which does not rule out a priori any entity whatever as the object of a religious interest. In this way we avoid the logical difficulties which arise, for example, from theories which make belief in God essential to religion. It yields a formula for basic religious questions ("What is most important?") which is logically independent of any particular answer (for example, "God" or "Nature" or "being itself" or "Nirvana"). This makes it possible to see how religious judgments might be genuinely synthetic.

3. *Patterns of subordination*

Now let us notice another sort of variability for which the theory leaves room. There are many patterns of subordination, many ways in which some m or other might be taken as more important than everything else. Religions differ not only in their choices of objects but also in the patterns of subordination they embody.

In world-affirming religions things other than God (or Nature or the Absolute) are given a positive value and sometimes even an intrinsic value. It is not necessary to deny that other things are good, nor even to deny that they are intrinsically good, in order to subordinate them to something m. Natural enjoyments and their objects may be taken as intrinsically good and yet be subordinated to God or to Nature or to the Absolute, being taken as gifts of God, or as modes of Nature, or as manifestations of the Absolute.

In world-denying religions, on the contrary, things other than something m are depreciated; their values are minimized or even negated. So these religions reflect a different pattern of subordination. To exalt m, in religions of this type, it is necessary to reduce other things. The limiting instance would be a religion in which other things were taken as unmixed evils, that is to say, simply rejected. This would be subordination by exclusion.

In some religions things other than *m* are valued only as means to *m* (for example, to heavenly bliss or to Nirvana). But not all religious subordination is teleological.[5] For example, in Stoicism, ancient and modern, particular things are viewed as parts of a whole. In this case the religious life consists not in subordinating things in action, using them as means, but in a contemplative life. Particular things are subordinated to Nature not in the way they are used, but in the way they are seen. The religious life then consists in seeing all other things as parts of a whole.[6]

The subordination involved in a particular religion may be systematic or unsystematic. It is not essential to being religious to have some systematic world view in which things non-*m* are assigned to categoreal types and related to one another and to *m* in accord with general principles of explanation. A particular culture may be relatively deficient in such categories and principles. For example, the subordination of all other things to Jahweh in ancient Hebrew religion is relatively unsystematic, in contrast with the Neoplatonism of Plotinus, which subordinates all other things to the One in a highly systematic way.

A certain minimal reflectiveness is indeed essential to religion. We do not suppose that subhuman animals are religious. There must be a judgment that something *m* is more important than everything else in the universe. But this judgment may be only implicit in the way *m* is actually

[5] It would follow that being religious does not entail having some *sole* end of action.

[6] "We see the world piece by piece, as the sun, the moon, the animal, the tree; but the whole, of which these are the shining parts, is the soul" (Emerson in *The Over-Soul*).

taken. Religious people vary widely in the degree to which they are reflective.

Even if there is a systematic scheme, this need not be a hierarchical scheme, as in Plotinus. It would be possible to think of the transcendence of God, for example, in such a way that things of all categoreal types are equally far from (e.g., unlike) God, instead of thinking that some types of things are by their natures nearer to God than others are. There are various ways of being systematic, in subordinating other things to a religious object. A systematic scheme may or may not be hierarchical.

4. *Problematical cases*

To see further how this theory might be applied, we ought to take some problematical cases, polytheism and intermittent religiosity.

It seems that a polytheist worships more than one thing and that therefore, for a polytheist, there is nothing to which all other things are in principle subordinated. So it seems that a polytheist is not religious. But this is paradoxical, for part of what we mean by saying someone is a polytheist is that he is religious. To deal with this objection we should distinguish different sorts of polytheism.

a. Collective polytheism. If someone worships more than one god at the same time, then the entity he takes as most important is *the gods*. Conceivably this might be a name for a *class* of beings, without any connective ordering relationships among its members, with only the common property of being a god to unite them in a class. Even so, beliefs can be held about them, and they might elicit certain emotions and require certain actions, moral and ceremonial. More usually in polytheistic cultures, "the gods" is not a name for a simple class of beings but for a nexus (Whitehead's term for a group of things with connective relationships among them). Ordinarily the gods are related by ancestry and in other quasi-human ways. They may cooperate or conflict with one another. Also, there may be an economy of functions, assigning to each some sphere of operation. Thus ordinarily what is denoted by "the gods" has a stronger unity than has a class.

b. Serial polytheism. If someone worships only one god at a time, but different gods at different times, then at any one time he takes only one entity as more important than everything else. We would say he is a polytheist when we sum up his religious experiences and activities into what we would ordinarily call "his religion." But any theory of religion has to allow for change in an individual's religion, however desirable it may be to have some unity and continuity throughout the episodes of a personal history.

c. Symbolic polytheism. In worshipping the gods someone may really be worshipping something else—perhaps the quality of divinity (or power or perfection or changelessness) that they all exemplify. Or he may really be worshipping the whole of Nature, whose parts and powers and interconnections the gods personify and symbolize for him. In this event it is simple enough to apply the theory we are considering.

A different problem is posed by intermittent religiosity. Most people are not religious most of the time, if being religious means having an active interest. When we say, "M is a religious man," we do not ordinarily mean that he always feels religious. We mean that religion plays an important part in his life.

We might feel justified in saying someone is always religious, meaning that his interests have a constant structure such that at all times something is more important for him than everything else. And we might maintain this in spite of evidence that at certain times he does not feel religious.

If his character is less constant, we could say there are times when he is religious and times when he is not. We would mean that sometimes his interests have a certain structure, such that something is more important for him than everything else, and at other times they do not. So we should ask how someone might fail to be religious.

5. *On not being religious*

Any good general theory ought to have ways of saying what it means not to be religious. For ordinarily we suppose that not everyone is religious all the time, and we can entertain the possibility that some people are never religious. This theory permits at least four ways in which someone might fail to be religious.

a. Someone might fail to be religious by not having any positive interests. He might be completely bored, thoroughly pervaded by a *taedium vitae.* Everything is trivial. If nothing is important, nothing can be more important than something else, and nothing can be most important.

b. Someone might fail to be religious by failing to be sufficiently discriminating. Suppose that, though some things are important, nothing is more important than something else. (For any *m* and any *n*, it is not the case that *m* is more important than *n*.) Nothing is subordinated to something else. This would be the case either if all objects of positive interests were equally important or if his experience were so unstructured as to give no basis for subordinations. Then he fails to be religious. If nothing is more important than something else, nothing can be more important than everything else.

c. Someone might fail to be religious in neither of the above ways which, as a matter of fact, describe relatively implausible cases. Let us say he has some strong positive interests. And he is discriminating, so that some things are more important than some other things. Then some of his interests are subordinated to others, which is to say that some objects are subordinated to others. He has several main interests, centered, for example, in his family, his profession, some artistic activity, and some political activity. But nothing is more important than everything else. (It is not the case that there is something m such that, for any n, m is more important than n.) This is so, let us say, because no suggestion to the contrary has arisen. He has not really considered the possibility that something is most important.

Then in this case he fails to be religious by failing to be reflective. The reason such a suggestion has not occurred to him in an effective way may lie in the character of his society. Its religious institutions may be weak and ineffective.[7] Or the reason may lie in his own constitution and in the course of his own experiences. Life seems less problematical for some people than for others. Perhaps he has not had to reflect much on his values and purposes.

d. But suppose some such suggestion has arisen for him, which in our own society is very likely to be the case. He has some strong positive interests, and he is discriminating, and he has considered whether there might be something more important than anything else (though he may not have put it in these words). Yet he does not accept this suggestion. He decides that there is in fact nothing in the universe which is in any way more important than everything else. Then he would deliberately fail to be religious; he would be deliberately adopting a nonreligious way of life. He would be adopting a policy of not putting anything before everything else.

In his view some things are more important than other things, and in this or that situation something m might be more important than the other things he finds involved in that situation. But always there are other things outside the situation over which m is not ranked in importance. At no time does he take something to be more important than everything else, unless he does so in spite of his resolution.

In these ways we might interpret and explain "M is not

[7] This could not be the whole story. Sometimes people come to be religious more or less independently of the religious institutions of their society.

religious." Other general theories would interpret this in other ways. For example, on a theory which construed "being religious" as believing some propostion p, not being religious would consist in not believing p. Analogously, if being religious is construed as having a feeling of a certain sort, or performing an action of a certain sort, then not being religious would mean not having such feelings or not performing such actions.

6. *Some uses of this theory*

A theory ought to be judged with a view to the ways in which it can be used. This theory would not be immediately useful for sociological analysis, though a certain theory of religious institutions can be derived from it, as suggested above. Nor would it be immediately useful in those psychological investigations which require more explicitly behavioral concepts. But it might be useful in the construction of devices for ascertaining attitudes. For this purpose it may have some advantage over other theories of religion.

In the next section I shall discuss its relevance to a theory of religious inquiry. But first let us consider how it might be used to interpret some concepts commonly associated with religion.

It is often implicitly assumed, and sometimes (as by Marx and Freud) explicitly stipulated, that religion always includes belief in something supernatural. But we encounter cases where we are inclined to say that M is religious even though we are doubtful whether he has any supernatural beliefs at all, for example, Theravada Buddhism, Spinoza, and Einstein.

The theory we have been considering can help us at this point. The something m to which (for someone M) all other things are subordinate is, by virtue of this very fact, of a different order from these other things. It is not only unique but extraordinary. It differs from all other things in a special way, and in this sense it might be said to be transcendent.[8] Now this relation between something m and other things has some similarity to the relation between a supernatural being (as ordinarily understood) and natural things. So we can see why we might be tempted to make belief in a supernatural being a necessary condition of anyone's being religious. At the same time we can see how we do not need to do this. We can take account of supernaturalistic varieties of religion, i.e., cases where the religious object is thought of not only as most important but, say, as being a person and having power to cause miracles. And we can also take account of nonsupernaturalistic varieties of religion. We can do justice to religious beliefs generally, without saying that the object of a religious belief is always a supernatural being.

Again, we can use this theory to interpret the role of worship in religion. In worship something is being taken as most important. But we could leave room for religious experiences and actions—for example, Zen Buddhist meditation—which do not amount to worshipping in the ordinary sense. For ordinarily "worship" is closely linked with "God" or "gods." So while we could give an interpretation of worshipping we would not need to say that anyone who does not worship is not religious.

Also, we can use this theory to interpret other theories of religion, for example, Rudolf Otto's theory. If something is taken as most important we can easily see how holiness, in Otto's sense, might be one of its attributes. It might be thought of as apart from all else, as The Other, and so on. Certainly many religious experiences involve numinous feelings. But we could avoid saying that all the components of numinous feeling, including feelings of self-abasement, are always characteristic of religious experience. Indeed, it

[8] On this theory there would be as many modes of transcendence as there are different patterns of subordination, some of which were mentioned above.

is not clear that they are true of all the forms of religion Otto mentions.

In such ways any theory should try to do justice both to the unsystematic meanings embodied in unsophisticated speech, and to the truths embodied in other theories of religious phenomena.

7. *An interpretation of inquiry*

This theory yields a predicate which can be used, along with comparable predicates derived from other theories, in formulating basic religious questions and proposals. "What is it that is most important?" would be a basic religious question. And a basic religious proposal in answer to this question would have the form, "*m* is most important."

I am not arguing that religious questions and proposals must be phrased in this way. Instead, I am suggesting that this theory can be useful in the *interpretation* of religious discourse. It might be used (*a*) to detect and state latent disagreements and (*b*) to formulate principles of judgment.

a. Let us take a hypothetical case. Suppose we read a Jewish prayer book and find it saying that God is "King of the Universe." And we read a Mahayana Buddhist scripture which speaks of Nirvana as the "True State." Now suppose it strikes us, as we examine these writings further, that some disagreement or other is involved in the different ways of life they express. But we find it difficult to express this disagreement by means of such phrases as those I have mentioned.

The reason is that the predicates are not interchangeable. It would not do to say either that God is, or that God is not, the True State. And it would not do to say either that Nirvana is, or that it is not, the King of the Universe. Neither of the predicates seems to *fit* the other logical subject. So the assertions do not meet head on; they miss and pass by one another. Yet some disagreement or other seems to lurk beneath the surface of what is being said. The concepts seem to overlap, and contrary assertions seem to be implied, but we do not know how.

The only way we can deal with this puzzling fact is to see what these predicates might mean, and in particular to see whether their meanings have some common element. If so, we could use the common element to construct propositions expressing an explicit disagreement. So we can ask whether part of what is meant by saying that something is the King of the Universe is that it is more important than everything else in the universe, and whether part of what is meant by saying that something is the True State is that it is more important than everything else in the universe. We would have to find this out by analyzing Jewish and Buddhist literature, by asking questions of Jews and Buddhists, and perhaps in other ways. Then, if we find that the concepts overlap in this way, we could express the latent disagreement as follows:

A. God is most important. / B. Nirvana is most important.

Then we could stay that *one* of the functions of "God is the King of the Universe" is to answer the question, "What is it that is most important?" and that *one* of the functions of "Nirvana is the True State" is to answer this question. But we would not be proposing to Jews that they adopt A as a Jewish doctrine, and we would not be proposing to Buddhists that they adopt B as a Buddhist doctrine, though they would be free to do so. We would be using these formulations in an analytical way.

If we are not successful by using this theory, we might try some other theory. For in a given case some predicates will be more useful for analysis than others. But suppose we are not able to produce any analysis of this sort. Then we would conclude either (1) that the assertions we began with in the Jewish prayer book and the Buddhist scripture make compatible (perhaps even complementary), not conflicting, truth-claims, *or* (2) that at least one of them does not make a truth-claim at all.

b. Now let us see how we could formulate rules of relevance and other principles of judgment in the frame of this predicate. Suppose we are asking, "What is it that is most important?" *Rules of relevance* might include:

(1) Consider those things which, speaking generally, have to be taken account of in life. This would exclude anything which, for the conduct of life, is negligible, if there is anything of this sort.

(2) Consider especially those things which have to be taken account of more than others. Many suggestions might occur, and some of these suggestions might point to something extraordinarily important. (We shall consider religious suggestions in Chapter VI.)

Then we would need some *procedure for judgment,* and this might be put as follows: Compare the most promising candidate (X) with other promising candidates. Is X more important than Y? Generally speaking, in the conduct of life does X have to be taken account of more than Y? Is it such that I have to give it more weight in making decisions, generally speaking? Continue in this way for all promising candidates. The final issue for judgment is, Is X more important than everything else?

In making and supporting judgments on this issue we would have to use *norms of judgment.* At least some of these norms would not be self-evident, but would be open to objections and in need of support. Such norms as the following might be offered as guides to judgment:

(1) Something that is actual (has power to effect change) is more important than a concept or imaginary counterpart of that thing.
This would count against something that existed only in imagination, or only as an ideal.

(2) The more powerful something is the more important it is.

(3) A source of all values (good things) would be more important than any particular value.

(4) A source of all values would be more important than the sum of values at a particular time.

Other norms could be offered and argued for as alternatives to these or in addition to these. I mention these only by way of illustration.

8. *"Is religion important?"*

Finally, for the sake of showing some things this theory does *not* say, let us distinguish three different propositions:

A. A religious interest is an interest in something taken as most important.

B. Religion is important.

C. It is important to be religious.

Then A, which states the theory we have been discussing, does not entail either B or C.

B says that religion has consequences of which we need to take account. For example, politicians had better take account of the church membership of their constituents; historians had better take account of the influence of religious institutions and individuals; psychiatrists had better take account of the religious beliefs and feelings of their patients; and I had better take account of my neighbor's religion. In general, M ought to take account of such facts as "N is religious."

Though B is true, on the whole, it does not necessarily follow from the theory we have been discussing. For it would be self-consistent to say that, while people do take something or other as most important, this is not an important fact about them. Indeed, this would be *true* if religious interests were relatively ineffective. And on this theory the effectiveness of religious interests is a variable.

C says that people ought to be religious. And this is quite a different proposition from either A or B. A tells us what religious interests consist in, but does not say whether they are effective (and hence important), or whether it is good to have them. B tells us that religious interests are effective, without telling us that they or their effects are good. C says it is good to be religious, that it is better to be religious than not to be. Now if A does not entail B, it seems clear that A does not entail C either.

C does not say what sort of religion people ought to have. It gives no answer to a basic religious question. So it is a moral proposal, not a religious proposal. Similarly, "It is important to have esthetic sensibility" would be a moral proposal. It calls for a moral judgment, not an esthetic judgment.

CHAPTER V

Religious Inquiry:
Basic Questions and Suppositions

1. *Curiosity and inquiry*

The object of this chapter and the next is not to give directions for answering religious questions, nor to give a genetic account of how religious beliefs are acquired. (Ordinarily religious beliefs are acquired through nurture in some particular religious community.) Instead, the object is to outline the logical structure of religious inquiry and to analyze the logical conditions involved in asking and answering religious questions. Incidentally we shall notice some structural analogies and contrasts with inquiries of other types.

A responsible proposal for belief is the result of inquiry. The proponent has seriously asked some question, more or less explicitly. He has found an answer, fortunately or ingeniously. And he thinks there are sufficient reasons for accepting it, which he can explain more or less well. Now he is placing the result of his inquiry in the public domain. So we ought to consider some general points about inquiry and their bearing on religious inquiry.

A sustained inquiry has a certain focus. A number of questions are interconnected and have some common central *point*. They are not isolated "spot questions"; they belong to a larger enterprise. This means that we begin an inquiry with a specific interest. Something has not only awakened but directed our curiosity.

Our curiosity may be disinterested or *pure*, in a moral sense of "pure." We may be genuinely interested in finding out what is true, wanting not to deceive ourselves and wanting to know more and understand better than we do. But an interest in truth does not of itself determine any particular subject matter of inquiry.

This (morally) pure curiosity need not be *idle* curiosity. Idle curiosity is a relatively passive attitude in which we are ready to notice almost any object that turns up and entertain almost any proposition that occurs to us. We have no active purposes; we are not seriously following up suggestions. But idle curiosity may turn into something more.

When we ask a philosophical question or a scientific question or a moral question or a religious question, we have been struck by some tangle of ideas that needs to be unraveled, some suspected regularity in nature that needs to be confirmed and stated with precision, some alternative in conduct that needs to be decided, or some claim for worship that needs to be weighed and judged. Our attention has been caught by some feature of the world which intrigues us and calls for sustained and systematic thought. Any serious interest in knowledge is something more than idle curiosity. So, to understand a certain judgment, we need to understand the sort of interest that prompts the question which the judgment decides. To understand religious judgments we need to understand religious interests.

Along with the specific interest which prompts an inquiry we may have a *general* curiosity. A physicist may have, along with his interest in the structure of atoms, a disposition to become interested in other problems as well, for example, the moral problems posed by nuclear weapons. But just as his scientific thinking is prompted by something more specific than general curiosity, so also is his moral thought. When we ask some particular question in a persistent way, we have geared our curiosity to a certain interest and it is now neither idle nor general, though it may be (relatively) pure.

It follows that religious inquiry cannot go on without a religious interest, any more than scientific inquiry can go on without a scientific interest, or moral inquiry without a moral interest. Of course there can be inquiry about religion (phenomenological or historical or philosophical inquiry) without a religious interest, just as much as (though no more than) there can be inquiry about science (historical or philosophical inquiry) without a scientific interest, or inquiry about morals without a moral interest. Having an interest in religion is different from having a religious interest.

Religious inquiry means asking religious questions seriously, just as moral inquiry means asking moral questions seriously. A serious discussion of what we ought to do about racial segregation or hydrogen bombs means that we are ready to do what we ought. So also a serious discussion of religious questions (not questions *about* religion) means that we are already religious, even if only incipiently and without full consciousness of the fact.

Inquiry is compatible with geniune convictions in morality or in science or in religion. We can be convinced that something is true and also be ready to reformulate the belief or give it up if necessary. The requirement is not that every formulation of belief must be actively doubted, but only that the believer be *ready* to revise any formulation *if* the facts, or logic, should turn out to count against it. This would not rule out genuine conviction but only a compulsive attachment to beliefs.

Let us take an analogous case. It is not necessary that a working physicist should actively doubt whether, say, Newton's laws of motion are accurate descriptions of functions of macroscopic bodies. It *is* necessary that he be ready to question this if some good reason for doing so should turn up. Again, to have a reflective morality we do not need to doubt all the moral precepts we have been taught. We do need to be ready to question any particular precept if, for example, obeying it should lead to some moral absurdity.

So this requirement is not that at no time shall we believe anything without questioning it. This is a weaker requirement. It would not ask gratuitous doubting but only a readiness to question beliefs.

2. *Basic religious questions*

Let us begin with the doctrinal schemes we find in various religions. These schemes are stated formally in the didactic parts of sacred scriptures, in creeds, records of dogmatic decisions, theological treatises, and in other places. They are stated informally in liturgies, prayer books, hymns, codes of religious laws of conduct, manuals of devotion, and in sermons and other sayings of holy men and teachers. And they are symbolically expressed in narrations of sacred stories, in enactions of rituals, and in many forms of art, architecture, music, and imaginative literature.

Now suppose we want to understand some such scheme, for example, that of ancient Egyptian religion or of Judaism or Christian Science or Comte's religion of Humanity. Then we might go about this in the following way: We could study the uses of important terms, for example, "Ra," "Torah," "mind," and "Humanity," in the scheme. This would lead us to investigate the internal logic of the scheme, to see how these terms are used in relation to one another and how various statements are interconnected. All along we would keep in mind the historical situation, we would be sensitive to various styles of expression, and we would look for underlying themes.

Beyond all this we would try to understand the enterprise in which these teachers and prophets are engaged, to see the point of the scheme they have produced, and what on the whole it asserts. So we would try to find some question to which the scheme as a whole could justly be taken as an answer (whether or not we think it is a good answer). This would be important also for understanding the terms and relations which make up its internal structure.

Now one reason we turned to general theories of religion

was to frame questions of this sort, questions to which various doctrinal schemes, epitomized in basic religious proposals, might be taken as relevant answers. Such questions would be of the form, "What is it that is——?" Filling in the blank with an appropriate predicate expression, we would have a basic religious question, for example, "What is it that is worshipful?" or "What is it on which we are absolutely dependent?" or "What is it that is holy?" If we substituted the letter P for the blank, "What is it that is P?" would be our formula for basic religious questions. These questions call for designation of some logical subject of which the predicate is true.

Clearly not all religious questions are like this. Indeed, most questions in ordinary religious discourse are not of this form. Let us consider two other sorts of questions and see how they are related to basic questions. These are: (a) religious questions about conduct (practical questions) and (b) religious questions about doctrine (doctrinal questions).

a. Religious questions about conduct have the form, "Taking account of s (for example, the will of God, the dictates of Humanity, the tradition of the church, the example of Gotama) what should I do about d (for example, making a pilgrimage, offering a sacrifice, choosing a profession)?" Such questions are not themselves basic, because they presuppose some answer to a basic question, in the following way: The standard (s) which is taken account of contains, explicitly or implicitly, some answer to a question of the form, "What is it that is P?" It is their reference to a standard of this sort which differentiates religious questions about conduct from nonreligious ones.

If the practical question involves a reference to some institutional authority like the tradition of the church, we look for the (presupposed) answer to the basic question by asking for the ground for the authority of the institution. If it involves some more autonomous principle of action, we ask for the ground for this principle. In some such way some answer to a basic religious question is presupposed in any religious question about conduct.

b. Doctrinal questions also are different from basic religious questions. The following are typical questions about doctrine: "Is the self annihilated in Nirvana?" "Is the Koran literally inerrant?" "Is God good? intelligent? personal?"

Questions of this form but quite different in intention may be asked not from a religious interest but from a historical or psychological interest. A historian or a psychologist may be interested in what Gotama taught and what Buddhists believe. Then the real question is not whether the self is annihilated in Nirvana but only whether Gotama taught this and whether Buddhists believe this. This would be a nonreligious question about doctrine.

Religious questions about doctrine ask about the attributes or characteristics of some religious object, or about its relation to other things. So there can be questions about the physical world, about historical events, and about human personality. What makes them religious is that they relate these topics to something taken as, for example, worshipful or holy or awe-inspiring.

Religious questions about doctrine can be marked off from nonreligious ones in another way. In any religion there are norms for deciding doctrinal questions, for example, sacred scriptures, tradition, the teaching of some magisterium, revelatory events in history, and the testimony of mystical experience. A doctrinal question is religious when it presupposes or mentions some religious norm of judgment. For example, "What is the nature of the soul?" would be a religious question if some addition like "according to the Bible" or "in view of the Inward Light" is being tacitly understood *and* if the Bible or the Inward Light is being taken as a norm of religious judgment. Explanation of the norm would have to include a reference to what is worshipped or aspired to in that religion.

So in one way or another a religious question about doctrine involves a reference to something which functions as a religious object for the questioner, this reference being involved either in the content of the question or in the ground for the answer. In these ways religious questions about doctrine presuppose answers to basic religious questions.

Doctrinal questions which presuppose that "God" is the answer to the basic question may be called theological questions. These are questions treated in systematic theology. By stretching the term we could speak of all doctrinal questions as theological questions. But this would do violence both to the etymology and the ordinary range of "theology." Perhaps we should be content to take theology as the systematic study of doctrine within some theistic religious community, so that theological questions belong to a larger class of questions, namely, religious questions about doctrine.

Almost any question might have a *bearing* on some religious question or other. For example, a scientific question like, "Do biological species evolve?" might have a religious import for Christians, though for Hindus it might have no religious import whatever. But even when it takes on religious import, it is not a religious question. The interest which determines its context and principles of judgment is a scientific interest, not a religious interest.

To sum up, religious questions are of different types, some questions presuppose answers to others, and some questions are such that questions of all other types presuppose answers to them, and are in this way basic or fundamental to religious inquiry. These are the questions we are mainly concerned to study.

3. *Basic suppositions*

It might be objected that the logically basic questions are not of the form, "What is it that is *P?*" but, instead, of the form, "Is there anything that is *P?*" For questions of the first form suppose there is something to which *P* truly applies. But this might not be so. Therefore, according to this objection, in religious inquiry we must begin without any basic supposition. We would ask first of all not, "What is it that is holy?" for example, but, instead, "*Is* there anything at all that is holy?"

This is a fair objection, for questions of this form have a certain significance. But they may or may not be real questions. An utterance may or may not express something the asker really wants to know. For example, it may be a rhetorical question. Whether it is a real question depends on the interest which prompts it.

Suppose a question of this form should be asked out of idle curiosity. It would have to be answered by a survey of the various items the world contains, including natural objects, human individuals and groups, supernatural objects, if any, and the various moments and features of experience. Perhaps nothing P will be found in this survey. What began as idle curiosity would end as such.

But suppose that in this idly curious survey of experience someone begins to sense that something or other is P. We would have to say that a religious interest has been discovered, or that one has been awakened. Perhaps (*a*) he has discovered something about himself that has been true all along. He has been religious without being aware of it. Or perhaps (*b*) he has become religious for the first time. In the former case, since he was religious already, the idly curious question was not the real question for him. In either case idle curiosity now turns into a serious inquiry. Now the real question is, What is it of which P is true?

So it is important to know whether "Is there anything that is P?" is being asked out of idle curiosity. Could the asker say not only, "For all I know there isn't any such thing," but also, "For all I care there isn't any such thing"? Does he care whether or not he finds an answer? If he cares, his caring is a religious interest and this is not the real question for him to ask, for if he has a religious interest he already supposes there is something of which P is true.

Someone might ask, "*Do* I have any rights and duties?" So we try to explain "rights and duties" by speaking of obligations, responsibilities, ideals, and moral aims. Now suppose he stubbornly—it may seem—fails to see the point of these concepts. So our explanations do not answer his question. We might conclude that either he is devoid of moral concern or has some moral concern without realizing it. So we could answer his question only indirectly, by introducing him to real situations where moral concepts are relevant, hoping either to bring his latent moral concern to consciousness or to induce one in him.

Or someone might ask, "*Are* there any precisely describable uniformities in nature?" Suppose that neither a phenomenalistic interpretation of "nature" nor inductive arguments for specific scientific laws succeed in answering his question. Then we can deal with it only indirectly, by introducing live situations where scientific concepts are relevant, in hope of eliciting a scientific interest.

Like these questions about morality and science, a question of the form, "Is there anything that is P?" is a limiting question. It is in *this* way that it is significant. It could be answered only indirectly, by evoking the relevant sort of interest in the one who asks it.

It follows that in serious religious inquiry there is an implicit supposition of the form, "There is something which is P." Whenever we are engaged in this way, we have been led by experience [1] to suppose there is something or other that is worshipful (*or* awe-inspiring, *or* holy, et cetera) and, proceeding on this supposition, we want to find out just what this is. Let us call these suppositions "basic religious suppositions."

In moral inquiry and in scientific inquiry analogous sup-

[1] For example, by numinous events, or by a sense of radical contingency, or by a sense of the possibility of a general ordering of life, or by some other intimation.

positions are made, as the instances above suggest. Anyone who is seriously asking a moral question has a moral interest, and in having this interest he is making some supposition, for example, that he has some duties and rights. Likewise anyone seriously asking a scientific question has a scientific interest, and in having this interest he is making some supposition, for example, that there are some uniformities in nature which can be exactly described. He has been led by experience to suppose that this is the case.

Thus the question, "Do Newton's laws express exactly and comprehensively some uniformities of nature?" has point by virtue of its supposition of natural uniformities, a concept which is logically prior to the concept of Newton's laws. Analogously, basic religious suppositions make religious questions possible.

A basic supposition in some inquiry does not function as a theory in that inquiry. A basic scientific supposition is not a scientific theory, and a basic religious supposition is not a religious theory.[2] Supposing that there is a supreme goal of life does not tell us what the supreme goal of life might be. Also, a basic supposition does not function as a conclusion, or as a preconclusion. It does not embody a fact which would support some one theory more than another. So basic suppositions are not substitutes for theories or for facts.

Most of the time we do not make our basic suppositions explicit. Nor, ordinarily, do we need to do so. But some such supposition is implicit in any basic question, and if the supposition were denied, the question would lose its point. In this way a basic supposition underlies the whole process

[2] So a basic supposition in science is different from, for example, the "supposition" that there is a monster in Loch Ness, and also different from the "supposition" that the radio-carbon content of the atmosphere in some past age was about the same as it is now. These are theories, which may or may not be assumed.

We shall consider theory construction in religion in the next chapter.

of thought by which theories are constructed and conclusions are reached. In calling attention to basic suppositions I am making a logical remark.

4. *Open commitments*

A sustained inquiry involves a basic commitment as well as a basic supposition. In speaking of these commitments I do not mean dramatic resolutions or promises sworn with furrowed brows. I am calling attention to a certain feature of the process of inquiring, in moral, scientific, artistic, and other inquiries, as well as in religious inquiry. Any inquiry makes its own demands, and a serious interest commits the inquirer to meeting those demands. For example, it would be absurd if someone said he had a strong scientific interest and yet, though he had opportunities to undertake scientific investigation, never did so. We make some commitment or other whenever idle curiosity turns into something more. When we inquire we are committed to finding the relevant facts, constructing theories, and treating as true whatever we may find to be true.

Let us notice one feature of commitments generally, including commitments in inquiry. A commitment may be relatively "open" in the sense that what we are committed to is incompletely specified. For example, we put ourselves in the hands of a doctor, or embark on the elaboration of a mathematical theory, or begin a sonnet, or set up an experiment in a laboratory, without knowing perfectly well what we are involved in. Indeed, it might be argued that most of our commitments are to some extent open. Their objects are incompletely specified. Often we do not know clearly and completely just what it is to which we are committing ourselves.

The open commitments we are concerned with occur in the initial stage, logically speaking, of an inquiry. In a religious inquiry this initial open commitment is to a serious search for what P is true of, and to taking as P what P is true of, whatever that may be. This is the natural complement of a basic supposition. Along with the supposition that there is something P is true of, there is a commitment to acting toward this, whatever it may turn out to be, in an appropriate way.

Analogous open commitments are implicit in other inquiries, and the character of the commitment varies with the interest that prompts the inquiry. In a moral inquiry the commitment is, for example, to doing what is right, whatever that may turn out to be. In a scientific inquiry the commitment is, for example, to faithfully and exactly describing uniformities in nature, whatever they may turn out to be.

The psychological function of these commitments is important. They are our only good defense against dogmatism. When we have made heavy investments in a theory which begins to incur our suspicions, we are tempted to repress our suspicions. We throw off such temptations by renewing our basic orientations, by reminding ourselves of the basic questions, suppositions, and commitments of our inquiry. Only if we understand ourselves in this way can we psychologically afford to question our own conclusions.

It can happen that disillusionment with the theory which guides a particular project may lead us to stop being scientists or artists or religious believers at all. I argue only that this need not be so. Disillusionment with a particular moral precept need not result in disillusionment with morality altogether. Disillusionment with a particular scientific theory need not result in disillusionment with science altogether. This is so because open commitments may operate in these domains. This is true also in religion. Somewhat as a scientist can remind himself, when a suggestion has led him astray, "What I am really after is the uniformities in this bit of nature, whatever they are," a religious inquirer might remind himself that what he is really after is what is holy, whatever that may be.

5. *The beginning of inquiry: a case in point*

Let us consider an instance which illustrates some of the points I have made about the logical beginnings of religious inquiry. Spinoza begins his *Treatise on the Improvement of the Understanding* in the following way:

> "After experience taught me that all those things which occur frequently in ordinary life are empty and futile . . . I finally decided to inquire whether something might be found (*daretur*) which would be a real good, and capable of communicating itself, and by which alone the mind might be affected, all other things being put aside (*rejectis*), whether, indeed, something might be found by which, having discovered and acquired it, I might enjoy continual and supreme happiness forever (*in aeternum*). I say, "I finally decided," because at first sight it seemed unwise to be willing to give up something certain for the sake of something which was at that time uncertain. I saw, without doubting, the advantages which are acquired from honor and riches, and that I would be forced to abstain from seeking these, if I wished to give earnest effort (*seriam . . . operam dare*) to something different and new." (*Opera*, Gebhardt ed., ii, 5)

Whether or not we want to call this a religious experience, it resembles religious experiences closely enough to illustrate some of their features. The points I call attention to are: (*a*) the fact that Spinoza begins with a specific interest, with something more than general curiosity and a great deal more than idle curiosity; (*b*) the presence in his mind of a basic question determined by this interest; and (*c*) the basic supposition and the open commitment which are implicit in his decision to inquire.

a. It would be too simple to say that the interest with which Spinoza begins is an interest in happiness, though this would be true as far as it goes. For the interest he has now is conditioned by a certain disillusionment or frustration. He has found that ordinary things, if taken as ends in themselves, are "empty and futile." So his interest has a sharper focus than a simpler and more innocent interest in happiness might have. He is interested now in something which would be a real good, a sharable good, and a good sufficient in itself. This would be the highest good.

b. So he must look for something to which this predicate truly applies. What is it that is "a real good, and capable of communicating itself . . ."? Suggestions are then in order. Is it God, as traditionally conceived? We know that Spinoza rejected this suggestion and adopted another. He came to think it is "knowledge of the union which the mind has with the whole of nature" (*ibid.*, 8), which he explains at length in the *Ethics*. But that would take us beyond the initial stage of his inquiry.

c. He says he decided to give earnest effort, to seriously devote himself, to the search for something different and new. This again is much more than curiosity. His decision was made with awareness of the risk he was running. When he made this final resolution to inquire (*inquirere*), he had come to see that it would be worth losing honor and riches to attain such a good. But he not only did not know *what* it is that is "a real good. . . ." (This is the object of his inquiry.) He also did not know whether he himself could attain some such good.[3] Yet *in spite of* this uncertainty he had begun to seek (*quaerebam*) it, not to ask *whether* any such good exists or not but to inquire *what* it is, abandoning the quest for honor and riches. Implicit in this decision, I suggest, is a supposition that some such real good does exist. And with the decision goes an implicit open commitment to that, whatever it may be, to which the predicate "real good . . ." truly applies. For he sees clearly that he cannot

[3] *incerto, non quidem sua natura (fixum enim bonum quaerebam), sed tantum quoad ipsius consecutionem (ibid., 6).*

both retain his earlier valuations and at the same time gird himself for a new principle of life (*ad novum institutum accingerer*).

In these ways Spinoza's experience [4] illustrates how a fundamental inquiry begins with a certain interest, which prompts a basic question and involves a basic supposition and an open commitment. This is true of religious inquiry no less than of inquiries of other types. And in a religious inquiry, as in any other, we may be more or less clearly aware of what we are doing.

[4] I do not say, "Spinoza's theory of knowledge." It is not clear to me that his theory of knowledge yields an adequate interpretation of his own experience.

CHAPTER VI

Religious Inquiry:
Suggestions and Explication

1. *Some examples of suggestions*

To introduce the role of suggestions in religious inquiry let us consider the following cases:

In *A Preface to Morals* [1] Walter Lippmann argued that traditional religious beliefs had been dissolved by the "acids of modernity" and were no longer live options. Those beliefs had served our civilization as a "preface to morals," and now some other preface to morals was required. So Lippmann proposed a view which he spoke of as "high religion," though his more specific term for it was "humanism." He says, "To replace the conception of man as the subject of a heavenly king, . . . humanism takes as its dominant pattern the progress of the individual from helpless infancy to self-governing maturity" (175).

Let us notice three points about this passage and its relation to Lippmann's proposal for a preface to morals: (*a*) It reports the rejection of one suggestion and the adoption of another. Now if the two suggestions are genuine alternatives, if one can logically replace the other, then there is some common question to which they give alternative answers. (*b*) These alternative suggestions are put not as propositions but as images. "The progress of the individual from helpless infancy to self-governing maturity" and "man as the subject of a heavenly king" are substantive phrases. Each evokes a set of memories, emotions, and ideals, all compressed into the form of a generalized image. (*c*) In his book Lippmann proceeds to explain, in various ways, how the main theses of "high religion" may be drawn from

[1] New York, Macmillan, 1929.

this "dominant pattern." He proceeds, I shall say, to explicate the suggestion he has adopted.

The next example is taken from an autobiographical essay by the novelist Ellen Glasgow.[2] She tells of her search for a faith, "or at least for a stable conviction," having rejected her father's God on account of the problem of evil. She was attracted by Jesus and by Buddha, but repelled by the "parasitic growths of human greed, stupidity, and ignorance" in the religions which sprang from them. Turning to mysticism, she read the Gita, Plotinus, Pascal, and Böhme. She says:

> "I remember an August afternoon high up in the Alps, when I persuaded myself that I had felt, if only for an infinitesimal point of time, that inward light which shone for Jakob Böhme when he looked through it into 'the essences' of the waving grass and herbs on the hillside. For an instant only this light shone; then it passed on with the wind in the grass; and I was never, in all the years that came afterwards, to know it again. The world and the time spirit together bore down on me. In the end, I recalled that moment of vision merely as a lost endeavor to escape from physical boundaries" (100).

Then later she says:

> "It is true, nevertheless, that even in my efforts and my failures, in my belief and my skepticism, I had arrived at the basis of what I may call a determining point of view, if not a philosophy. In my endless curiosity about life, I had fallen by a happy accident (how else could this occur in my special environment?) upon a strayed copy of *The Origin of Species;* and this single book had led me back, through biology, to the older philosophic theory of evolution. The Darwinian hypothesis

[2] In *I Believe*, C. Fadiman, ed., New York, Simon and Schuster, 1939.

did not especially concern me, nor was I greatly interested in the scientific question of its survival. . . . What did interest me, supremely, was the broader synthesis of implications and inferences. On this foundation of probability, if not of certainty, I have found—or so it still seems to me—a permanent resting place; and in the many years that have come and gone, I have seen no reason, by and large, to reject this cornerstone of my creed.

"All this, precipitate as it appears in print, was by no means within the nature of a revelation, though it is true that my discovery of the vast province of ideas was not without the startled wonder, and the eager awakening, of a religious conversion" (101–102).

Three questions might be asked:

a. How was it that the mystical experience in the Alps had no lasting importance for her? One way of putting the answer is to say that this experience did not convey to her an effective suggestion. It did not convey a starting point for thought; it lacked illuminative power. In particular it failed to throw light on the spatio-temporal structure of her life. As a result she "recalled that moment of vision merely as a lost endeavor to escape from physical boundaries." So the experience became an *interpretandum*, not an *interpretans*. It did not yield concepts that were powerful enough to do what needed to be done.

b. What was the "basis of . . . a determining point of view" at which she finally arrived? What suggestion did she get through reading Darwin's book? It was not the biological theory itself which satisfied her concern for a "stable conviction." Darwin's theory was only the vehicle of the suggestion she adopted. "What did interest me, supremely, was the broader synthesis of implications and inferences." This was, perhaps, a vision of cosmic evolution as a dynamic process subject to natural necessities. Perhaps Spinoza would have had a good deal to say to her.

c. How did this interest her? What function did this suggestion have for her? She came upon it with "the startled wonder, and the eager awakening, of a religious conversion." It gave her "a determining point of view," "a permanent resting place," the "cornerstone" of a "creed." That is why this suggestion interested her "supremely."

For a third example of the part suggestions play in inquiry I refer to Augustine's treatment of the opening verses of the book of Genesis. In his commentaries on Genesis, in his *Confessions,* in *The City of God,* and elsewhere he dwells on these verses, especially on the first verse, "In the beginning God created heaven and earth."

He adduces this passage in discussions of many different topics: the Stoic theory of time, the Neoplatonic view of the soul, the origination of new forms of life in the course of time, the Trinity, the importance of historical events, and others. His use of it is not to give a final answer to the question at hand. Rather he draws from it new suggestions, which put both the question and familiar answers in a new light. Pondering on these verses, he begins to see distinctions he had not thought of, and new ways of doing justice to the facts.

The conclusions he comes to are not simply deduced from the passage. Between the passage and his conclusions there comes a process of imagination and conception. The passage suggests themes and categories which then have to be thought out and applied. It is as though the meaning of the passage comes tightly knotted and has to be unloosed, or, like a piece of cut glass, refracts the light and sends it in unexpected directions.

Now, turning from these examples of suggestions, let us ask why suggestions are needed, how they occur, how they are adopted, and how they are explicated.

2. *Why suggestions are needed*

Some questions can be answered directly and simply, for example: "What is the product of 11 and 12?" "What is

Armstrong's telephone number?" and "Who is the tallest person in the room?" There are clear and sufficient rules for answering these and many other questions. We follow the rules and we find the answers. A procedure for judgment is all we need.

Other questions cannot be answered so simply and directly. The available rules are less explicit and complete, for example, when we ask who committed the murder, what is the cause of some strange disease, what is the best way to get to the top of the mountain, whether Baker would make a good doctor or a good teacher, what gives a particular novel its unity and strength, or how to develop the next movement of a quartet. In these cases we do not see our way straight to the answers. We have to puzzle them out.

Answers to these questions do not come all at once, at least not usually. We find clues, we follow up indications, we explore possibilities, we try out combinations. Before we get an answer we go through a stage where we adopt and explore suggestions.

It is true that sometimes religious questions are answered in a simpler way. Clear rules are found at hand, such as, "Ask your father" and "Ask the priest," which lead directly to answers explicitly stated as propositions. But many religious questions cannot be answered by appeals to procedural rules. In many perplexities no such rules are available; the problem is not how to deduce a conclusion from clearly formulated premisses but how to formulate the premisses.

Such questions must be answered by beginning with non-propositional suggestions, by making decisions between alternative suggestions, and by working out suggested meanings. And all this requires constructive imagination. In this way religious inquiry is like a detective following up a clue, like a public health officer tracking down a strange disease, like trying out a particular route to the top of the mountain, like looking for the key to Baker's character. We begin with something which suggests more than it says, and hence with something more concrete than a proposition.[3]

This is not peculiar to religious inquiry. The following examples illustrate the functions of suggestions in other sustained inquiries also.

In a letter to Haeckel,[4] Darwin tells how he got the idea of natural selection. He says that, as he pondered the observations he made during the *Beagle* expedition and compared them with similar phenomena, "it seemed to me probable that closely related species might spring from a common ancestral stock. But for some years I could not understand how each form could be so admirably adapted to its environment. Thereupon I began to study systematically the domestic animals and cultivated plants, and perceived clearly after a time that the most important modifying force lay in man's power of selection and in his use of selected individuals for breeding. . . . When, by a fortunate chance, I then read Malthus' *Essay on Population* the idea of natural selection suddenly rose to my mind." Cassirer comments, "But more than two decades passed before the idea had taken shape sufficiently for Darwin openly to propose it."

Freud tells in his *Autobiography*[5] how he arrived at his theory of primitive culture. He had been studying totemism and had been reading Frazer and Robertson Smith. He says, "When I further took into account Darwin's conjecture that men originally lived in hordes, each under the domination of a single, powerful, violent and jealous male, there rose before me out of all these components the following hypothesis, or, I would rather say, vision" (138). Then he describes this image, which is explicated in his theory of primitive culture.

[3] This is the point of Owen Barfield's remark that the poet does not make judgments; "he only makes them possible—and only he makes them possible." *Poetic Diction*, 2nd. ed., 113n., London, Faber and Faber, 1952.

[4] As given in E. Cassirer, *The Problem of Knowledge*, Woglom and Hendel, tr., 161, New Haven, Yale University Press, 1950.

[5] J. Strachey, tr., New York, W. W. Norton, 1935.

Most suggestions occur in less dramatic ways than these. Also, some suggestions are less fruitful than others. There is some disagreement, for example, about Freud's theory of primitive culture. But when we are dealing with problems which cannot be solved by quasi-mechanical procedures, we have no option but to adopt some suggestion. Otherwise we have no starting point for developing a theory. And without a theory we can throw no light on the facts.

3. *How suggestions occur*

Any natural object (like a vine, the sun, a stone), any human relationship (like sexual love, physical combat, parenthood, political authority), or any historical event (like a flood, the Exodus, Gotama's enlightenment, the death of Christ) might, logically speaking, function as the vehicle of a religious suggestion. And in the history of religion a great variety of things have functioned in this way. Such objects, relations, and events introduce, in a concrete way, answers to basic religious questions. They become paradigmatic symbols.

This has an important consequence for the phenomenology of religion. To understand a particular religion and compare it with others we need to study not only the propositions of its doctrinal scheme but also its symbols, and particularly those symbols which convey the suggestion to which that faith is a response. This is an enterprise to which historical study, literary analysis, and psychological theory all contribute.

One feature of suggestions is the contingency of their occurrence. We cannot produce promising suggestions just when we need them. As in other perplexities—moral, scientific, artistic—there are times when our learning does not tell us what we want to know. We have to wait for the illuminating idea.

Also, suggestions are not made to order. Sometimes when they occur they are not what we looked for. For example, according to the *Majjhima-Nikaya,* the venerable monk

Malunkyaputta asked certain questions of Buddha, adding that if they were not answered he would abandon the life of a monk and return to the life of a layman. One of these questions was whether or not the world is eternal. Another was whether or not the saint exists after death. Buddha not only refused to answer these questions; he rejected the assumption that a monk needed to know the answers. Malunkyaputta had confused religious questions with speculative ones. This confusion needed to be cleared away. Part of the reply is as follows:

> "Pray, Malunkyaputta, did I ever say to you, 'Come, Malunkyaputta, lead the religious life under me, and I will explain to you either that the world is eternal, or that the world is not eternal . . . or that the saint neither exists nor does not exist after death'?" [6]

So sometimes we revise our questions. Beginning with one formulation in mind, as Malunkyaputta did, we encounter a suggestion which "speaks to our condition" but does not lend itself to our formulation of the question. It promises an answer to a better question (more answerable, more apt and proper to our situation, more profound) than the question we were asking.

This enables us to do some justice to a criticism of philosophy made by certain Christian theologians and, in a different way, by Zen Buddhist teachers. The theologians say that instead of answering our own questions we ought to answer the questions God puts to us. We ought to leave room for the divine initiative. The Buddhist teachers say it is precisely our attachment to thinking things out which keeps us from the nonattachment and openness in which salvation consists.

---

[6] Sutta 63 (H. D. Warren, tr.), from E. A. Burtt, ed., *The Teachings of the Compassionate Buddha,* 34, New York, The New American Library, 1955. Burtt substitutes "explain" for "elucidate" (Warren).

We can agree that religious questions often need correction. But this is true also of other questions including moral and scientific questions. It is not only in religion that we find ourselves barking up the wrong tree. And it does not follow that we should not ask questions but only that we need to learn to ask better questions.

Illuminating suggestions cannot be produced at will, and when they occur they may have the shock of novelty. Are there conditions which are necessary for the occurrence of religious suggestions?

We can say that having a religious interest is a condition of the occurrence of religious suggestions, though we would have to add that the event which conveys a suggestion may itself also awaken such an interest. For a historian of religion the vine of Dionysus or the parable of the Sower might illuminate Greek religion or early Christianity in a powerful way without functioning for *him* as religious suggestions. These symbols might have only a historical meaning and convey not religious suggestions but suggestions about religion.

So there must be some openness toward religious truth for a religious suggestion to be significant.[7] For example, someone might hear the story of Gotama's enlightenment and make one of the following comments: "What became of his wife and child?" "A clear case of narcissism." "You often get that sort of flight from the world among members of a privileged and unproductive aristocracy." Or, to take another example, the story of the death of Christ might evoke one of the following reactions: "A miscarriage of justice." "An example of religious intolerance." "He must have had a very strong death instinct." In these cases the teller of the story, who meant to convey a religious suggestion, might say, "But you haven't gotten the *point*."

[7] "Nothing is so incredible as an answer to an unasked question." Reinhold Niebuhr, *The Nature and Destiny of Man*, ii, 6, New York, Scribner's, 1947.

The story is not being taken as the vehicle of a religious suggestion but in some other way. So it has not struck home.

The occurrence of illuminating suggestions is bound to be both wonderful and mysterious to those to whom they occur. And this also is not peculiar to religion, as the legend of Archimedes reminds us. This is the reason for talk about "inspiration" in poetry and in religion. And this is the basis in human experience for theological theories of revelation in general.

I say "in general" because what gives unity to some particular religious community is a common response to some particular illuminating suggestion. Indeed, we can identify and distinguish various faiths by identifying the suggestion to which each responds. For example, in formulating its faith Judaism starts with the history of the people Israel; Christianity starts with Jesus Christ; and Buddhism starts with Buddha. Similarly, Neoplatonism starts with a certain mystical experience, and Stoicism develops its doctrines from experiences of accepting limitations. This gives some general understanding of the theological dictum that faith is a response to revelation. But each community has to develop its own doctrine on this matter. For the content of the suggestion, and the way it is conveyed, vary from faith to faith.

I offer one further observation about the occurrence of suggestions. In religious literature we find allusions to a kind of experience called "dryness" (*siccitas*). This might be regarded as a reflection, in emotional life, of the non-occurrence of illuminating suggestions. There are analogies with moments of discouragement and frustration in other inquiries.[8]

---

[8] With his permission I add a comment by Professor H. H. Price: "The discouragement and frustration may have their good side, somewhat like the apathy and depression which often occur in recovery from a physical illness (preventing energetic activity which would interfere with the healing process). The 'message,' so

4. *How suggestions are adopted*

If anyone undertakes an inquiry he has some focus of his attention and he is committed to some general line of action. If someone has a serious interest in reconstructing the history of ancient Crete he will take the trouble to look at monuments and read books on the subject. The adoption of a suggestion carries the focusing and engagement still further. We decide to explore the subject in a certain way, not in other ways, and commit ourselves to a specific line of action and thought, like the climber who decides on a certain route to the top of the mountain.

We do not have to be irrational in making these decisions. Indeed, we cannot be rational without making them. We would be irrational if we refused to try to answer significant questions, or if we were confused about our questions, or if we assigned to our conclusions an undeserved finality. But for a wide range of questions a certain kind of rationality—the rationality of calculations—is not possible. When we try to answer questions which require investigation, not simply calculation, the only kind of rationality we can have requires us to adopt and explore clues which are luminous but not transparent.

In science, in morality, in historical explanation, and in other inquiries adoption of suggestions is necessary also, as well as in religion. The difference is that in religion, vis-à-vis other human interests, more of the self is engaged. I do not say the self is engaged more, but that more of the self is engaged. In principle a religious interest engages the self centrally.[9] Its function is to relate the whole self to its source or ground or goal. This peculiarity of religious in-

to speak, of the discouragement and frustration is 'Leave the sub-conscious processes of gestation alone for the time being, and do not interfere with them by untimely conscious activities.' "

[9] See Henry M. Rosenthal, "On the Function of Religion in Culture," in *The Review of Religion*, 5:148–171, 290–309 (1941), esp. 167–171 on "centrality."

terests is reflected in the way religious suggestions are adopted. It is appropriate and natural that adoption of a religious suggestion be taken as a matter of utmost moment and treated with solemnity.

By speaking of "decision" and the "adoption" of suggestions I have stressed the element of conscious intention more than it deserves. We make many decisions without thinking, "I am now making a decision." We take one fork of the road and not another; we go to one doctor and not to another; we act on one business policy and not on another—all this without much conscious weighing of alternatives.

Thus we may adopt some suggestion because, we would say, "At the time it seemed the natural thing to do," even at important turning points in our lives. We know that what we are doing is important, and we are not being irresponsible, and yet we have no hesitation in doing what we do. In these cases the action is the ripe fruit of many previous actions. The action fits our character as a glove fits a hand. In speaking of decisions I mean to include such actions as these. I do not mean to suggest that all decisions are made in anguish or even in anxiety, though some (far too many indeed) undoubtedly are.

Also, ordinarily the relevant question in religious inquiry is not, "What suggestion can I find?" but rather, "What *does* illuminate life supremely?" Instead of looking for something we do not have, we come to know better what we already have, as Bunyan's pilgrim found the key to his dungeon in his own bosom.

5. *Explication of suggestions*

An intense attachment to religious symbols may generate strong resistance to explicating those symbols by stating propositions. This depreciation of propositional meaning in religion may take several forms:

a. Sometimes it takes a romantic form. Only in concrete

feeling do we apprehend the truth. Only what "the blood" tells us is true. We murder to dissect; in analytical and conceptual reasoning we kill the goose that lays the golden eggs. John Henry Newman's words in "The Tamworth Reading Room" (1841) [10] might be appealed to:

> "The heart is commonly reached, not through the reason, but through the imagination, by means of direct impressions, by the testimony of facts and events, by history, by description."

The meaning we find in the direct impact of a symbol, by "direct impressions," is the only meaning—a conclusion Newman did not draw—that matters. If we reframe this meaning in discursive language and abstract categories, we falsify it. Hence a recurrent evangelical suspicion of theology.

b. Resistance to explicating suggestions takes another form in transcendental mysticism. The intellect mounts from worldly things to a vision of something beyond being. Since the object of this apprehension is utterly transcendent, it is not only futile but positively misleading to form propositions about it. Meister Eckhart says: "Why dost thou prate of God? Whatever thou sayest of Him is untrue." Again, from a Buddhist teacher:

> "When Mind and each believing mind are not divided,
> And undivided are each believing mind and Mind,
> This is where words fail,
> For it is not of the past, present or future."

c. Another way of depreciating the explication of symbols into propositions is expressed in Kierkegaard's Christian existentialism. This is by insistence on the absurdity of the revelatory event, the occurrence of the eternal at a particular point in time. Kierkegaard is not just saying that a

[10] In *Grammar of Assent*, 89, New York, Christian Press Association, n.d.

particular historical fact is unique. He seems to mean that the paradoxes in which we are driven to speak of this fact are irremediable and unmitigated. As a consequence, the truth that is possible in religion is not propositional truth about the fact but only the truthfulness or authenticity of our personal relation to it. Truth is subjectivity.

d. One other variety of religious depreciation of propositional truth might be mentioned. Its motive is to protect and maintain the authority of a particular revealed doctrine. This is different from the interest of Kierkegaard, if I understand him. For example, against the Mu'tazilites, who interpreted the Koran's references to God's throne and hands and eyes in a figurative way, al-Ash'arī says: "We confess that God is firmly seated on his throne. . . . We confess that God has two hands, without asking how. . . . We confess that God has two eyes, without asking how. . . ." [11]

We can understand and appreciate some of the motives behind this resistance to explication of religious symbols. It arises in part from knowing the difference between propositions and nonpropositional meanings, and wanting to keep the contrast clear. It is like Cleanth Brooks' rejection of "the heresy of paraphrase." We should not suppose, he says, that a paraphrase of a poem is equivalent in meaning to the poem itself. Similarly, religious people rightly insist that abstract systems of thought cannot substitute for concrete experience. But one might insist on the secondary and subordinate character of propositional explication of meaning without rejecting it altogether. And this is the generally accepted view in most religious traditions.

Granting that concrete experience (imaginative, intuitive, paradoxical, personal) is primary in religion, still, when we inquire, this is not enough. We cannot be content with images and figures and symbols, though we cannot do without them. We cannot be content with them because we

[11] In A. J. Arberry, *Revelation and Reason in Islam*, 22, London, G. Allen and Unwin, 1957.

have to understand what we experience, and for this purpose "reason" in the sense meant by Newman is essential
(which Newman was by no means denying). No doubt the
"heart" is not reached by reason; but we need to understand
—and be able to say—what is in our hearts.

Explication of religious symbols is important, first, for
the sake of self-knowledge. We may accept too easily a
familiar explanation of the meaning of a suggestion, failing
to think subjectively in Kierkegaard's sense. A firsthand
experience may be clothed with a secondhand interpretation. New wine is poured into old bottles. So every man
must be his own theologian. If he is a member of a religious
community (and for most people religion is not an altogether solitary enterprise), he will learn from its other
members and take full account of its tradition. Nevertheless
in doing so he cannot responsibly delegate the interpretation
of his experience to anyone else.

Second, without a concern for truth religious experience
would degenerate into sentimentality. A religious suggestion is a promise of truth. To adopt it is to undertake to
explore its meaning, and the object of the exploration is to
obtain what it promises. The exploration looks forward toward a judgment. But for a good judgment we must know
what truth-claim is put forward in the symbol.

A third reason for explicating what symbols suggest is
to help us explain our proposals. When we make proposals
responsibly and in good faith, we want to make them as
clear as we can. One motive for clarity is charity. When we
are asked for explanations, we want to offer something more
than a figure of speech.

For these reasons, which are all connected, we need to
construct a set of propositions which together express, as
nearly as possible, the meaning of the suggestion. These
propositions can be compared with one another, to see
whether they are consistent and coherent. Then they can be
compared with the relevant facts and tested for their ap-
plicability and adequacy to experience.

We need not assume that the meaning of a suggestion, as conveyed by a symbol, can be completely funded into propositions. It may be that, though many propositions can be formulated as partial expressions of its meaning, the total set of these propositions cannot be substituted for the symbol, as an equivalent vehicle. If so, the propositions must be so framed and stated as to retain a direct allusion to the symbol itself. This, I take it, is why Karl Barth says that Christian theology should have a vital connection with the direct presentation of the Christian gospel.

At this point we can gain a perspective on the formulation of doctrines in religious communities. Christian theology, for example, is to the Christian church what the interpretation of his own starting point is to the individual believer. Biblical theologians and systematic theologians state, at different levels of abstraction, propositions drawn from the paradigmatic suggestion to which the faith of the church responds. In nontheistic religious faiths a strictly analogous discipline is in order. For example, when Lippmann explains the principles of "high religion," applies them to family life and economic morality, and relates them to modern science and philosophy, what he is doing is similar in function—though very different in his point of view, his method, and his conclusions—to what John Calvin does in the *Institutes of the Christian Religion.*

The unity of a doctrinal scheme results from the suggestion it explicates. A scheme may be more or less complete, depending on how far the meaning of the suggestion has been thought out; some schemes are more rudimentary than others, some are more elaborate. Also, a scheme may be more or less systematic, depending on the extent to which systematic categories [12] have been devised and developed.

---

[12] Such as, in Christian theology, for example, "person" (as in "the persons of the Trinity"), "incarnation," "atonement," "creation," and others.

A basic religious proposal,[13] then, is an epitomization of the truth-claim made by a doctrinal scheme as a whole. It condenses the scheme's answer to a basic religious question. It gives a blunt answer to a basic question. And, since the scheme explicates some paradigmatic suggestion, we may say that a basic proposal states the meaning of the suggestion summarily.

Finally, the explication of suggestions is not peculiar to religious inquiry. In any inquiry construction of theories is important for reasons strictly analogous to those mentioned above. What guides the scientist,[14] or the moralist, or the artist, in his construction of a theory is the suggestion he has adopted. In any sustained investigation a theory grows out of the explication of a suggestion.

6. Wholeheartedness and certainty

A suggestion is not a conclusion but a promise of truth. It has to be made clearer in thought, and its practical implications have yet to be explored. So adopting a suggestion is not the same as coming to a conclusion and making a judgment.

Still, even here a certain wholeheartedness is desirable. If we say "yes" together with a lurking inward "no," this double-mindedness will result in confusions. If we assent from some inner compulsion we involve ourselves in self-deceptions. So we must ask, How sure must we be that the suggestion will give what it promises if we are to be wholehearted in adopting it? We do not have to be absolutely certain, in a strong sense of "absolutely certain," which can be explained by the following steps:

[13] For example: "The God and Father of our lord Jesus Christ is the maker and ruler of all things," or "Nirvana is the True State," or "We find the meaning of life by living in harmony with Nature."

[14] See, on the use of models in science, Stephen Toulmin: *The Philosophy of Science*, ch. II, esp. 34–35 (New York, Harper, 1960) and R. Harré, *Theories and Things*, sect. 3 (London and New York, Sheed and Ward, 1961).

a. Does the adoption of a religious suggestion commit us to making a prediction that we will never fail to adhere to it? By a "prediction" I do not mean an intention or a resolution. I am asking whether, when we adopt a religious suggestion, we must be in position to make a certain descriptive assertion, namely, that at no time as long as we live will we cease to act on the suggestion we adopt.

Now certainly many religious people, including many earnest believers of many faiths, have not supposed that such an unqualified prediction was required. The possibility of "falling away from the faith" has often been admitted. And with due regard for the hazards of life a prediction to the contrary, excluding this possibility, might well seem rash to many pious minds.

b. Does adoption of a religious suggestion commit us to making a prediction that no experience will ever *with good reason* lead us to exchange it for another? This prediction would be weaker than that in *a.* That prediction would be falsified by our becoming insane, for example. Such cases are excluded here. This would still yield a very strong sense for "absolutely certain." We could say that someone is absolutely certain of something he believes if he is in position to assert that there could never be any good reason for him to disbelieve it. Now, though some religious believers have seemed to assert this, there are two ways in which an assertion of this type might turn out to be untrue. One way is by ignorance of future experiences. Do we know for certain that we will have no experiences in the future which would, with good reason, count decisively against the suggestion we are adopting? Do we know the limits of possible experience in *this* way? Another way the assertion might turn out to be untrue is by ignorance of alternative suggestions. Do we know for certain that no suggestion will ever occur which would have more warrant for adoption than this one? In other words, to sum up, is our survey of possible experiences and possible alternative suggestions complete?

By ordinary standards it would be unreasonable to require this prediction, because we would need more than human foresight and perspicacity to justify it. Ordinarily we assume that qualifications like "as far as I can see," supposing that we are trying reasonably hard to see as far as we can, are compatible with good faith and genuine conviction.

It would follow that adoption of a religious suggestion might fail to be "absolute" in both of the following ways and yet be wholehearted: (1) It need not require an unqualified prediction of perpetual adherence to the suggestion adopted; (2) it could admit the possibility of experiences which might, for all one knows, require the rejection of this suggestion and the adoption of another.

The venture of inquiry, like all other ventures, would be ruled out if we should resolve to run no risks. We act with the understanding that action is risky, yet we are often wholehearted in doing so. That which makes it rationally possible, in religious inquiry as in other inquiries, to accept the normal risks of being wrong is an aim at truth. "What is truth?" asked Meister Eckhart. "Truth is something so noble that if God could turn aside from it, I could keep to the truth and let God go." It is not enough to affirm this primacy of truth over all particular conceptions only in a general way. It has to be applied within the framework of the specific inquiry in which we are engaged. This involves knowing the supposition which is implicit in the interest which prompts that inquiry, an interest awakened by some experience of the world within and around us. Then we might know in a specific and effective way what it means to subordinate some particular concept we have (for example, a particular conception of God) to truth.

We can accept the possibility of change in the direction of our thought if we have a continuing objective and if we know what that objective is. So a normal apprehension of the risks of inquiry need not become an inhibiting anxiety, and it is possible, in principle at least, to respond freely and wholeheartedly to whatever illuminates most that which we dimly discern.

CHAPTER VII

Judgments

1. *Introduction*

In the past two chapters we have been considering the logic of religious inquiry. In the chapters following this one we shift our focus to the logic of religious discourse, to see what can (logically) be said in religious conversations and arguments. In this transition chapter we consider the place of judgments in religious inquiry and discourse. Judgments are decisions belonging to a later stage of inquiry than the decisions made in adopting suggestions. They are expressed in appraisals of proposals for belief.

Suppose someone adopts some promising suggestion. He then explores its meaning in thought and action. Finally, after reflection on the results of this exploration—after "experience," we might say—he decides whether the suggestion has given what it promised. He is making a judgment.

Sometimes we use the term "judgment" to cover decisions —and expressions of decisions—of many sorts, so that all evaluations are judgments. But I shall use it here in a more specific way, to mean a decision of a truth-claim. So when we express judgments, in this narrower sense, the appropriate appraisal terms all belong to that large family of which the following (in some of their uses) are members: accurate, adequate, correct, exact, fair, justifiable, probable, proper, reasonable, right. "True" is the most prominent member and, we might say, the father of this family. Judgments are expressed in appraisals of a specific kind.

To illustrate this restricted sense of "judgment" let us distinguish judgments from some appraisals which might be classed with judgments as logical appraisals. For example, when we say an utterance is *unclear* we are appraising the utterance in a certain way but not making a decision on the truth or untruth of that utterance. We are unsure what is being said, so we are not in a position to make a judgment.

Again, when we say an utterance is *irrelevant* this is not a judgment in the restricted sense. We understand what is being said, but it is not to the point. The speaker is (deliberately or inadvertently) talking about something else than the matter at hand. Here again we are appraising an utterance but not deciding a truth-claim.

Again, when we say an argument is *invalid* or *inconclusive* we are not deciding whether any statement in the argument is true or untrue. Even if the speaker is proposing its conclusion we are not judging the proposal when we appraise the argument. The conclusion may or may not be true. Again, this is an appraisal but not a judgment.

With this sense of "judgment," if no religious proposals make genuine truth-claims, then there are no occasions for religious judgments. We can leave open the question whether some of the prima-facie truth-claims we find in religious discourse are genuine. We can ask, "If there are religious judgments, what would they be like?" And we can consider how appraisals of religious truth-claims would be different from appraisals of some religious utterances which do not purport to make truth-claims, namely, injunctions and confessions.

2. *Basic religious proposals again*

First let us compare basic religious proposals with some nonreligious proposals for belief,[1] to see how different sorts of issues arise. Let us take as an explicit statement of a basic religious proposal:

iA. Nirvana is the supreme goal of life.

And let us begin by comparing this with:

iB. The earth is spherical.

[1] Some of the sentences I shall discuss here might be used in informative utterances, but let us take them as proposals for belief.

Notice two points about iA and iB:

a. They are alike in that either could be judged negatively without inconsistency. In some circumstances it would be right to say the earth is not spherical. And even if the issue were narrowed down by saying, "Well, roughly spherical," this could still be denied without inconsistency, though wrongly. But there are other proposals which could not be judged negatively without inconsistency. For example:

iC. The product of 46 and 23 is 1058.

The religious proposal iA might be denied without inconsistency. It would be self-consistent to say, "No, the supreme goal of life is to glorify God and enjoy him forever," or to say, "No, there is no supreme goal of life." One might make either of these negative judgments on iA without contradicting oneself.

b. iA and iB are dissimilar in that the logical subject of iB is ostensible and the logical subject of iA is not. This is not to say that Nirvana cannot be referred to at all. But it is clear that no one can point to what is meant by "Nirvana" in the way one can point to what is meant by "the earth."

Now let us take a nonreligious proposal of a different sort:

iD. It is better to submit than to resist.

Suppose this is said by one United Nations soldier to another in a Chinese prison camp in North Korea. The problem is whether to give information about their fellow prisoners, or to resist the demand. Suppose the penalty for resistance is death, and that both prisoners are convinced there is no way through the horns of the dilemma. Then notice four points of comparison about iA and iD.

a. In both—but not in iB and iC—a preference is expressed. In each case something is ranked above something else. Submitting is ranked above resisting; Nirvana is ranked above all other goals.

b. A difference appears when we consider how these preferences are related to injunctions (proposals for action). In iD, we might say, an injunction lies just below the surface of the preference. A particular action is virtually enjoined. The injunction, "Let us submit," follows quite simply and directly [2] from iD. In contrast, any injunction to a particular action would follow much less simply and directly from iA. The reason for this lies in the following difference: iA ranks objects and iD ranks actions.

There are indeed many religious injunctions, like the Ten Commandments in Judaism and Christianity, and the Noble Eightfold Path in Buddhism. But these injunctions are not directly and immediately derivable from utterances like iA. For example, the injunction against killing in the sixth commandment does not follow immediately from saying that it is God that is holy. It would have to be introduced in some way, for example, by saying that God has revealed that killing is wrong, either by an explicit command or by revealing his own character (in his dealings with Israel, say) so as to show that murder is inconsistent with devotion to him.

Similarly, the Buddhist injunction to a middle path between self-indulgence and self-torture does not follow simply and directly from saying that Nirvana is the supreme goal of life. It needs to be introduced (as in the Four Noble Truths) by consideration of (1) the consequences of self-indulgence and self-torture, and (2) the possibility of avoiding both and attaining Nirvana, a possibility suggested by the figure of the Enlightened One himself.

Thus, to sum up this point of difference, iA yields injunctions less directly and immediately than iD does.

c. Another difference appears when we consider some other injunctions customarily derived from religious prefer-

---

[2] Assuming that submission is feasible. If there were no opportunity to submit, iD would still be a significant proposal. It is not a proposal for action but for ranking actions.

ences, for example, the commandment to keep the sabbath day holy and the injunction in the Eightfold Path to "right concentration." These enjoin ritual actions or actions aimed at self-discipline and not, in one common meaning of the term, moral actions.

d. Another difference is that while iD ranks two definite actions, submission to these captors and resistance to them, iA is open at one end. Nirvana is ranked over any other goal. The contrast in iA is not between Nirvana and some definite alternative; Nirvana is being marked off from any object whatever which might be a goal. (This need not mean excluding other goals. One might aim at many other goals too, but above all at Nirvana.)

This open-endedness is characteristic of basic religious proposals. Something proposed as a religious object is being contrasted with any other candidate for that function. This implicit negation of alternatives is consistent with appreciating certain values in them. A Jew or a Christian or a Moslem might say that God gives a kind of deliverance from anxiety that is in some ways *like* the attainment of Nirvana. Or a Theravada Buddhist might conceivably say that, at one stage of the religious life, the conception of a creative reality might have a provisional use. It might help in detaching attention from the self and its desires.

The intrinsic intention of a basic religious proposal is not polemical. It is true that most highly developed religions have been scarred by conflicts through which they have passed in their histories. But negation of particular alternatives is only incidental to the positive intention of a religious proposal, which is to point to some source, ground, or center of the meaning of life.

Let us take another nonreligious proposal for contrast with iA:

iE. The universe is a single substance.

Suppose this is meant as a direct logical alternative to "There are many real things in the universe." Then let us ask how iE is like, and how it is unlike, iA. First notice some relatively superficial points:

a. It is like iA (and also like iB) syntactically. A predicate is applied to a subject, and the issue for judgment is whether it properly (truly) applies.

b. iE looks, at least, like iA (and like iB, but unlike iC) in that, it seems, either might be contradicted without inconsistency. Like iA, iE seems a matter of fact, not a matter of logic.[3] Whether or not the universe has the unity of a substance seems an arguable question.

c. The logical subject of iE like that of iA (but unlike that of iB) is not ostensible. It might be argued that the universe can be referred to more successfully than Nirvana can be. But counterarguments could be produced on this point. Certainly the universe (as meant in iE) is not ostensible in the same way the earth is. It cannot be referred to in *that* way.

d. Unlike iA (and also unlike iD, but like iB and iC) iE is not an explicit expression of a preference. There is no explicit ranking of the universe in contrast with something else, for example, its "accidents" or "modes." There are no doubt latent overtones in the notion of substance that might have this effect. But strictly speaking no comparative valuation, as between the universe and something else, is expressed.

To bring out some further contrasts between iA and iE, let us ask whether iE is strictly speaking a positive alternative to iA and, if not, how it might be transformed into one. For this purpose let us ask first how a Theravada Buddhist would treat iE.

A Theravada Buddhist might deny both iE and its direct contrary—i.e., "There are many real things in the universe"

---

[3] Though sometimes dialectical arguments are offered to show that it is in *this* sense a matter of logic.

—since all things including the universe itself are only transient aggregates. But he would not treat iE, taken by itself, as a positive alternative to iA. As it stands, it fails to give practical guidance for life.

How then might iE be transformed into a positive alternative to iA? How might it become a basic religious proposal? It might become a basic religious proposal if it should be used to say there is something even more important than Nirvana, namely, that One Nature in which all things consist. Then Nirvana might be treated as a subjective correlate of the One Nature, the experience of the individual mind when it is united to the One Nature. It is the One Nature that makes Nirvana possible. This is indeed something like the proposal made in Mahayana Buddhism, which Theravada Buddhism rejects.

And now let us ask how a Jew or a Christian or a Moslem would treat iE. We have ample historical evidence on this point. In general, allowing for certain variants, iE would be treated as inconsistent with certain important doctrines of those faiths. It would be inconsistent with the doctrine of creation to deny that there are many real things in the universe. Furthermore—and more to the point—with certain historical episodes in mind (the Stoics and Spinoza, for example) adherents to those faiths might be inclined to look on iE itself as an alternative basic religious proposal. What would justify their doing so?

They would be justified if—but only if—iE were developed in a certain way. Suppose this universal substance were marked off from and contrasted with its "modes" (and whatever else could be mentioned), including, for example, one's passions. And suppose all these other entities were ranked below the universe in a certain way. This is, in fact, what the Stoics and Spinoza did. Developed in this way, iE might become a logical alternative to the basic proposals of Hinduism, Judaism, Christianity, and Islam.

Let us take one more nonreligious proposal:

iF. A hydrogen atom is composed of one proton and one electron.

There is one interesting way in which this is like iA. Both contain systematic terms. Both "Nirvana" and the terms in iF belong in special contexts and get their meanings in those contexts. The risks of taking terms like "atom" out of their systematic contexts in scientific theories are often mentioned. Similar warnings about terms like "Nirvana" are also in order, and in our own culture we might need this reminder even more about "God." Both "God" and "atom" are often used unsystematically. But where a proposal about God is made on a reasonably high reflective level, the term has its meaning in the context of some doctrinal scheme. The meanings given the term by such doctrinal schemes as those developed by Thomas Aquinas, Soren Kierkegaard, and Paul Tillich, to take some contrasting examples, have to be taken into account.

These conceptual systems are not natural occurrences like the patterns of crystals and biological systems. Human inventiveness has been at work, whether in physics or in theology. To understand the point of such a scheme, and thus to understand its concepts, we need to know what prompts its production. In particular, what questions are the schemes designed to answer? It follows that, to understand both iA and iF, it is especially important to understand the interests which generate the schemes.

I have not given labels to the types of nonreligious proposals I have illustrated. We might call iB a descriptive assertion, iC an analytical statement, iD a moral assertion, iE a speculative or metaphysical assertion, and iF a scientific statement. Or better names might be found. But giving such labels might tempt us to think we have drawn clear boundary lines between the types. All I have done is to compare a particular religious proposal with some nonreligious proposals, to indicate roughly the sort of issue which basic religious judgments would decide.

3. *Appraisals of injunctions*

Now let us distinguish proposals for belief like iA-F from utterances of certain other sorts. This will help us see how judgment terms are different from some other appraisal terms. Let us consider injunctions and, in a later section, confessions. Consider the following:

iiA. Come into the garden.
iiB. Don't cross the picket line.
iiC. Put some incense on the altar.

These belong to a large class of utterances I shall call injunctions, including invitations, appeals, requests, admonitions, prescriptions, commands, and similar proposals. They are proposals, but not proposals for belief; they are proposals for action. Let us see what sorts of appraisals are appropriate to them.

To decide to accept or reject a proposal for action is to decide to do or not to do what is proposed. We decide whether or not to go into the garden, to cross the picket line, or to put incense on the altar. These decisions are matters for "good judgment." But using good judgment in these decisions is different from making judgments. In deciding whether to accept or reject a proposal for belief we decide whether what is proposed is probable or correct or accurate or, more generally, true. What is proposed in an injunction is an action; what is proposed in a proposal for belief is a proposition.

We appraise injunctions in various ways. We may say that iiA is a friendly invitation or a welcome suggestion, for example. But these appraisal terms ("friendly" and "welcome") properly apply to the intention of the proposer and to our own reaction to the proposal. They do not properly apply to what is proposed (the action enjoined) in the way "probable" properly applies to what is predicted. More specifically, they do not directly express decisions about doing or not doing the act enjoined. Even though I say it is a friendly invitation I might (logically) not accept it. I am not announcing that I do (or do not) accept it.

Again, we may say that iiB is a justifiable request or a morally intolerable interference with personal liberty. But these predicates properly apply not to the action enjoined (what is proposed) but to the act of enjoining.[4] More specifically, again, these appraisals do not announce decisions about what is proposed in the injunction. Even though it is a justifiable request I might (logically) not comply with it (though in this case I might be acting unreasonably). Incidentally, these particular appraisals of iiB depend for their weight on prior or implicit judgments about moral principles, claims to authority, and the consequences of actions.

Now when we appraise injunctions are we really either (a) appraising the intention of the enjoiner ("a friendly invitation"), or (b) appraising the act of enjoining ("a justifiable request"), or (c) saying something about our own reaction to the injunction ("a welcome invitation")? Or may we also say something which is directly about the action enjoined (e.g., putting some incense on the altar)? Let us take another kind of appraisal.

We may say (by metonymy) that iiC is an idolatrous temptation or a pious admonition. We mean the injunction is a temptation to do an idolatrous act or an admonition to a pious act. And this shows not only that the injunction is being appraised in the light of some religious belief but also that it is being interpreted as conveying a proposal for belief. For example, the early Christians refused to put incense on the altars of the imperial cult because (a) they regarded

---

[4] The distinction between (x) something proposed (an action, or a proposition), and (y) the act of proposing x, is worth noticing because terms like "proposal" and "injunction" may bear either sense, though the distinction is not always important.

the action as symbolic of a particular religious belief and because (b) they rejected this belief. Similar cases in point are the refusal of Jehovah's Witnesses to join in flag salutes in schools, and the problem whether Japanese Christians should take part in Shinto ceremonies. So some utterances expressing injunctions implicitly convey proposals for belief also.

This suggests one way of saying something which is directly about the action enjoined. A Roman might say, "That would be a pious action," adding in support of this proposal for belief about the action, "because the emperor shares the divinity of the gods." Or a Christian might have said, "That would be an idolatrous action," adding, "for worship belongs to God alone, the maker of heaven and earth." Each is making, and supporting, a proposal for belief about the action enjoined. In these cases judgments, both on the proposals for belief about the action and on the supporting proposals, would be in order.

However, we might imagine a sceptical Roman administrator saying to the pious Roman, "Not really, but do it anyway." And he might say to the Christian objector, "I know, but do it anyway." His own business is to get the act done or, if not, to impose penalties. As far as he is concerned the injunction does not depend on the truth of any of these proposals for belief. This suggests that, when we make proposals for belief about the action enjoined and judge proposals for belief which are implicit in the injunction, we are not giving a complete response to the injunction proper. The injunction is not itself a proposal for belief. Some other response is called for.

We make a complete response to the injunction proper only if we say (explicitly or implicitly) that we will, or will not, do it. This might have the force of a prediction. Or it might have the force of a performative utterance: "I hereby do it," or "I refrain from doing it," or "I promise to do it," or "I refuse to do it."

Now predictions would not answer to the injunction as

clearly and directly as performatives would. "I refuse to do what you suggest" would be a more direct *response* to an injunction than "I will probably do what you suggest" *if* the latter should mean only "It will probably turn out that way." An injunction calls for [5] a commitment, one way or another, not for a prediction.

This teaches us something about the difference between proposals for action (injunctions) and proposals for belief. In both cases decisions are called for, but there is a crucial difference in the way these decisions are announced. The right way to announce a decision about a proposal for belief is by an appraisal of what is proposed, specifically by an expression of a judgment, in which we use the appraisal terms which are appropriate to judgments. We announce the decision by saying that what is proposed is true or untrue, adequate or inadequate, and the like. The right way to announce a decision about an injunction, on the contrary, is not by appraising what is proposed, but by uttering (by one form of words or another) a performative.

4. *Injunctions to believe*

The injunctions considered above enjoin some overt action or other. But are there not injunctions to inward action also? Indeed, are we not sometimes enjoined to believe or disbelieve certain propositions? It seems there are some injunctions in which believing something is the sort of action enjoined. This calls for special attention. Consider the following:

iiD. Please believe I did not do it.
iiE. Don't believe what he says.
iiF. Believe that the Lord is good.[6]

These expressions might suggest that, instead of distin-

[5] Of course injunctions can be ignored, or evaded, and many injunctions should be.

[6] Suppose that this does not mean the same as "Trust in the Lord."

guishing proposals for belief from injunctions, as we have been doing, we should look on the two sorts of proposals as overlapping classes, or that we should look at proposals for belief as a subclass of injunctions. These suggestions would lead to confusion, as I shall try to show.

Let us ask what kinds of appraisals, and other responses, these peculiar utterances call for. This will help us see more clearly the difference between judgments and responses to injunctions. And this will throw light on the difference between believing and other actions.

The most direct and explicit function of these utterances is to express (*a*) an injunction. Someone asks or tells someone else to do something. I shall call this the injunction proper, and I call attention to three of its features: (*ai*) the intention of the enjoiner, (*aii*) the act of enjoining, and (*aiii*) the act enjoined. These features call for different sorts of responses. Some appraisals apply directly to the enjoiner's intention, for example, of iiE, "That was a friendly warning." Others apply to the act of enjoining, for example, of iiD, "That was needless; I know you did not do it" or, of iiE, "That is offensive; I can make up my own mind." The problem is, What responses, if any, would be appropriate to the act enjoined in these utterances? For example, suppose someone says of iiD or iiF, "That is hard to do." What might this mean?

Along with the injunction proper, an utterance of this sort conveys (more or less explicitly)[7] (*b*) a proposal for belief, expressing some proposition. The act enjoined in the injunction proper involves this proposition in some way.

Consider first the injunctions proper, in injunctions to believe, and especially certain points about the enjoiner's intention. Then we shall turn to the act enjoined. There are

[7] Consider, for example, the following series: "Seek Nirvana"; "Take Christ as your savior"; "Know that you are one with the Infinite"; "I hope you will come to realize that Humanity is the only thing worth living for."

four kinds of situations in which injunctions to believe might be uttered:

(1) Suppose first that the enjoiner believes the proposition in question, which is ordinarily the case. Then the injunction to believe would convey an *honest* proposal for belief. The enjoiner wants the proposee to believe the proposition in question. And one reason he wants the proposition believed is that he himself believes it is true.

(2) But suppose the speaker does not believe the proposition in question. Suppose that in iiE the speaker thinks or knows that what "he" says is true. Suppose that in iiF the speaker either does not think that "the Lord is good" makes sense, or is undecided whether it is true, or thinks it is not true. Then the proposal for belief the utterance would convey is a *fake* proposal for belief.

The speaker might have one or more of several reasons for genuinely wanting someone to believe the proposition: (*a*) He might think it would be good for himself if the proposee believed it (for example, an accused man addressing a jury). Or (*b*) he might think it would be good for the proposee (a parent or teacher talking to a child). Or (*c*) he might think it would be good for some third party or for the community (a statesman interpreting history on a television broadcast). Conceivably the speaker might have no reason at all for genuinely wanting someone to believe the proposition. He might be merely a mischief-maker.

(3) A third sort of case needs to be taken into account. Suppose that, in an injunction to believe, the speaker makes it clear that he does not believe the proposition p and that he is not proposing that p is true. "Believe p, though p is not true." This is not so bizarre as it might seem.

Something like this would be the case in appeals to "make-believe." "We know there really aren't any fairies, but let's make believe there are." Making-believe, however, is not the same as believing, and in cases of this sort what we have is not exactly an injunction to believe. What is asked for is something less than believing but something more than entertaining some proposition. The force of the injunction is that we be receptive to what is mentioned. We should dwell on it. It means something. There is something in it. Consider, for example:

iiG. Think of the way Micawber waited for something to turn up.
iiH. Consider how Lucifer rebelled against God.
iiJ. Remember what Prometheus did.[8]

Such appeals for "suspension of disbelief" or, we might say, for heuristic belief, may be more or less sophisticated. We may be asked to think of the world "as if" certain categories properly and truly applied to it. We may be invited to adopt certain myths, though the statements by which they are expressed are not strictly true. Poets, novelists, and dramatists tremble on the verge of making similar injunctions. And even scientists sometimes present simplified and imaginative models of the physical world.

What is the point of such injunctions? It is important to be clear about this; for if we are not, then they might encourage indifference to truth. Certainly this is not the usual intention of such injunctions. The intention may be to use the untrue proposition as a means of suggesting some true proposition. For example, although there aren't any fairies, many unexpected and delightful things happen. Or the intention may be to create an image for adoption as a guide to the formation of true propositions, for example, Bohr's model of the atom, or the character of Hamlet in Shakespeare's play,[9] or the image of God as a heavenly king. If

[8] Perhaps in these cases "the way" and "how" and "what" are signals that belief in the *occurrence* is not the point of the injunction.

[9] We do not need to attribute this intention to Shakespeare or to deny it of him. The point is only that Hamlet as a dramatic character might be used in this way, for example, by a moralist.

these intentions are carried out successfully, then these injunctions would not promote indifference to truth.

There is a real danger, however, that this positive and constructive function of untrue propositions may not be understood. In that case the injunction will be either puzzling or misleading.

So we would need to add that, while propositions believed to be untrue may be used as vehicles of suggestions, it is also possible to convey suggestions by means of propositions believed to be true.[10] Some current uses of "myth" may mislead on this point. For we are likely to think of a myth as a narrative of events which in fact did not occur. So, when we are told that religion cannot dispense with myths, this seems to imply that fictive narratives are necessary for conveying religious suggestions. I am not denying they may do so; I am only denying they are necessary for conveying religious suggestions. Further, there will be an important difference between what is suggested when fictive narratives are used in this way and what is suggested when the vehicle is a story believed to be true. When the Stoics mentioned the actions of the Olympian gods they were suggesting something different from what Homer's stories suggested to a Greek of his time. Also, Christianity and the Hellenistic mystery cults were different in this way.

(4) Finally, consider a fourth sort of situation. Consider "Believe p," uttered as a brusque command, or "I wish you would believe p," uttered as a plea. And suppose the utterance is intended directly to cause—that is to say, to force or induce—someone to believe p. In this case threats or promises are implied. This might be the case whether the proposal for belief being conveyed is honest or fake.

[10] Compare the following remark by a contemporary theologian: "In the field of religion, any statement which is literally true has no particular significance." It might be argued that, unless *some* statement in a given system is literally true, no other statement in the system will be true in any *other* important sense of "true."

Here we verge on a large topic, a range of topics, indeed, including hypnotic suggestion, autosuggestion, the will to believe, and "self-verifying beliefs," among others. Exploration of these topics would take us into important psychological questions and moral questions. I leave them to one side, remarking only that this residual function would be both psychologically and morally problematical. But a brief remark on the ethics of persuasion is in order.

Suppose M wants N to believe *p*. But this is not all he wants. He wants N to be true to himself, let us say. So he wants to avoid confusing N, to avoid encouraging N to deceive himself, and to avoid making N less critical. This will limit the range of considerations which M is willing to offer N as reasons for accepting *p*. It will make him unwilling to offer N, as a reason for believing *p*, (*a*) any proposition which he knows or thinks is irrelevant or inconsistent or untrue and (*b*) any argument which he knows or thinks is invalid.

Now let us turn to the act enjoined in an injunction to believe, for the peculiarity of these injunctions comes out most clearly at this point. The acts enjoined in them are different from the acts enjoined in ordinary injunctions. In the previous section we saw that, although we can make proposals for belief about an act enjoined in an ordinary injunction ("That would be an idolatrous act"), injunctions call for decisions about doing or not doing the action. Such decisions are announced by means of performative expressions such as "I will do it," "I hereby do it," and "I refuse to do it." So injunctions call for performatives. The question we have to consider is whether performatives are appropriate to the act enjoined in an injunction to believe.

At least some of these injunctions ask for other acts, overt or nonovert, along with the act of believing. These actions may be thought to lead to believing, or to follow from believing. For example, we are asked to give serious and thoughtful attention to the proposition in question. Or steps which seem to go beyond believing may be called for, along with the call for belief. Very often, as in "Seek Nirvana" and "Take Christ as your savior," we sense a surplus meaning of this sort in religious injunctions to believe.

Of any of these actions other than believing which we are being asked to do it is fair to ask, "How do I do it?" For this would help us understand just what we are being asked to do. In answer, we might be told to engage in meditation, or to read the Bible. But the specific point of an injunction to believe is to call for a decision about the proposition in question, that is, for a judgment. The enjoiner could claim that the point of the injunction is being evaded[11] if no decision one way or the other is announced.

At this point, however, the relevant question is not "How do I do it?" but instead "Is is true?" For while we may learn how to perform certain overt actions, and how to contemplate certain objects, and even perhaps how to have certain attitudes,[12] we cannot learn how to believe something. The reason is not that this would require a degree of effort or skill which is in fact impossible. The reason is that this is not the sort of thing one learns or fails to learn to do. The only way we can come to believe something is by seeing whether it is the case.

Yet this may be too simple. There is a sense in which we learn to make up our minds and come to decisions about proposals for belief. In the course of life we learn that some

[11] And I am arguing, in effect, that it is *right* to evade the specific points of such injunctions, because very often suspense of judgment is justified. Furthermore, when a judgment is justified it is not made in *compliance* with an injunction to believe, though the process of deciding might be stimulated by some such injunction.

[12] The discussions of interests in earlier chapters suggest a limitation on injunctions to attitudes. If someone should ask, "How do I become religious?" or "How do I become scientific?" and if these are *real* questions, much can be said in either case, but only obliquely. Interests cannot be commanded (and are in this way like beliefs), though they may be evoked.

decisions are more urgent than others. It is a matter of practical wisdom to know when suspense of judgment is called for and when judgments must be made. And if practical wisdom can be learned this can be learned.

Also, perhaps we can learn how to inquire. We can learn to think what we are doing and thus acquire some practical clarity as we try to answer questions. Also, perhaps experience may ripen our estimates of the facts with which we deal. We learn to weigh one fact against another, and to tell fruitless questions from fruitful ones. So perhaps we can learn to formulate better questions and proposals.

All this is evident from the fact that on a given question we are likely to trust the judgments of some people more than others. But all this is not learning how to believe in the same sense in which we can learn how to behave. We can learn when to make decisions, and we can put ourselves in position to make more intelligent decisions. But whether, when we decide, the right decision is an affirmative or negative one—this depends not on anything we can do or learn to do but on what happens to be the case.

Consider, as possible direct replies to iiD-F, which ask someone to believe some p: (R1) "That is hard to do" and (R2) "That is impossible." And consider the reasons which might be given for these replies. Any plausible interpretation of the replies would have to include, among the reasons for them, some logical appraisals of p. Reasons for R1 would have to include something like "Because what you are asking me to believe is not clear" or something like "Because there is much evidence against p." [13] Reasons for R2 would have to include something like "Because p is self-contradictory" or something like "Because p is clearly incompatible with the evident facts." Further, these logical appraisals would be sufficient reasons for the replies.

Now suppose these replies were given to the ordinary in-

[13] Similarly, reasons for "It is easy to believe p" would have to include something like "p is clear and evident."

junctions iiA-C. Then reasons for them would have to include statements like, for R1 to iiA, "Because the gate is
locked and I would have to climb over it" and, for R2 to
iiC, "Because I am resolved to be faithful to God." And
such statements would be sufficient reasons for the replies.

In the replies to iiA-C the difficulties and impossibilities
are physical or psychological or moral difficulties and impossibilities; the replies to iiD-F refer to logical difficulties
and impossibilities. Hence in the replies to iiA-C the essential and sufficient reasons are physical or psychological or
moral facts; in the replies to iiD-F the essential and sufficient
reasons are logical facts.

For this reason the act which is the specific point of an
injunction to believe cannot be enjoined in the way ordinary acts can be enjoined. Beliefs, like interests, cannot be
commanded. Nor can they be enjoined, strictly speaking,
in milder ways than by commands. For we cannot try to
believe in the way we can try to behave. Logical difficulties
and impossibilities cannot be overcome in the way physical,
psychological, and moral difficulties can be overcome.[14]
And we cannot decide, or learn how, to comply with an
injunction to believe something in the way we can decide,
or learn how, to comply with an injunction to do something.

So one result of this examination of these peculiar utterances, injunctions to believe, is to reinforce the distinction
between proposals for action and proposals for belief and
to show that they call for decisions of different kinds. In
responding to proposals for action, we decide whether or
not to do what is proposed; in responding to proposals for
belief, we decide whether or not what is proposed is true.
And this helps to show how judgments are different from
appraisals of other sorts.

[14] Though we can cope with them in various ways, for example,
by making concepts clearer or by discovering or inventing new
concepts.

Another conclusion is that injunctions to believe are logically and morally problematical, for they seem to ask us to do something which cannot be done. So the right response to such an utterance is to disregard its specific point and to respond in the appropriate ways to (*a*) the legitimate injunctions to various actions associated with believing and (*b*) the proposal for belief which it implicitly conveys.

5. *Confessions*

We have been distinguishing judgments from appraisals of other sorts by marking off proposals for belief from injunctions. Now we need to distinguish proposals for belief from another important class of utterances in religious discourse.

First let us distinguish various functions of first-person utterances. (*a*) Some are *performatives*, for example, "I refuse to put incense on the altar." (*b*) Some are *informative utterances*. For example, a psychologist is investigating religious behavior and asks M whether he went to church last Sunday (or whether he ever had a mystical experience). M replies, "Yes, I was in church last Sunday" (or, "Yes, once I had a mystical experience"). Ordinarily we would not take these as religious utterances, though they are about religious phenomena. They simply report certain facts which M (but not the psychologist) is in a position to know. Arguments about their truth are possible but not, in the circumstances, in order. (*c*) Some are explicit *proposals for belief*, for example, "I attained Nirvana" and (by a fanatic) "I am the Creator." In these cases arguments about their truth are not only possible but in order. But many first-person utterances are (*d*) *confessions*, deliberate [15] expressions of emotional states or of attitudes, using this term to cover acknowledgments, admissions, avowals, declarations,

---

[15] Thus distinguishing these utterances from those which inadvertently reveal something about the speaker. The latter may be true of any utterance whatever.

disclosures, professions, and similar kinds of utterances. Consider, for example:

iiiA. I am in the depths of despair.
iiiB. We fast on Fridays.
iiiC. I bow to the will of Allah.
iiiD. I believe the body of Jesus was reanimated after death.

Let us take iiiA-D in such a way that they are not performatives or informative utterances or explicit proposals for belief. Thus suppose the point of iiiB is not to report but to declare. Again, suppose iiiC and iiiD are said not liturgically or in private devotions, where they might have a performative force, but in conversations. Also, they are not meant to introduce discussions of whether or not M *does* bow to the will of Allah or believe in the bodily resurrection.

Then these utterances are not themselves explicit proposals either for belief or for action (injunctions). Still, such utterances often convey implicit proposals for action or for belief. For example, said in a certain way iiiB might convey, "And *you* ought to fast on Fridays too." We might call this an implicit injunction. And iiiD might be used in such a way that a proposal for belief lies just below the surface of the utterance. In this case we would have an implicit proposal for belief.

Indeed, whenever a confession declares some referential attitude, as in iiiC and iiiD, it is fair to hold the speaker responsible for some implicit proposal for belief. If referential attitudes are confessed, proposals for belief are implied. For these attitudes (unlike moods) have objects, and a conscious relation to some object involves some belief about it. This would be true of attitudes describable as "knowing" or "believing" or "seeing" or "obeying" or "having a sense of" or "having a feeling that" or "having an intuition of" or "being in harmony with" or "having an encounter with" and many others. For example: "I take refuge in the Dharma" and "I see the hand of God in all this."

So if someone utters a confession and does not wish to be held responsible for some belief but wishes, instead, to disavow any claim to truth, he ought to make it clear that he is not declaring any referential attitude but only a mood or an emotional state. Thus for problematical concepts like "authentic existence" it is necessary to pose a dilemma: either the concept applies to a state involving some relation between the speaker and the world, in which case truth-claims are involved, or it applies to an emotional state, in which case they are not.

In consequence, when a referential attitude is declared it is not enough to appraise the confession by using terms which apply directly (*a*) to the speaker himself, like "naïve," "frank," "insincere," and so on, or (*b*) to our own reactions, as when we say a confession is "embarrassing" or "welcome," or (*c*) to the circumstances in which it is made, as when we say it is "damaging" or "timely." And it is not enough to appraise the confession itself (what is explicitly said) as "interesting," "irrelevant," "trivial," and so on. When a confession conveys an implicit proposal for belief, then we ought also to judge what is implicitly proposed. For example, it is relevant to say of iiiD: (i) that the speaker wants us to believe what he says he believes, (ii) that it is true that he really does believe it, and (iii) that what he says he believes is not true.

6. *"Noncognitive" theories*

Now we are in position to consider some theories of meaning in religion which parallel "noncognitive" theories of moral discourse.[16] Instead of using the term "noncognitive" we can put the issue more clearly in another way. Let us consider theories which hold that religious utterances do

[16] For a well-constructed "noncognitive" theory of moral discourse see Charles L. Stevenson, *Ethics and Language*, New Haven, Yale University Press, 1944. For some searching criticisms see the discussion between Stevenson and Richard B. Brandt in *The Philosophical Review* 59: 291–318, 528–540 (1950), and Richard B. Brandt, *Ethical Theory*, ch. 9, Englewood Cliffs, N.J., Prentice-Hall, 1959.

not make proposals for belief and hence do not make truth-claims.[17]

These theories admit that some religious utterances seem to make truth-claims but argue that this is only specious. Insofar as religious utterances are significant at all, they can be analyzed into utterances which do not purport to make truth-claims, such as injunctions, confessions, and conjunctions of these. They mitigate this conclusion by granting that religious utterances may, incidentally, convey truth-claims of other types, for example, historical or scientific or speculative claims, though usually these theories regard speculative claims as specious also. But, they say, religious utterances do not make religious truth-claims.

It would follow that there are no proper occasions for religious judgments in our sense. The only appraisals which religious utterances call for are those appropriate to pure injunctions and pure confessions. "True" and "untrue" would be inappropriate.

We can disagree with these theories without denying the great importance of injunctions and confessions in religious discourse, to which they have rightly called attention. But I believe they have failed to see the full significance of religious injunctions and religious confessions.

R. B. Braithwaite has sketched a theory of this sort in his Eddington Lecture.[18] He says: "A religious assertion . . . is the assertion of an intention to carry out a certain behaviour policy, subsumable under a sufficiently general

[17] For a survey of recent literature including some "noncognitive" theories see Frederick Ferré, *Language, Logic and God*, New York, Harper, 1961. See Ronald W. Hepburn, *Christianity and Paradox*, London, Watts, 1958, and John H. Randall, *The Role of Knowledge in Western Religion*, Boston, Starr King Press, 1958.

[18] *An Empiricist's View of the Nature of Religious Belief*, Cambridge, Cambridge University Press, 1955. See also "Religion and Empiricism: IV" in *The Cambridge Review*, 10 March 1956. Paul Schmidt proposes a theory similar to Braithwaite's in *Religious Knowledge*, Glencoe, Ill., Free Press, 1961.

principle to be a moral one, together with the implicit or explicit statement, but not the assertion, of certain stories. . . . a religious belief is an intention to behave in a certain way (a moral belief) together with the entertainment of certain stories associated with the intention in the mind of the believer" (32–33). (He is aware that these are not the ordinary meanings of "assertion" and "belief," but he thinks they are the only senses in which they can be applied to religious utterances.) For example, "God is love" primarily declares a resolution to follow an agapeistic way of life both inwardly and in overt conduct. It also tells a story—of a supernatural person (in the sky, perhaps) who loves everyone—which is associated with the resolution. But there is no logical connection between the policy and the story. The story gives no logical support to the resolution but only a psychological reinforcement. So there is no need for the story to be true.

Let us begin with the stories. Their relation to the life policies cannot be simply an external causal connection. If this were so, then any story might effectively reinforce any policy. Hindu stories (like "Atman is Brahman") might reinforce Christian policies, and Moslem stories (like "Allah inspired Mohammed") might reinforce Zen Buddhist policies. But this is not plausible. So there must be some internal connection between stories and policies.[19] One possible connection is that stories *suggest* policies.[20]

[19] As Braithwaite seems to acknowledge when he says that a story describes the behavior policy "in a new way" (31). If this is so, there is a logical connection, not just a causal connection, between telling the story and declaring the policy. Braithwaite's main point here is that the stories do not logically *justify* the policies, which for the moment I am not denying. Certainly they could not justify anything at all if they are not asserted.

It is worth noticing that the stories Braithwaite cites as examples would be doctrines, not basic proposals.

[20] See, on the roles of narratives, fictive and historical, in section 4 of this chapter and in section 1 (under "Mode D") in chapter x.

How does a story suggest a policy? Usually, in the history of religion, both directly and indirectly. Religious systems usually *include* moral tales, like the parable of the Good Samaritan, which directly suggest moral policies. But they usually include also distinctively religious stories, which suggest moral policies only indirectly. These stories directly suggest some object which is given a distinctively religious valuation, an object to which some basic religious predicate applies. This object may be some ideal state of things, for example, Nirvana or the Kingdom of Heaven, which becomes the goal of a policy. Or it may be some real condition, for example, Allah or *Deus sive natura*, with which policies must be congruent. Religious life policies arise in view of some religious interpretation of the goal or of the setting of human life.

How could Braithwaite introduce such concepts into his analysis? They themselves might appear in story form, instead of being suggested by stories. Some image of a goal or of the setting of human life might occur in a story. But since the stories are only entertaintained, not asserted, no claims about objects of these concepts would be made. So it seems that if these concepts should be taken seriously they would have to be expressed as aspects of policies, that is to say, as "intentions to behave." So let us turn to the declarations of moral policies.

These are "assertions of intentions." But it seems that no claims are made in these utterances either; for a moral utterance by some speaker "is not used to assert the proposition that he has the attitude" (11–12). They are neither reports (informative utterances) nor proposals for belief. So these are not assertions in the ordinary sense. Rather they express or show forth or evince attitudes. In our terminology they are confessions.

Further, since religious stories do not make any claims, it seems that on Braithwaite's analysis no serious claims whatever are essential to religious utterances. But surely, in view of the conflicts and arguments which abound in the history of religion, this is so implausible that it verges on absurdity.

At this point Braithwaite's theory could be made more plausible in two ways. In the first place, having an intention to live in a certain way is different from finding oneself living in a certain way. Further, to the extent that the intention is the result of reflection, it involves a decision. Some alternatives have been considered and rejected. Now if someone declares some policy he has adopted in a reflective way, he should be willing to give his reasons for adopting the policy. And some of these reasons would make claims about the policy and its consequences.

In the second place, if anyone adopts a policy for himself, he ought to be willing to propose it (or some generalized version of it) to others also, in appropriate circumstances (however mildly). For we are all involved in a common search for practical wisdom. Further, if someone not only declares a policy ("I intend to live agapeistically") but also proposes it ("It is good to live agapeistically" or "I suggest that you consider living agapeistically"), he ought to be willing to give reasons why others should adopt it. These reasons have to be more than "personal" reasons for the policy. (As a matter of fact, Braithwaite seems to admit that declarations of policies convey implicit injunctions, for he says there is room in religious discourse for arguments about the practical consequences of policies.)

Now reasons for a policy, whether they appear as reasons for the speaker's own adoption of the policy or as reasons why others should adopt it, must include something more than a description of the policy. Otherwise they would not be reasons for the policy. It can be argued that utterances of reasons for policies implicitly convey intentions to behave (more general behavior policies, perhaps), but this cannot be their sole or even their primary function. They must be assertions in some stronger sense also, if they are to be reasons.

On this extension of Braithwaite's theory, religious utterances would make some serious claims. But so far the only claims which would be essential to religion are moral claims. He grants that other claims may occur incidentally, for example, historical claims ("Gotama sat under a bo tree"), but these claims are not essential to religious discourse. The stories need not be true. Religious claims would be, essentially, moral claims, claims that policies have or lead to moral values.

Now let us take another step beyond Braithwaite. It is not plausible to say that religious intentions differ from moral intentions only by virtue of the fact that the former involve the entertainment of stories [21]—without going beyond Braithwaite's treatment of stories in the way suggested earlier, which introduces specifically religious claims. Moralists have used stories to reinforce policies throughout history, for example, Plato's image of the charioteer and his two horses, and various utopias. Moral tales abound in novels, poetry, popular "inspirational" literature, and in the folk wisdom of fables, legends, and proverbs by which moral precepts are mainly conveyed. So we ought to find some other way of distinguishing between religious utterances and moral utterances.

When does a moral policy have religious import? Ordinarily, we would say, only if it is related to something which is religiously valued. So, if some declaration of policy or injunction to a policy is a religious utterance, its religious character can be determined from the reasons for the policy. If the reasons include no distinctively religious valuations, we should conclude that the policy is not a religious policy.

[21] He suggests three other distinctive features of religious assertions: (*a*) policies are specified not by isolated assertions but by systems of assertions; (*b*) concrete examples are given; (*c*) policies concern internal behavior (intentions to "feel in a certain way," to have a certain frame of mind) as well as external behavior. But these are clearly not distinctive of religious utterances and he does not seem to take them seriously. I shall return to the point about frames of mind.

A policy might be related to a religious valuation in various ways. For example:

A. Have compassion for others, because in this way you will attain detachment from your selfish concerns, and this will lead you to Nirvana, the supreme goal of life.
B. Love your neighbor, because this is the will of God for you.
C. Maximize mutuality, because the rich pattern of human interactions you will thus share and nurture is the supreme good, more important than anything else in the universe.
D. You ought to love your neighbor with no ulterior end in view. This is an unconditional imperative. You will be able to do so if you are reconciled to God and put your destiny in his hands, for he is the determiner of destiny. Then you can love your neighbor without an anxious eye to consequences.
E. Live according to your station in life and content yourself with fulfilling what it requires, for the totality of stations is one harmonious whole, and this is the only true reality.

The relation between the policies and the religious evaluations in these cases is not a completely external relation. The valuations tell us not only *why* something is to be done but also *how* it is to be done (with an aim at Nirvana, in obedience to God, with a sense of its ultimate value, by entrusting one's own destiny to God, with a view to the whole). So the religious valuation is integral to the injunction as a whole, and distinguishes a religious injunction from a nonreligious injunction. A religious injunction depends on a basic religious proposal for its significance. So, if "God is love" is a religious utterance by virtue of some policy it enjoins, the policy is connected with something *m* to which some basic religious predicate is implicitly applied.

In this way we could explain how serious claims are made in specifically religious discourse. On Braithwaite's view there are no distinctively religious *claims*. At most, religious

utterances convey moral claims, along with incidental historical and other claims. But if this is the case, why should
anyone say these things in such roundabout ways?

Finally, moral policies are not equally prominent or important in all forms of religion. And this raises the question
whether having a moral policy is essential to being religious.
This is different from asking whether or not a religion
ought to have a moral policy. Certainly, if by "a moral
policy" we mean only a general plan of life, then any well-
developed religion involves a moral policy, though we
would have to leave room for religious *experiences* of an
ecstatic sort which do not. (Hence we would have to leave
room also for expressions of religious experience which do
not include resolutions to behave.) But if, on the other
hand, a moral policy is a way of acting toward other persons
and involves duties to them, then there have been religions
in which moral policies are not essential, for example, some
of the mystery cults in the Hellenistic world and those
strains in various historical religions where a life of solitude
is counseled.

So far we have been mainly concerned with religious
injunctions. Now let us consider religious confessions further. When someone deliberately expresses some religious
state of being, he is not just expressing an emotional state
like euphoria or depression or unhappiness or complacency
or rage. Emotional states are not in themselves either religious or nonreligious. Religious states of feeling include a
relational element. Religious joy is, for example, "joy in
the Lord" and religious despair is despair of attaining some
religious goal. Religious states involve referential attitudes.
This seems abundantly evident from the phenomenology of
religion. It follows that intentions to have certain frames of
mind or to feel in certain ways (Braithwaite), if they are
religious intentions, are intentions to have referential attitudes.

Some religious confessions, it might be said, are meant to

show some state of the subject's own existence which is nonemotional but at the same time nonreferential, for example, enlightenment or bliss or "authentic existence." But, if these are religious confessions, then these states themselves are being valued in a religious way and are expressed (and implicitly proposed) as objects of religious attitudes. They can be alluded to, desired, aimed at, or "leaped to" by those who are not in them. And it is reasonable to ask the speaker to make the point of his utterance clear by saying how the state is valued.

Therefore a religious confession includes an implicit or explicit reference to something m, other than the emotional state of the speaker, to which he is related in a religious way. So, to make the point of his utterance clear, he should be willing to say of m that it is the supreme goal of life, or that it is the ground of being, or that it is holy, or something else of this sort. In this way religious confessions presuppose basic religious proposals for their significance.

In these remarks on "noncognitive" theories I have argued that religious confessions and injunctions of various sorts involve basic proposals. In this and earlier chapters I have taken some steps toward showing how these proposals might make truth-claims. Much remains to be shown. But one point seems reasonably clear from the history and phenomenology of religion: religious utterances are meant to make more serious *claims* than these theories permit, claims which are liable to disagreement and to argument and call for appraisals which are not appropriate to pure injunctions and confessions. These claims seem to call for judgments.

7. *Proposals for belief*

Compare now some different ways in which a proposal for religious belief might be made. It might be conveyed (*a*) in a direct assertion, (*b*) in an injunction to believe, or (*c*) in a confession of belief. For example:

Pi. Nature is the whole of which our lives are parts.
Pii. Look at yourself and everything else as parts of Nature.
Piii. I am content to be a part of Nature.

These are three ways in which the same proposal for religious belief might be conveyed. For the reasons explained above, it would be conveyed less directly and explicitly in Pii and Piii than in Pi, for Pii might be used to propose a heuristic belief, and Piii might be meditatively uttered. Pi raises an issue for judgment more explicitly and clearly. It asks more clearly to be judged as true or untrue. It is an explicit proposal for belief.

Just as (explicit) injunctions and confessions can convey (implicit) proposals for belief, so (explicit) proposals for belief can convey (implicit) injunctions and confessions. Indeed, we might ask whether proposals for belief do not always convey (implicitly) some injunctions and confessions.

One injunction is implicit in any proposal for belief, namely, an injunction to serious consideration of the truth-claim of some proposition. In this respect proposals for belief differ from idle (irrelevant) or playful or humorous remarks. The context of a proposal for belief is a serious inquiry.

Similarly, a confession is implicit in any honest proposal for belief. The proposal deliberately expresses the interest which prompts the inquiry. A moral proposal expresses a moral interest; a scientific proposal expresses a scientific interest; a religious proposal expresses a religious interest. Anyone who makes a genuine proposal for religious belief is acknowledging (implicitly) that he himself is involved in religious inquiry in some way or other. And this means, as we saw in Chapter V, that he is making some basic supposition and commitment. This is part of what it means to say that he believes what he is proposing.

Although, in making a proposal for belief, the proposer conveys an injunction and a confession, the point of his remark is not to admonish nor to reveal his own experiences and attitudes. These functions of the utterance are subordinate. The point of his remark is to present a proposition for judgment.

8. *The finality of religious judgments*

What sort of finality may a judgment have? In making a judgment: (*a*) we are more or less *sure* that we have settled the issue, and (*b*) we *do* settle the issue more or less. Let us look briefly at these two dimensions of the finality of a religious judgment, its certainty and its stability.

a. Certainty. In adopting a suggestion we accept a promise of truth. In an affirmative judgment we declare, in effect, that we have what was promised. The mood of adopting a suggestion is expectation; the mood of an affirmative judgment is satisfaction. But this satisfaction can be more or less complete. The decision is made with more or less certainty.

In any particular situation two questions about certainty arise: How certain does one have a *right* or warrant to be? and How certain does one *need* to be in making the judgment? A short answer to both questions might be, "Reasonably certain." What would this mean? Roughly speaking, this means, in reply to the first question, as certain as the situation permits one to be and, in reply to the second question, as certain as the situation requires one to be. And from this short answer two general questions then arise: (1) Do we ever have *sufficient* warrant to make an affirmative religious judgment? (2) Is it ever reasonable (warranted) to have *absolute* assurance in making a judgment?

We shall return to these questions later, but a word about each is in order now. Whether there is sufficient warrant for some judgment depends on both (1) the strength of the evidence and (2) how urgently the situation requires a decision. All issues are not equally urgent, and the more urgent an issue is, the less conclusive the evidence has to be for a decision to be reasonable.

If some religious proposal were known to be necessarily true, it would be reasonable to have absolute assurance in making a judgment. But, if knowing a proposition is necessarily true requires knowing it has no consistent alternative, then basic religious judgments cannot be made with absolute certainty. For it is always possible to state a self-consistent alternative to any basic religious proposal. It follows that, while we might be reasonably certain, we cannot be absolutely certain in *this* sense,[22] in making a religious judgment.

b. Stability. Whether or not someone's belief remains stable does not strictly depend on how certain he is in making his judgments. He may continue to believe something even though he is not absolutely certain it is true. It is a fact that we do settle religious issues more or less—sometimes more, sometimes less. But since some people do change their minds and come to deny what they previously affirmed, for example, in conversions, a prediction that M will never change his mind cannot be absolutely certain. Such a prediction may be especially hazardous if made by M himself.

Thus we have two senses in which a basic religious judgment cannot be absolutely final. It cannot be final in the sense that we can be absolutely certain about it, if this means knowing it is necessarily true. And it cannot be final in the sense that it would be reasonable to predict, with complete assurance, that we shall never cease to hold it. But these limitations do not exclude the possibility of religious judgments which are reasonably certain and stable.

[22] There may be other good senses of "absolutely certain," but this is the only one about which I am clear. I am not objecting to saying we are absolutely certain in some other sense than this, if we can be reasonably clear what we mean.

CHAPTER VIII

Religious Arguments

1. *Introduction*

The conditions of making truth-claims explained in Chapter II determine the kinds of arguments required to support a religious truth-claim. To restate those conditions, a proposal makes a significant truth-claim only if: (*a*) it can be given a self-consistent formulation, and (*b*) it permits the formulation of a self-consistent alternative, and (*c*) it permits a reference to its logical subject, and (*d*) it permits support for the assignment of its predicate to this logical subject.

The initial use of these conditions is to see whether a prima-facie truth-claim is a genuine truth-claim. They do not tell us whether: (*a*) there is sufficient reason for an affirmative judgment, or (*b*) there is sufficient reason for a negative judgment, or (*c*) suspension of judgment is called for. As stated, they are minimal requirements a proposal must satisfy to be qualified as a candidate for being true or untrue. But they also indicate ways in which its strength or weakness as a candidate must be appraised.

To qualify as a truth-claim, a proposal must permit *some* reference to its logical subject, but the references it permits may be more or less successful and adequate. It must permit *some* support for its predication, but this support may be strong or weak. Whether a proposal is self-consistent and permits self-consistent alternatives are not so much matters of degree. But even here there are degrees of strength and weakness. For as the proposal is elaborated into a doctrinal scheme we may find the scheme more or less coherent. And as we compare the proposal with its logical alternatives we may find it is more or less powerful in doing justice to the elements of truth which its positive alternatives contain.

It would follow that, once a proposal has been admitted as a candidate for truth, arguments (for and against it) of four sorts are in order, as follows:

a. Arguments about the consistency and coherence of the developed proposal;

b. Arguments about its power to interpret its alternatives;

c. Arguments about the adequacy of the references it permits;

d. Arguments about the adequacy of the support for its predication.

In this chapter I discuss arguments of the first two sorts, and introduce some preliminary considerations about the latter two sorts. I shall discuss references in the next two chapters and predications in Chapter XI.

An argument against a proposal might go so far as to show it is utterly inconsistent, or that it is merely a tautology, or that no reference to its logical subject is possible, or that no support for its predication is possible. In any of these cases the right conclusion is not that it is untrue but that it does not even make a genuine claim to significant truth.

2. *Arguments about consistency and coherence*

Often we find good uses for paradoxical expressions. We use them to bring out alternatives which are being overlooked. "Did he do it or not?" "Well, he did and he didn't." Or we mean to call attention to a distinctive quality. "He is both proud and humble at the same time." In general we use these rhetorical devices to force an awareness of the uniqueness of something. We pose contrasts which stretch the imagination and prevent a too simple conception of some action or quality or thing.

So it is not surprising that paradoxes often occur in religious discourse. For one general feature of religious discourse is that something or other (God, Nature, Nirvana,

Humanity, the One, the Way, for example) is being distinguished from all other subjects of discourse. For example:

"Arjuna, I am the cosmos revealed, and its germ that lies hidden."

"The Good is everywhere and nowhere."

"The Way is always still, at rest,
And yet does everything that's done."

"Lord of all being, throned afar,
Thy glory flames from sun and star:
Center and soul of every sphere,
Yet to each loving heart how near!"

Though we can make good use of paradoxical expressions, we cannot assert propositions which contradict one another. So when we encounter a paradoxical-sounding utterance we need to ask whether we do indeed have a real contradiction on our hands or only an apparent one. For example:

A. Instead of giving our devotion to some supernatural being which we conjure up out of fanciful wishes, we should devote ourselves to mankind. . . . We should have reverence for the source of our being, and since we are children of nature, it is to nature that our reverence is due.

B. The God revealed in Christ is the creator of all things. . . . It is as true to say that God does not exist as to say that God exists.

Suppose the author of A is presenting a new form of religion for the modern world, and that B occurs in a theological text. Then problems about consistency would arise in different ways. In A the point to be explained is the compatibility of religious devotion to mankind and reverence for nature as the source of our being. Are these possible together, and, if so, how? Is there some (unstated) unifying interest, for example, in cosmic evolution, so that mankind is nature's noblest work? Or is one of the objects, mankind or nature, subordinated to the other in some way? The suspicion of inconsistency can be dispelled either by showing (*x*) how both mankind and nature are subordinate to something else or by showing (*y*) how one of them is subordinate to the other.

In B the point to be explained is how God can be the creator and yet be said not to exist. For if creation is an activity, whether a single act "in the beginning" or a continual activity, it must be truer to say God exists than to say he does not. So we would need to know how "creator" is used in Christian theology.

In cases like A we wonder whether two different religious objects are being proposed. Are we faced with two incompatible basic proposals? In cases like B only one object is proposed, but the nature of this object is not clear. It seems that incompatible doctrines are being asserted. So we have two sorts of apparent inconsistencies, calling for different sorts of explanations.

Now notice a different kind of inconsistency:

C. Nature is the source of our being; nevertheless we cannot live according to nature.

D. God inspired the prophets, but he did not tell them what to say.

A and B look like pairs of incompatible proposals. But in C we seem to have both a basic proposal and a retraction of it, assuming that the source of our being is that according to which we live. Similarly, in D we seem to have both a doctrinal proposal and a retraction of it. C and D are puzzling because they seem to take back with one hand what they offer with the other. We wonder whether any proposal is really being made.

So these latter inconsistencies have to be cleared up in a

different way. It could be explained that "source of our being" in C is not to be taken as a basic religious predicate but as a historical predicate (We have a natural historical origin), as, for example, an Orphic might say he is a child of earth as well as of starry heaven. And someone might explain what meaning of "inspired" the adversative clause in D is not meant to retract. But if no such explanation is possible we must conclude not that we have incompatible proposals but that we do not really have proposals.

Sometimes we are puzzled not by feeling that statements conflict but by not knowing how they hang together. We suspect not that the statements are inconsistent but that they are incoherent. They are not clearly connected with one another, yet they are offered together as parts of one proposal. This might be our feeling about A above. Let us take some extended examples.

In *Reason in Religion*,[1] Santayana says:

"Piety, in its nobler and Roman sense, may be said to mean man's reverent attachment to the sources of his being and the steadying of his life by that attachment. . . . The true objects of piety are, of course, those on which life and its interests really depend: parents first, then family, ancestors, and country; finally, humanity at large and the whole natural cosmos" (179).

In the next chapter he says that along with piety religion has a higher and nobler and unworldly side, namely, spirituality, which he explains as follows:

"A man is spiritual when he lives in the presence of the ideal, and whether he eat or drink does so for the sake of a true and ultimate good" (193). . . . "For it is religion that knows how to interpret the casual rationalities in the world and isolate their principle, setting this principle up in the face of nature as nature's

[1] New York, Scribner's, 1905.

standard and model. This ideal synthesis of all that is good, this consciousness that over earth floats its congenial heaven, this vision of perfection which gilds beauty and sanctifies grief . . ." (212).

This makes us want to ask how the ordered set of "objects of piety" is related to the "ideal synthesis of all that is good." We do not seem to have an explicit contradiction. "Piety" is not identified with "spirituality," so the objects of piety do not have to be the same as the object of spirituality. Yet piety and spirituality are said to be two sides or aspects of religion.

This would not be a problem if Santayana were merely describing religious phenomena. In that case he would not need to exhibit a logical unity among the features he described. If the phenomena exhibited disconnections it would be enough to leave it at that. But it is reasonably clear that Santayana is not merely describing religious phenomena. Along with such cues in the quoted texts as "nobler" and "really depend," the general tenor of the book suggests that he is making a religious proposal and thus saying what religion ought to be. So it is fair to ask how coherent his proposal is.

For another example let us take some texts from *The Human Enterprise*,[2] by Max Carl Otto. Much of the book is a plea not only for disbelief in the existence of God but for "an affirmative faith in the nonexistence of God" (334). The correlative of this faith is "a marching interest in the well-being of mankind, material and spiritual" (335). Indeed:

> "The deepest source of a man's philosophy, the one that shapes and nourishes it, is faith or lack of faith in mankind. If he has confidence in human beings and believes that something fine can be achieved through them, he will acquire ideas about life and about the world which

[2] New York, Crofts, 1947.

are in harmony with his confidence. Lack of confidence will generate corresponding ideas" (366).

Now along with faith in mankind there are certain attitudes historically associated with faith in God which are prized by the humanist. These are: (*a*) "a feeling of oneness with the unending procession of living forms" (341); (*b*) "the primitive, elemental sense of community with the all-sustaining earth" (341); and (*c*) a conscious awareness of "an unexplored beyond" (342). And, Otto says, these will provide "a positive source of inner renewal analogous to that found in the best forms of theism" (342).

Here again we are presented with a number of objects: mankind, the procession of living forms, the all-sustaining earth, and an unexplored beyond. And we are not sure how to take all these together, though they seem parts of a single proposal, a positive alternative to faith in God.

In both cases the problem of coherence arises only if we take the statements together as parts of a whole. We would not be puzzled in this way about remarks taken at random from the course of a casual conversation. So the way to reply to the objections is to show the point of the proposal. This would mean formulating the question at issue and showing how the parts of the proposal fit together in answer to this question. This is the general form which arguments for the coherence of a developed proposal must have.

It would be wrong to foist on Santayana or on Otto some question he does not really mean to answer. This is why it would be wrong to look for some single general theory of religion to replace all others, and derive some basic religious question to replace all others. But it is fair to ask for *some* question to be stated, so we could understand the point of the proposal and thus see more clearly how its various parts contribute to making this point.

Finally, let us consider paradoxes again. First we should distinguish paradoxical expressions from the propositions they might be used to convey. A proposition may be conveyed in various ways. It may be stated explicitly by a declarative sentence; it may be conveyed by gestures and other nonverbal symbolic actions; or it may be conveyed by verbal expressions which fail to state explicitly what is meant, including paradoxical expressions. So a paradoxical expression might be used as a device to convey a self-consistent proposition.

Further, we should distinguish statements of contradictory propositions like "God is a person/ God is not a person" from statements of contrasts like "God is our Refuge and Strength." For a contrast is not a contradiction, and even a great multiplicity of contrasts, as in Krishna's self-description in Chapter X of the *Bhagavad-Gita*, might be stated without contradiction.

Sometimes it is held that paradoxes are essential in religious discourse, and we should examine this view, of which a mild version and a strong version are possible.

a. The mild version is that paradoxical expressions are necessary to suggest the extraordinariness of what is being alluded to in religious discourse. But it might be added that, though such expressions are necessary vehicles for suggestions, it is also possible to explicate these suggestions in nonparadoxical ways and thus to mitigate the paradoxes. On this view the use of paradoxes is not to convey pairs of contradictory propositions; they convey contrasts which enlarge our vision of what is being suggested.

b. A stronger version would be as follows: Religious suggestions must be conveyed by paradoxes, and these suggestions cannot be explicated in nonparadoxical ways. Now from this it would seem to follow that either (1) paradoxes are not being used to convey propositions or (2) they are being used to convey pairs of contradictory propositions. In either case it would follow that there could be no self-consistent proposals for religious belief. And from this it would follow, according to the argument in Chapter II, that no religious proposals make significant truth-claims. But this is a result which defenders of this version might hesitate to accept.

What reasons could be given for holding that paradoxes are necessary in religion? It would seem that anyone who defends this view must know some fact from which this necessity follows. Let us consider two sorts of facts which might be thought to imply it.

A defender of the view might appeal to some fact about the inner states of religious people. To support the strong version it might be claimed that all religious people are in a peculiar state of inner conflict such that its expression must involve assertion of contradictory propositions. This would be a psychological theory about religion, and it would have to be tested by examination of the phenomena of religious experience.

Or it might be claimed that what is alluded to in religious discourse is of such a character that it cannot be suggested without use of paradoxes, and (on the stronger version) such that we can formulate no self-consistent propositions about it. This would be claiming a fact about the object of religious experience. This way of defending the necessity of paradox concerns us more directly, and I have two comments about it.

First, by claiming something about the object of religious experience, namely, that it has just this character, either version of the view would show that it is not a general theory of religion but a religious proposal. It proposes as the religious object something which has the character mentioned. (So it would be better to claim this for Christianity, say, or for Buddhism than to make the claim for "religion.") But, logically speaking, disagreements about this are possible. It might (logically) be held, for example, that the religious object is such that while symbols are necessary, paradoxes (though useful, perhaps) are not necessary.

Second, if the proposal thus made in the stronger version

is wrong, it is wrong not by being inconsistent, in the way A seemed wrong, but in some other way. It does not ask us to accept two incompatible proposals at once. The trouble with A was that it seemed to say too much; this proposal, like C, would seem to say too little.[3]

3. *Dialectical arguments*

Although it may not be unreasonable to accept a paradoxically stated proposal, it is unreasonable to accept a proposal which is in itself inconsistent. On the other hand, when we consider positive reasons for accepting a basic religious proposal, its consistency is not sufficient reason for accepting it. For there might be a number of self-consistent basic proposals. Then a choice among alternative consistent proposals would be a matter for good judgment, to be supported by arguments of other sorts.

One matter for good judgment and argument is, as we have seen, the degree to which a proposal is coherent, the degree to which, as the proposal is developed and explained, its parts form a whole. Another sort of argument is in order when rival proposals are compared and contrasted with one another. I shall call these dialectical arguments.

First, is it possible to argue that there is only one consistent religious proposal? This would mean showing that all basic proposals but one are inconsistent. It would not have to mean that there is no truth in other proposals, but it would have to mean that any elements of truth embodied (inconsistently) in other proposals are consistently embodied in the proposal in question.

I do not see how it could be shown a priori, by some *unrestricted* argument, that all basic proposals but one are not self-consistent. For this would mean that there are a priori norms of religious judgment, norms such that they cannot be disavowed without self-contradiction. And, as I have argued in the discussion of Kant, Schleiermacher, and

[3] The mild version would be relatively harmless in this respect.

Rudolf Otto in Chapter III, the notion that such norms are possible arises from a confusion of general theories of religion with religious proposals. Only if we begin with a special theory of religion, such that a particular proposal is built into the theory itself, could we seem to derive norms of judgment which are valid a priori. This sort of argument depends on smuggling conclusions into premises.

Any such norms would have to be deducible from a quite general theory of religion, since they are meant to govern all religious judgments. But it is of the essence of a general theory of religion that, while it gives a certain value to P (for example, "holy") in expressions of the form, "It is m that is P," so that rules of relevance can be deduced, no special value is given to m. So if norms of judgment, which restrict the values of m, are deducible from some theory of religion, this shows that the theory is not a general theory but a more or less explicit religious proposal, to which counterproposals are logically possible.

While it is essential to religious inquiry and argument that rules of relevance be deducible from a general theory of religion, it is essential to a general theory of religion that no norms of judgment be deducible from it. It follows that there can be no norms of religious judgment such that their rejection entails a contradiction. In this sense there are no completely neutral norms of religious judgment. And if such norms were the goal of the search for "the religious a priori" earlier in this century, it was a hopeless quest.[4]

This can be illustrated by recurring to Anselm's ontological argument for the existence of God. Two assumptions are required by the argument as it is ordinarily (and no doubt correctly) understood. It must assume (A) that God is "that than which nothing greater can exist or be conceived." And it must assume (B) that it is greater to

---

[4] But not a fruitless one, for it produced some useful general theories of religion and also some interesting and important religious proposals.

exist both in the mind and in reality than to exist in the mind alone.

Although assumption *A* was not likely to be challenged by a medieval atheist, it might be questioned—by a Theravada Buddhist or by a humanist, for example. Such an opponent might say: "There does exist in my mind the conception of something than which nothing greater can be achieved. But this conception is not a proposition but only a predicate. I understand this predicate, and I think there is something of which it is true. But I do not agree that it has to be applied to God. In my own judgment, that than which nothing greater can be conceived is Nirvana." Or Auguste Comte might have challenged assumption *A* by saying that nothing greater than Humanity ("the Great Being") can exist or be conceived.

What might Anselm's rejoinder be? In reply to the Buddhist, he might speak of God's function as creator and ruler of nature, and of the importance of the world of nature and substantial things. He would be suggesting that a substantial reality is greater than a state of mind. Here assumption *B* would come into play, to be explained and justified. In reply to the humanist, Anselm might speak of the power of God to create and redeem, and its superiority to human power. In these and other ways Anselm might aim at justifying the challenged assumption. In doing so he would be explicating the "greater than" in the predicate.

The issue then joined between Anselm and his opponent is about the scale along which "greater than" is being construed. Arguments on this issue are then in order.[5] It is possible to say, "I grant you that *m* is greater than *n* in *that* way; but being greater in *this* way is more significant than being greater in *that* way. So *n* is really greater than *m*." This means that, though assumption *A* may look like a

[5] For example, see Charles Hartshorne, *The Divine Relativity*, 18–22, 41–49, New Haven, Yale University Press, 1948, and *The Logic of Perfection*, La Salle, Ill., Open Court, 1962.

definition, and might be taken as such by Anselm and his contemporary opponents, it must become something different once it is challenged. "*Is* it God that is 'that than which nothing greater can be conceived'?" It must then become a proposal, to which alternative proposals are possible. So, if it were challenged in this way, the ontological argument would have to be extended into an argument in support of a basic proposal in which the predicate, "that than which nothing greater can be conceived," is applied to God, the reference of the term "God" being given by its traditional use or in some other way.

A challenge like this might be met in another manner. The term "God" might be taken as a name for whatever the predicate properly applies to. Then asking what it applies to would be asking what God is. And if a case could be made for saying that Humanity or Nature or Nirvana is that than which nothing greater can be conceived, then it would be proper to say that Humanity (or Nature or Nirvana) is God. Sometimes, indeed, the term seems to be used in this way.[6] But it is fairly certain that Anselm would not have taken this tack. And this supports the view that assumption *A* was for Anselm something more than a formal equivalence.

The point of this excursion is to show how consistent alternatives to a basic religious proposal are always possible. If this is so, an unrestricted dialectical argument is not possible. But we might hesitate to look on such a priori arguments as being genuinely dialectical. A genuine dialectical

[6] As in Gandhi's remark, "Rather than say that God is Truth I should say that Truth is God." Another interesting example occurs in an essay by H. Richard Niebuhr: ". . . the important question for religion is not the question, whether a god exists, but rather, what being or beings have the value of deity. . . . The true query of religion is, 'Which among the available realities has the value of deity or has the potency of deity?'" ("Value-theory and Theology" in J. S. Bixler, R. L. Calhoun, and H. R. Niebuhr, ed., *The Nature of Religious Experience*, 114, New York, Harper, 1937).

argument, we might think, restricts itself to comparisons of particular proposals, and arguments of this latter sort are always in order.

It is always in order to try to show how some proposal conserves, and expresses in a more consistent and coherent way, the values of another. For example, modern philosophical analysts can argue that they are doing better what ancient and medieval philosophers were trying to do. Similarly, the early Christians could argue that the law and the prophets were fulfilled in Christ. And Hindu philosophers [7] can try to show that the *advaita* Vedanta philosophy contains in a clearer and purer form what is true in theism.

For another example, in discussing the triumph of Christianity in the ancient world the historian Guignebert says:

"Christianity supplanted Neoplatonism and Manicheism during the decay of the old world because it could express their own tendencies better than they could themselves and also express the one not to the exclusion of the other, but together balancing and harmonizing them." [8]

Guignebert does not mean this as an argument for the truth of Christianity; he writes here as a detached historian. But it exhibits the form of a dialectical argument. It implies that both Neoplatonism and Manicheism were inconsistent, that each had a certain value, that the value of each was better expressed in Christianity, and that these values were expressed in Christianity in a self-consistent way.

Again, sometimes it is argued that all nontheistic forms of religion are implicitly or "virtually" theistic. Then, as a next stage, it is argued that all other forms of theism than some particular one (for example, Christian theism) are

[7] And others, for example, Aldous Huxley in *The Perennial Philosophy* and Alan Watts in *The Supreme Identity*.

[8] Charles Guignebert, *Christianity, Past and Present*, 197, New York, Macmillan, 1927.

adumbrations or undeveloped forms of that one. On these premises it is then argued that, to the extent that any religious proposal is inconsistent with Christianity, it is also inconsistent with itself.

In these cases the argument aims to show that without the higher form the lower forms are inconsistent in themselves. Taken in themselves, the lower forms contain elements that conflict with their main intentions.

But I urge that arguments of this sort have to be made good for each particular rival proposal. One might, indeed, argue that some proposal is more consistent and coherent than any other and that it expresses the elements of truth in all others. But this has to be shown for *each* rival, by analysis of its structure and implications. Only by a fair and detailed analysis of particular proposals could it be shown that all but one entail contradictions and are therefore internally unsatisfactory. We cannot, simply by understanding some one proposal alone, see that all others must fail to be self-consistent.

It follows that dialectical arguments are deficient in finality. For suppose that someone has shown, by detailed analysis, that proposals X, Y, and Z are lacking in consistency, and that proposal R salvages and conserves their main positive intentions. This does not yet amount to an absolutely and finally decisive argument for R, because there may be other proposals which the dialectician has not thought of. Some of these might be similar to X or Y or Z yet also different in subtle but important ways. So one limitation of dialectical arguments is that we cannot be sure we have taken account of all alternative proposals.

One feature of dialectical arguments is that, insofar as they are arguments for some religious proposal and not merely negative arguments, they contain implicit appeals, beyond the proposals they consider, to the facts of life. Consider the argument of Second Isaiah (Isa. 44:9–20) against the pagans of his time. An idol, he says, is made of wood from the same tree that provides fuel for hearth fires. The idol and the firewood are made of the same stuff and both are made by human hands. Now it is obviously impossible for the idol maker, who is a human being, to endow his part of the timber with properties which would justify worshipping it. So it is inconsistent to propose that we worship an idol. It is obvious that we ought not to worship anything made with our own hands. Yet it is proposed by the pagans that we worship the idol. So the proposal reduces to an absurdity.

This *reductio ad absurdum* is a purely destructive argument and might be employed with equal force by someone who rejects all other religious proposals also. In order to construct a dialectical argument with a positive religious conclusion, negative arguments have to be supplemented in one of two ways. Either way requires an appeal, beyond the proposals being considered, to the facts.

One way to give positive content to a dialectical argument is to accept certain components (though not others) of the allegedly inconsistent proposal. For example, Second Isaiah agrees that we ought to worship something not made by human hands. This is a premise he assumes the pagans accept. Or a Hindu Vedanta philosopher might agree with Christians that God is eternal, though not agreeing about how God is related to the temporal world.

The other way to give positive force to a dialectical argument is to propose something not envisaged in the allegedly inconsistent proposal. Thus Second Isaiah proposes that there is a divine creator of heaven and earth. In either case, whether he is agreeing with one of his opponent's premises or whether he is adding a premise of his own, the dialectician makes himself liable for giving reasons for believing what he proposes. What reasons can he give?

He may be able to show that his proposal is self-consistent, that its main alternatives are not self-consistent, and that it embodies their values. But something more is needed if in doing this he means to stake out a claim in the public domain. *Ad hominem* arguments would not be enough. He needs to appeal to facts of one sort or another.

4. *Appeals to facts*

It needs to be said, as a reminder, that the business we have in hand is not to construct an empirical argument for some religious proposal. Our business is rather to see how appeals to facts might be made in support of religious proposals. In speaking of appeals to facts I am not assuming that there are any pure or utterly uninterpreted facts. I am referring to a certain sort of move that is made in the course of arguments. "Facts," as we ordinarily use the term, may also be noticed or overlooked, established, and weighed. "Fact" is tightly linked to "theory" in ordinary use. Theories fit, or do not fit, the facts; facts support, or do not support, theories.

To distinguish different purposes for which appeals to facts are made in the course of religious arguments, let us recall three features of basic religious proposals: (*a*) a logical subject is mentioned; (*b*) a certain predicate is said to be true of this logical subject; and (*c*) this implies that the predicate is not true of alternative logical subjects.

So one purpose for which facts might be appealed to (or, we might say, adduced) is to support a reference to the logical subject of the proposal. Facts may be brought in to help answer the question, "What is it to which you are referring?" For example, "When you talk about God, what is it that you are talking about?" Answer: "I am talking about the being who gave the Law to Israel." Fact adduced: "Israel got the Law."

Another purpose for which facts might be adduced is to support a predication. Granting that the reference is reasonably successful, so we know reasonably well what is being talked about, we want to know whether the predicate is true of this logical subject. For example, supposing that we understand what is meant by "Nirvana," we want to know whether it is true that Nirvana is the supreme goal of life. So we ask for reasons for saying this of Nirvana. With a similar intent we might ask, "Why should we say that God is the ground of being?" And facts might be adduced in aid of answers to questions of this second type. For example: "Because all evils come from craving" or "Because new values continually come into existence."

More or less incidentally to these two purposes, facts may be brought into religious arguments to support negative judgments about alternative proposals. They may be appealed to in aid of answers to questions like "Why is nature more important than mankind?" and "Why is it God and not nature that is holy?" So facts might be used to support a comparative judgment. And this would bring us again to the use of dialectical arguments in religion.

I shall not give a separate treatment of the use of facts in dialectical arguments, though some of the specimen arguments in the succeeding chapters will illustrate this use. I shall deal with the use of facts in references in the next two chapters, and with the use of facts to support predications in Chapter XI. But some preliminary points should be made.

In addition to distinguishing different purposes for which facts are adduced, we have to distinguish different sorts of facts. Further, we must distinguish different sorts of proposals. For I hope to show that some proposals rule out facts of certain sorts from being relevant to them, and rule in facts of other sorts. In this way we shall get some light on the limits within which a particular proposal may be supported by facts. A proposal cannot be supported by facts which it rules out from relevance.

It does not seem possible that any religious argument could be absolutely decisive in the sense that it would establish beyond any conceivable doubt that some basic religious proposal is true and all others untrue (though it is conceivable that an argument might establish its conclusion beyond *reasonable* doubt). One reason is that a priori norms of judgment, norms such that if anyone failed to accept them he would be convicted of irrationality, are not available in religion. Norms of judgment must be proposed and supported along with the proposals to which they are meant to apply. A second reason is that we cannot be absolutely sure that an argument has taken account of all the relevant facts. A third reason is that in dialectical arguments we cannot be absolutely sure that an argument has taken account of all the alternative proposals. So it is not possible for religious arguments to be absolutely decisive, though some might be convincing.

So, while the least we should hope for is to show that a proposal is as consistent and well grounded as its main alternatives, the most we could hope for is to show it is more consistent and better grounded than its main alternatives. We cannot achieve strict proofs in religious arguments.

How serious would this consequence be? Would it rule out the possibility of being reasonable in religion? Of course not. Being reasonable does not depend on being able to give coercive proofs of the propositions we maintain. There are many propositions which we reasonably believe but which we do not know to be true.

What, then, would it mean to be reasonable in religious arguments? (*a*) It would mean being aware of the antecedent conditions of basic religious judgments, namely, the suppositions on which they are made and the questions they mean to decide. Put negatively, this means not making category mistakes of a certain sort, not confusing religious questions with scientific or moral or metaphysical questions. (*b*) It would mean also, if there are no a priori norms of judgment, not arguing as though there were some. Put positively, this means proposing our norms of judgment as subject to analysis and comparison with counterproposals. (*c*)

CHAPTER IX

Some Types of Basic Proposals

Requests for references, like "Help me direct my thought to what you are talking about," are requests for explanation, but they are unlike requests for explanation of predicates. In particular, requests for references arising from basic proposals are unlike requests for explanation of basic predicates. We might ask, "Just what are you saying of m when you say m is worshipful?" And an explanation would have to include giving rules of relevance and a procedure for judgment in the frame of "worshipful." But even a complete explanation of the predicate "worshipful" would not amount to a reference to m.

References may be objected to, and therefore have to be supported. For example, in reply to the request, "What are you referring to when you speak of God?" it might be said, "God is the cause of the world." Objections to this reference are familiar, in the form of objections to the cosmological argument for the existence of God. If the reference is to be successful the objections have to be met, and the reference supported, in two different ways. (*a*) The fact ("the world") used as the starting point for the reference must be explained and established if challenged. It would have to be shown that finite things are a totality and that the existence of this totality is contingent.[1] (*b*) The category ("the cause of") used to move from this starting point to the goal of the reference would need to be explained if challenged. It would have to be shown how this category applies to the fact. So one sort of religious argument is about the validity of references.

[1] Or "the world" might be interpreted in some other way, in answer to the question, "What are you referring to when you speak of the world?" Requests for references are in order here too.

Requests for references might be met in various ways, depending on what is being proposed. In the next chapter I shall distinguish various modes of referring. But first we should look at some different types of basic religious proposals, for the nature of the object referred to determines what modes of referring are available. It would not be strange if the ways in which Second Isaiah could refer to Jahweh should differ from the ways in which Cleanthes the Stoic could refer to Zeus.

The following points will explain how these types are constructed and how they are to be used. First, in constructing the types I am drawing on the phenomenology of religion. But, in order to distinguish categoreal questions from historical questions, I begin in each case by framing a hypothetical proposal as an instance of the type. Then I make some allusions to historical forms of religion which might be assigned to the type. Thus the types may have a certain diagnostic value. But the arguments in which I make use of the types later on do not depend on the aptness of the historical allusions.

Second, I do not offer this as an exhaustive list of types of basic proposals. There might well be proposals which are not classifiable according to these types. There are bound to be border-line instances. Also, other schemes of classification are possible. But this one will be useful for showing how modes of referring are related to types of proposals.

Third, I do not claim that the terms I use for these types are used in the proposals to which they apply. A proposal does not need to classify itself, though it might do so. Monsieur Jourdain spoke prose without saying (or knowing) he was speaking prose. To anticipate, for example, we need not suppose that the hypothetical proposer of the first type below would call wisdom a quality, though he might do so. I only suggest it would be fair to call it a quality.

Fourth, some of these hypothetical proposals will be unconventional. By ordinary standards some may seem too primitive; some may seem too sophisticated. Some readers may wish to reserve the term "religious" for a narrower range of proposals than this. I only point to some family resemblances among proposals of these types. My later argument about correlations between types of proposals and modes of referring would not be affected in principle by narrowing the range of types.

Proposals of the types I shall discuss have as their logical subjects, respectively, entities which might be called:

1. Qualities
2. Relations
3. Particular natural entities
4. Particular human individuals and groups
5. Nature
6. Mankind
7. Pure forms
8. Pure being
9. A transcendent active being

TYPE 1. QUALITIES

Consider the following hypothetical proposal:

"In my judgment, instead of believing in some transcendent being you call God, and instead of devoting yourself to humanity, you would do well to seek wisdom above all else. Wisdom is more important—holier, if you like—than God, who is after all only a fiction. Humanity is also a fiction, since there are just a number of particular human beings—and they are a very mixed lot. Wisdom is the only thing for which the world is well lost. It means a peace and an inner freedom, without which nothing else is worth having and with which nothing else is needed."

Consider also, as logical subjects of other proposals of this type: detachment from desire; love, or unity (integrity), or freedom, or creativeness, as qualities of feeling and action; and life as a quality of things (which would be one way of interpreting "reverence for life").

Consider also the following instances from the history of religion, about which we might ask whether they propose some quality or other: Confucianism; the subjectivistic strain in primitive Buddhism; the Biblical book of Proverbs, though not of course those passages which personify Wisdom as a transcendent being or principle; Walter Lippmann's treatment of "maturity" in *A Preface to Morals*; and Baker Brownell's naturalistic mysticism in *Earth is Enough*. The following passage from Cicero is relevant also:

> "O philosophy, thou guide of life, thou discoverer of virtue and expeller of vices, what had not only I myself, but the whole life of man been without you! To you it is that we owe the origin of cities; you it was who called together the dispersed race of men into social life; you united them together, first, by placing them near one another, then by marriages, and lastly by the communication of speech and languages. You have been the inventress of laws; you have been our teacher in morals and discipline; to you we fly for refuge; from you we implore assistance; and as I formerly submitted to you in a great degree, so now I surrender up myself entirely to you. For one day spent well and agreeably to your precepts is preferable to an eternity of error." [2]

To what is Cicero referring? Is he personifying a complex quality of human life (sociality, social inventiveness, social wisdom)? Or is he invoking a Platonic essence, as in Type 7?

[2] As given by S. J. Case in *Experience with the Supernatural in Early Christian Times*, 301, from *Tusculan*, v. 2, New York, Century, 1929. See, on "philosophy," A. D. Nock, *Conversion*, chapter 11, London, Oxford University Press, 1933.

TYPE 2. RELATIONS

Consider the following:

"Nothing in the world is better than harmony. What I mean by harmony is things existing together in such a way that they do not threaten or detract from one another's existence but instead contribute to and enhance one another's existence. This is the supreme good and the source of all other good things. This is indeed the source of that inner peace and freedom you call wisdom. If and only if you stand in this sort of relation with other things, then as a subjective consequence you have that quality of experience. The relation is the parent of the quality.

"I agree that entities like God, Humanity, and Nature are either fictions or otherwise inadequate for the function we have in mind. But the quality you propose is also inadequate. One thing about harmony is that it doesn't leave anything out. 'God' leaves you out. Humanity leaves Nature out. Nature leaves out the distinctive features of human life. And your proposal of a quality of mind leaves out the world beyond ourselves, natural and human. But harmony, as a pattern of things, doesn't leave anything out except what doesn't exist—and that should be left out, of course."

Consider also, as logical subjects of proposals of this type: the classical conception of justice; love or unity (integration) as a relation among persons and things.

We could ask whether the following instances amount to proposals of this type: some of the sayings of Empedocles about Love and Strife; certain sayings in the *Tao Tê Ching* about the Way; Martin Buber's saying that "God is in the relation." Consider also this passage in John Steinbeck's *The Grapes of Wrath* in which Casy, the ex-preacher, says:

"Sometimes I'd pray like I always done. On'y I couldn' figure what I was prayin' to or for. There was the hills, an' there was me, an' we wasn't separate no more. We was one thing. An' that one thing was holy. . . .

"An' I got thinkin', on'y it wasn't thinkin', it was deeper down than thinkin'. I got thinkin' how we was holy when we was one thing, and mankin' was holy when it was one thing. An' it on'y got unholy when one mis'able little fella got the bit in his teeth an' run off his own way, kickin' an' draggin' an' fightin'. Fella like that bust the holiness. But when they're all workin' together, not one fella for another fella, but one fella kind of harnessed to the whole shebang—that's right, that's holy. An' then I got thinkin' I don't even know what I mean by holy" (Modern Library ed., 110).

TYPE 3. PARTICULAR NATURAL ENTITIES

Consider the following hypothetical proposal:

"The sun is the ultimate source of our life. It makes the corn grow; it gives us warmth. Also its brilliance blinds us. It surpasses all other things in power."

Consider, as other logical subjects of this type: the earth, the sky, the moon, a river, a mountain, light, animals, et cetera.

Consider this Egyptian hymn to the sun-god, where the Aten (the solar disk) is addressed as follows:

"O creator of what the earth brings forth, Khnum and
    Amun of mankind! . . .
Excellent mother of gods and man, good creator who takes
    the greatest pains with his innumerable creatures . . .
He who reaches the ends of the lands every day and be-
    holds those who walk there . . .
Every land adores him at his rising every day, in order to
    praise him." [3]

Consider also this Babylonian hymn to the moon:

"O Lord! Who is like unto thee? Who is equal to thee?
Great hero! Who is like unto thee? Who is equal to thee?

[3] In W. F. Albright, *From the Stone Age to Christianity*, 219, Garden City, Doubleday, 1957.

Lord Nannar! Who is like unto thee? Who is equal to
thee?
When thou liftest up thine eyes, who can flee?
When thou drawest near, who can escape?" [4]

(For other instances see van der Leeuw, chs. 5–8.) On a
more sophisticated level we might ask whether life, as in
"reverence for life" and in "the life force," might appropri-
ately be taken as a particular natural entity, though a very
complex one.

TYPE 4. PARTICULAR HUMAN INDIVIDUALS AND GROUPS

Consider the following as a possible religious proposal:
"What we need, as an object of reverence and devotion,
is something concrete, not some abstract quality or relation. We need something that is really *there* and has real
power. To this extent, even the sun worshippers were on
the right track. But of course they were very primitive and
naïve, and did not understand what they were doing.
Really, they were projecting onto a part of nature the
values generated by a human community.

"They realized this sometimes, though unclearly, when
they identified the king as a descendent of the sun and worshipped him. They were recognizing that it is the state, a
particular social organization, which is the source of our
values. What would we be without it? We are born into it
and by its laws and by the subtle and powerful influence of
its life we become what we are. So if we realize the true
spiritual source of our being, we will give our devotion to
our country. We will live for it and die for it."

Consider Alexander Meiklejohn's interpretation of Rousseau in an essay significantly entitled "From Church to
State." For it is fair to ask whether he is making, implicitly,
a religious proposal and, if not, whether what he says is
misleading.

[4] From H. Zimmern, *Babylonische Hymnen und Gebete*, II, 1911,
6, in G. van der Leeuw, *Religion in Essence and Manifestation*, 66.

"The peculiar significance of Rousseau for our Western culture lies in the fact that he leads the way in the substitution of the state for the church as the primary institution of human brotherhood. . . . The state is, for him, the agency of fellowship. It is, therefore, the source of all morality. And, for the same reason, it is the source of intelligence."

He quotes from *The Social Contract* as follows:

"Each of us puts his person and all his possessions in common under the supreme direction of the general will, and, in our corporate capacity, we receive each member as an indivisible part of the whole."

And he says:

"And the striking fact is that the meaning which that theology [i.e., medieval theology] tried to express remains unchanged. The 'Christian' tradition is maintained. . . . 'Whosoever will lose his life for my sake shall find it' was the old doctrine. It is now replaced by the assertion that each of us, in a well-organized society, yields to the state *all that he is, all that he has,* and that, in doing so, each of us becomes a free person." [5]

As other possible objects of this type consider: the king, the dead, the tribe. (See van der Leeuw, chs. 13–14, on the king and the dead. On nationalism see van der Leeuw, ch. 37; Carlton J. H. Hayes, *Essays on Nationalism*; D. C. Holtom, *Modern Japan and Shinto Nationalism*; and Stanton Coit, *The Soul of America*.)

The next two types of proposals are not types in quite the same sense as the others in this list. They might be taken as types with but a single instance each. But in each case the entity may be conceived in different ways, being endowed

[5] In *Religion and Education*, 18, 21–22 (italics mine), Cambridge, Harvard University Press, 1945.

with different qualities and attributes. In this way there may be various proposals of each type even though the same name is given the object proposed.

TYPE 5. NATURE

Consider the following hypothetical proposal:

"It is true enough that we must conceive the ultimate, that on which we are absolutely dependent, as concrete and not as abstract. But it must also be something universal, not something particular like the sun or a king or a nation. Otherwise religion declines into superstition.

"Also we must avoid that form of superstition which projects particular natural things and qualities and relations into a transcendental realm. Supernaturalism of any sort, whether centered on an ideal quality, on an ideal principle of law, or on an ideal person or persons, is only a more sophisticated form of superstition.

"The true source of our being is nature, that system of things of which we and all other things are parts. Here each of us has his place. This is, for each of us, our home. Here and here only can we be true to ourselves. Nothing is alien to nature except what is unreal. And when we turn from our private dreams and fancies and wishes, to this reality, we find both an inward freedom and an outward productiveness. This is, indeed, the way of salvation."

The ancient Stoics, especially the early Greek Stoics, seem to have made proposals of this type. And Spinoza might be interpreted as the great exponent of Stoic religion in modern times. Consider also the following passage from Holbach's *Système de la Nature*, ch. 14:

"O Nature, sovereign of all beings! and ye, her adorable daughters, Virtue, Reason, and Truth! remain forever our revered protectors! it is to you that belong the praises of the human race; to you appertains the homage of the earth. Show us then, O Nature! that which man ought to do, in order to obtain the happiness which thou makest him desire. Virtue! animate him with thy beneficent fire. Reason! conduct his uncertain steps through the paths of life. Truth! let thy torch illumine his intellect, dissipate the darkness of his road. Unite, O assisting deities! your powers, in order to submit the hearts of mankind to your dominion. Banish error from our mind; wickedness from our hearts; confusion from our footsteps; cause knowledge to extend its salubrious reign; goodness to occupy our souls; serenity to occupy our bosoms." [6]

Similar strains of thought can be found in the writings of many other writers in modern times. When the term "God" is used in proposals of this type, then "pantheism" is an appropriate characterization.

But it is not always easy to say just what is being proposed in these historical instances. Many passages in Stoic literature, especially in the later Roman Stoics, present God as a transcendent personal being. Again, Spinoza's *Deus sive natura* is sometimes taken to be closer to the medieval conception of God than to naturalistic pantheism. And Holbachs' "assisting deities" do not fit neatly into the framework of this type. Indeed, we might ask whether for Holbach Nature (as well as Virtue, Reason, and Truth) was really an *ideal*. Fortunately we do not have to solve these problems of historical interpretation. The point of this list of types is only to suggest some of a variety of possible conceptions of the religious object.

TYPE 6. MANKIND

I use this term instead of "Humanity" because the latter might suggest a quality (the quality of being rational or creative or sympathetic), an essence, or a class (human beings), whereas it is a community or nexus (in White-

[6] In J. H. Randall, Jr., *The Making of the Modern Mind*, 279, Boston, Houghton Mifflin, 1926.

head's sense) that I have in mind here. But often the two terms are used interchangeably. Consider the following hypothetical proposal:

"It is true enough that our existence as human beings has a natural basis. But if we make nature the object of reverence, then we seem to deny the radical importance of moral distinctions, and we lose sight of the distinctive values of human life. For nature is neutral on moral issues and unconcerned for human welfare. But we cannot be neutral on moral issues, and we cannot be unconcerned about human welfare, without ceasing to be human. We cannot be content with a religion which gives no moral inspiration and guidance.

"At the same time, in this age of science, we cannot believe in any transcendent being, beyond the world. While we ought to be loyal to the particular human communities we belong to, they point beyond themselves to a larger community, the community of mankind. And in this community we find an object of reverence from which we draw inspiration and spiritual strength, and to which we can devote all our energies."

Religious humanism has to be taken seriously as an alternative to which, in the modern period, many earnest minds have tended when traditional faiths have lost their power. In van der Leeuw's words, Humanity was "the sole entity worthy of worship that remained to thousands after the fierce conflagration of potencies in the nineteenth century" (271). Consider this passage from Auguste Comte's *Positive Polity:*

"By it [the conception of Humanity] the conception of God will be entirely superseded; and a synthesis be formed, more complete and permanent than that provisionally established by the old religions. . . . Towards Humanity, who is for us the only true Great Being, we, the conscious elements of whom she is composed, shall henceforth direct every aspect of our life, individual or collective. Our thoughts will be devoted to the knowledge of Humanity, our affections to her love, our actions to her service.

"Positivists then may, more truly than theological believers of whatever creed, regard life as a continuous and intense act of worship; worship which will elevate and purify our feelings, enlarge and enlighten our thoughts, ennoble and invigorate our actions." [7]

(See also the writings of Frederic Harrison, Felix Adler, Stanton Coit, J. A. F. C. Auer, M. C. Otto, Lewis Mumford, and others, *Humanist Sermons*, Curtis Reese, ed., and the journal *The Humanist*.) Many versions of this type appear. Some are in a stoical, some in a romantic mood. Some attach themselves to scientific method and scientific theories; some are detached from and even somewhat critical of the influence of modern science on human values. There are literary, philosophical, and psychological versions.

I hesitate to set off the next three types from the preceding ones in a special way, though I want to make the features of each type clear. My reason is that the characterizing terms which might come first to mind are likely to be misleading if we apply them to the logical subjects of all proposals of these types. Certainly "supernatural" would not be a good term for all of them, though it might characterize some of them. Again, we might be inclined to speak of all these entities as "transcendent," to contrast them with entities referred to in proposals of the preceding types. But one function of a basic proposal of any type is to mark off its logical subject from all else in a special way. So any entity proposed as a religious object is in this sense transcendent. It might be said that entities of the next three types are epistemically transcendent also, since they are

[7] *System of Positive Polity*, 1 (J. H. Bridges, tr.), 263, 264, London, Longmans, Green, 1875.

not given in experience as directly as those of the preceding types. But this is a matter for argument. It can be argued, on one hand, that Nature and Mankind (and perhaps other entities referred to in the preceding types) are not given directly in experience and, on the other hand, as by mystics and others, that some of the entities to be mentioned below are given directly in experience. So I shall simply present these types without any common characterization of all the entities referred to in them.

TYPE 7. PURE FORMS

Consider this hypothetical proposal:

"What is really worthy of our reverence is the multiplicity of pure forms. For these, and these alone, may be contemplated with unmixed satisfaction, and contemplation is the highest activity of man. It is wrong to attribute actuality or activity to pure forms. They are not active, or even actual. They are just themselves. They are the Good and they are Beauty, not for any extrinsic reason—not, that is to say, because they affect the world and change the course of events, but intrinsically. Their value consists simply in their being what they are. So they are wrongly loved if they are loved for the sake of ourselves or of our fellow men or the state. In this contemplation we rise above the world without ceasing to live in it. This realm is timeless and ageless. Eternity is always near."

Other possible proposals of this type might have as their logical subjects selected forms or ideals or essences instead of the realm of pure forms as such, for example, the Good or Beauty or Humanity or Truth.

It would be in order to consider, as possible instances of this type: some of Plato's dialogues, the Ideas in Schopenhauer's system, the essences in Nicolai Hartmann's *Ethics*, and Santayana's conception of spirituality as the contemplation of essences. (See, in van der Leeuw, chapter 95 on the "religion of form.")

Consider Sterling P. Lamprecht's discussion of "the religious insight of Hellenism" in *Our Religious Traditions:* [8]

"It inquires concerning the ultimate before which men ought to stand in reverence. Is that ultimate a power which, by the very compulsion of its fiats, creates the distinction between good and evil? Or is the ultimate rather a value by which all the powers that there may be, small and great, finite and even infinite, may, indeed must, be judged, and to which those powers, whether they conform or fail to conform to its moral demands, are alike subject in principle?" (86).

"Hellenism accepts joyfully the other alternative, namely, that certain values are in principle supreme, whether or not these values are espoused by powers that sponsor and secure them" (88).

Consider also the following:

"But there are other frames of mind, to which we shouldn't deny the name 'religious,' which acquiesce quite readily in the non-existence of their objects. (This non-existence might, in fact, be taken to be the 'real meaning' of saying that religious objects and realities are 'not of this world.') In such frames of mind we give ourselves over unconditionally and gladly to the task of indefinite approach toward a certain imaginary focus where nothing actually is, and we find this task sufficiently inspiring and satisfying without demanding (absurdly) that there should be something actual at that limit. . . .

"And I, for my part, should be willing to accord to my *focus imaginarius* that same attitude of unquestioning reverence, that my critics accord to their existent God: it is, in fact, *because* I think so highly of certain

[8] Cambridge, Harvard University Press, 1950.

ideals, that I also think it unworthy to identify them with anything existent." [9]

In the context Findlay appeals for support to Plato, Plotinus, Erigena, Fichte, and Samuel Alexander.

TYPE 8. PURE BEING

A possible proposal:

"You are very near the truth. But you present something abstract. You say the object of reverence is a set of forms. And you say this is good in itself. But this 'in-itself' relation is hardly possible in an ideal entity. Should we not think of that which we contemplate and reverence as *being* in a fuller sense?

"Certainly what we need to turn to is beyond the world. I agree also that it is not active; indeed if it were active it would not be beyond the world. It would then be one of the things that make up the world. But at the same time it is something more than ideal. It is more than pure form; it is beyond form.

"This ultimate does have a kind of power, though it does not exert its power. It is Power without Will. Though it does not act, yet in some utterly mysterious way it is the source of finite being. It is the One, and simply by being itself it gives unity and being to all things. The true goal of life is to be one with it."

(See Aldous Huxley's *The Perennial Philosophy*, Alan Watts' *The Supreme Identity*, and W. T. Stace's *Time and Eternity* as recent proposals of this type.) We could ask whether, along with the religious philosophy of Plotinus, proposals referring to the Tao, Brahman (in *advaita* Vedanta Hinduism), the Buddha-nature (in Mahayana Buddhism), the Godhead (in Eckhart), and "being itself" (in Paul Tillich's theology) are of this type.

[9] J. N. Findlay in A. Flew and A. MacIntyre, ed., *New Essays in Philosophical Theology*, 56, 74, New York, Macmillan, 1955.

We might consider whether the Form of Good, in the sixth book of *The Republic*, comes nearer to this type than to the previous type. In this passage, does Plato's religious proposal amount to "logical realism" or to Neoplatonism? Similarly, we might ask whether Spinoza's *Deus sive natura* belongs to this type instead of Type 5. We might ask an analogous question about Aristotle's conception of God, and, indeed, about the Aristotelian and Neoplatonic strains in medieval Christian theology. Do they belong to this type, or do they belong to the next type we shall notice, or do they effect some synthesis of the two?

Many varieties of religious mysticism seem to be of this type. One eccentric variety of religious experience, relevant to this type, might be mentioned. Reporting his experience after inhaling nitrous oxide, Benjamin P. Blood says, "I know—as having known—the meaning of Existence: the same center of the universe—at once the wonder and the assurance of the soul." [10]

TYPE 9. A TRANSCENDENT ACTIVE BEING

Consider the following as a possible religious proposal:

"The being who is the source of all things is not a 'pure' being in either of the senses you have proposed. He is a being who acts. He creates all good things—and all things that have some unity of being are insofar good. In every situation of life he is, so to speak, at work. The end of life is to enjoy his works and obey his will. True joy is found in his service.

"This is what makes our activity as well as our thought significant. You are right that we cannot really worship and center our lives on stars and trees or kings and nations. There is something more ultimate than things and persons, namely, the creator of them all. But when you move from the world of nature and human history to some realm of

[10] As quoted by William James in *The Varieties of Religious Experience*, 389, n. 2, New York, Longmans, Green, 1902.

pure form or pure being, you value this world at less than its worth. This is the real world God gives us to live in together. We serve God best when we too, in our finite ways, are productive."

This hypothetical proposal, like the others given above, is not meant as a paradigm of its type but only as an illustration. Consider as possible logical subjects of this type: the hero gods in primitive religion, Shiva, Homer's Zeus, Jahweh, the Best Soul in Plato's *Laws*, the savior gods of the mystery cults, and Allah. Consider the conception of God in the Apostles' Creed and in the main line of Christian theology, in the theology of Judaism, and in theistic Hinduism.

Many forms of theism have been proposed within the theological traditions of Hinduism, Judaism, Christianity, and Islam. And if we include conceptions falling more or less outside those traditions the range of variation is even more impressive.[11] It would not be true to say that the term "God" always means a person. Nor does it always mean a supernatural being.[12] Consider the following:

"What is God? God is the integrating process at work in the universe. It is that which makes for increasing interdependence and cooperation in the world. . . . To seek to enter more deeply into conscious appreciation of this interdependence, and to live according to its requirements, is to practice religion." [13]

"We are in the presence neither of ideals completely embodied in existence nor yet of ideals that are mere rootless ideals, fantasies, utopias. For there are forces

[11] See C. Hartshorne and W. L. Reese, ed., *Philosophers Speak of God*, Chicago, University of Chicago Press, 1953.

[12] E.g., a being such that he can do miracles, in the modern sense of "miracle" (namely, an event which cannot be explained by any discoverable laws of nature).

[13] H. N. Wieman, *Methods of Private Religious Living*, 46–47, 79, New York, Macmillan, 1929.

in nature and society that generate and support the ideals. They are further unified by the action that gives them coherence and solidity. It is this *active* relation between ideal and actual to which I would give the name 'God.' " [14]

"We must conceive the Divine Eros as the active entertainment of all ideals, with the urge to their finite realization, each in its due season. Thus a process must be inherent in God's nature, whereby his infinity is acquiring realization." [15]

So we should leave room within this type both for conceptions of God as a supernatural person and for other conceptions of God.

In concluding this list of types of religious proposals, I repeat some earlier words of caution. I do not suggest that this list exhausts the possibilities. There may well be proposals of other types than these.[16] Nevertheless we can find a good use for this list. It will give us a context in which we can discuss various modes of reference to the logical subjects of basic proposals.

[14] John Dewey, *A Common Faith*, 50–51, New Haven, Yale University Press, 1934.

[15] A. N. Whitehead, *Adventures of Ideas*, 357, New York, Macmillan, 1933.

[16] See van der Leeuw, Part I, and F. H. Smith, *The Elements of Comparative Theology*, New York, Scribner's, 1937.

CHAPTER X

References

1. *Modes of reference*

I shall discuss five possible ways of referring to logical subjects of basic religious proposals: by ostension, by giving examples, by assigning regular effects, by assigning extraordinary effects, and by interpretation.

MODE A. OSTENSIVE REFERENCE

Often the simplest way of referring to something is to point to it, or to give a definite description locating it in relation to something to which we can point. For example, we can say, "It is the next street beyond this one." Is there any use for references of this kind in making religious proposals?

The only likely candidates for being referred to in this way are those of Types 3 and 4, particular natural entities or human individuals and groups. You can point to a sacred cat or to a sacred king. But this is not so simple as it seems. In the case of the cat, it is not just a cat that is being proposed. It is a cat plus something less easy to refer to—some power cats possess, or which possesses cats. And, in the case of the king, it is not just this man, who happens to be the king, that is being proposed. You would not point to Ramses in his sleep or when he is putting on his shoes or playing with his children, but when he is on the throne in his royal robes. It is not a particular physical object as such that is being proposed.

Still, the pointing is not misleading if it is done in the right way—at the right time and place and with the right purpose understood by all concerned. Maybe the pointing would be less ambiguous and misleading in the case of the sun or the earth or the sky. But here also one would have to guard against misunderstanding. Would it be just as appropriate to point to the sun when a cloud is passing over it or when it is sinking beneath the horizon or going into an eclipse, as when it is rising or when it is high in a clear sky at midday?

Pointing to human groups would be more difficult than pointing to a divine king. How would one point to a tribe? With a sweep of one's arm in the midst of a village when people are engaged in domestic tasks and diversions? Or when the fighting men are assembled before a raid, or when the elders sit in judgment?

One answer to difficulties of this sort is to produce a symbol of the object proposed. In the absence of the king one can point to the palace or the throne or the royal mace. If the sun is obscured one can point to the polished brass on the altar in the temple. So military standards and banners can be symbols of the tribe. But this step takes us farther away from direct ostensive references. Instead of pointing to the object proposed, something else is found to stand for it and mediate it.

MODE B. GIVING EXAMPLES

From our list of types of proposals, the best candidates for reference by example are qualities, relations, and pure forms. One might ask about the proposal under Type 1 above, "Give me an example of what you mean by wisdom." The proposer could then mention some acquaintance or historical figure. "Socrates was a wise man. He had the quality I mean." To distinguish this quality from others Socrates also had, attention would be called to particular actions which manifest it. Also, these actions would be contrasted with unwise actions to make the example clear. Perhaps a number of examples would be needed.

Using hypothetical cases would be in order, such as, "If someone consistently made intelligent choices, was not excessively perturbed by the evils he recognized, and had a source of lasting satisfactions, we would call him a wise man." But these would be subordinate to the elucidation of the examples themselves. For a reference by example supposes that someone has actually had the quality.

Similarly, one might ask about the proposal under Type 2, "Will you give me an example of harmony, so I will know what you are talking about?" Then the proposer might mention a family, or a larger community, whose members are living together harmoniously. Or he might give a biological example, taking some healthy organism and showing how it is maintained by a balance of functions. Or he might take as an example the way several musical notes sound together. Or he might even take a case of equilibrium in an inorganic physical system. Since the relation of harmony holds not only among human beings but also among things of other sorts, examples may be drawn from a wider domain than examples of wisdom. Other relations might be interpreted as applying only among human beings, for instance, love. In that case examples would be drawn from a narrower domain.

One feature of qualities and relations should be noticed. A quality like wisdom is proposed as something one can actually have. It is not an ideal in the sense in which a pure form (Type 7) can be an ideal,[1] though it is a goal. It is a desideratum, but the important point is that it may be not only desired but possessed. An ideal cannot be possessed. Nor do we speak of instances of an ideal. Similarly, harmony is a relation in which one can actually stand, a satisfiable condition of enjoying things in a certain way. It is not an (unreachable) ideal. Ideals have to be referred to in a somewhat different way, as we shall see. Entities of Types 1 and 2 can be actualized in a way those in Type 7 cannot.

Consider proposals of Type 7. Would it be appropriate

---

[1] Pure forms need not function as ideals. An essence can be contemplated without being aimed at.

to ask of the proposer of an ideal like Beauty, "Will you give me an example of what you mean?" Is it logical to try to give an example of Beauty, where Beauty is not an experienceable quality but an ideal? Not exactly. For what the proposer would be doing, when he mentions this or that beautiful thing, as Plato does in the *Symposium,* is to set the stage for the appearance of Beauty. This is not really giving examples. It is not actually bringing the thing itself onto the stage. Here we must anticipate discussion of Mode E below.

What could be done is like giving examples, in that particular beautiful things would be mentioned. But what is meant by Beauty is not exactly the quality these things have. The examples of the quality are being used to refer to something that is not itself a quality. This is done in two ways which dovetail together. The first way is to arrange the examples in a series such that successive contrasts, as attention moves from one member to the next, suggest a scale. Then it is suggested that the scale extends even beyond the highest member of the series and even beyond the maximal imaginable instance of the quality. Thus the mind is carried toward Beauty itself.

The second way of using examples of qualities or relations to refer to something which is not itself a quality or a relation is a version of the mystical *via negativa.* Indeed, this has already been introduced in principle as a feature of the more positive way mentioned above. What is meant, it is said, is *not* the quality present in the examples mentioned. And this can be conveyed by drawing attention to the imperfections of the instances. The bloom of youth soon fades, it is said, and so for any example of beauty that might be cited. Each has defects, and these may be brought out so as to suggest something that has no such defects—pure Beauty. This is a negative way of pointing to the ideal. It is like moving away branches in a thicket, to clear the way for a view beyond the thicket. But these ways of referring are different from giving examples. Insofar as they are not merely suggestions, they are references in Mode E.

MODE C. ASSIGNING REGULAR EFFECTS

Now we come to another way of adducing facts in aid of references. The proposer might call attention to some regularity in the course of events, for example, the regular succession of the seasons, or the rise and fall of empires. Then he might mention the logical subject of his proposal as the cause of this series of regular events. He points to something by assigning to it this set of effects. "What do you mean by m? (What are you talking about?)" "I mean by m the cause of E_1, E_2, E_3. . . ."

This way of referring is not in order if the proposal is of Types 1 or 2 or 7 or 8. Qualities, relations, pure forms, and pure being are not causes in this way. Nor would entities of Types 3, 4, and 6 be referred to in this way, though it is not categoreally impossible. Certainly it might be said that the sun causes the recurrence of spring. But this fact would be adduced to support a predicate, to show the sun is worthy of reverence and devotion, not to refer to it. For referring to it, a more direct and obvious alternative is open —ostension.

So the entities most naturally referred to by assigning regular effects are Nature and a transcendent active being. In each case there is a problem. The problem about Nature arises from an ambiguity. If "Nature" means the system of natural objects and events, this cannot be the cause of some particular series of events, at least not in the required sense. What we then have is a whole-part relation, which falls under Mode E. It would be strange to speak of a part as an effect of the whole.[2] But if "Nature" means an entity

[2] We might say that a whole affects its parts. But this would be different from saying the parts are themselves the effects of the whole. A whole might be said to affect (be a necessary condition of) its parts without causing (being a sufficient condition of) them.

which transcends the system of natural objects and events in some way, then the relation would be different from a whole-part relation. Then we might have a proposal of Type 8 or 9. The central problem about Spinoza's conception of *Deus sive natura*, namely, in what way infinite substance transcends its modes, stems from his uses of "whole" and "cause."

Now we come to the problem about referring to a transcendent active being as the cause of a series of regular effects. Here the traditional objections to the cosmological argument for the existence of God are relevant. (Indeed, considering the traditional theistic arguments as complex references may put them in a new light.) The main question is, In what way is the entity transcendent? If it is *utterly* beyond the world,[3] we cannot refer to it as the cause of some regular series of effects in the world. For in causal explanations our minds are not carried utterly beyond the world. I do not object to finding various analogous meanings for "cause." Even in ordinary discourse we do not use the term in one way only, to say nothing of its scientific and quasi-scientific uses. But the farther we extend the meaning of "cause" and use it analogically, the more difficult it is to use the concept in *referring* to something.

These problems would not arise if (*a*) the being were conceived as not utterly beyond the world, so that *some* categories would apply in an unambiguous way,[4] and if (*b*) causal explanation of regular events were explicated in a systematic way by means of some metaphysical scheme. Then by using the scheme we might be able to refer to a transcendent being as a necessary (perhaps crucially necessary)

[3] In most conceptions of God he transcends the world but is not utterly or absolutely transcendent, since he is immanent in the world also.

[4] See C. Hartshorne, *The Divine Relativity*, New Haven, Yale University Press, 1948.

condition of the series of events. This would be a reference of a different sort, falling under Mode E.

MODE D. ASSIGNING EXTRAORDINARY EFFECTS

One way we make references is by assigning to something certain extraordinary events as its effects. We introduce some entity m into discourse by mentioning some extraordinary event and saying that m produced it. Instead of some regularity or other in the course of events, we mention an event which is marked out in some way from the ordinary course of events and is thus extraordinary. And we say, for example, "m is the inventor of the flying machine."

This involves something like historical explanation, since it involves explanation of unique events. But in making the reference we are using the explanatory process backward, so to speak, as in Mode C. The immediate interest is not in explaining the event but in using an explanation of the event to introduce us to the agent.

Events of many sorts might be used in this way, including "miracles." But extraordinary events are not limited to miracles in the modern sense of that term. To be in principle inexplicable by scientific laws—the ordinary modern conception of a miracle—is not the only way an event may be extraordinary. Certainly many events have been used as starting points for religious references without being extraordinary in *this* way. In primitive societies extraordinary events are contrasted not with scientifically defined regularities but only with regularities evident in common experience. For example, suppose the laws governing eclipses of the sun are not even suspected. Then though an eclipse of the sun would be an extraordinary event it would not be thought of as a miracle in the modern sense.

In more sophisticated societies also, extraordinary events may be starting points for religious references without being miracles. For example, a modern Jew might give a strong meaning to the Biblical saying, "I am the Lord thy God, which have brought thee out of the land of Egypt, out of the house of bondage" (Exod. 20:2), without supposing that the Exodus involved any contradiction or suspension of laws of nature. The Exodus is an extraordinary event because of its crucial importance in the history of Israel.

The factual starting point might be a private event instead of a public event (as the Exodus). A reference might start with some turning point in the inner history of an individual, an experience of deliverance from desire or from sin or from spiritual ignorance, for example. And Buddha or Christ or Rama might be referred to as the one who brought about the deliverance.

Like Mode C, this mode would be inadmissible for proposals of Types 1 and 2. Qualities and relations are not causes or agents. Though not inadmissible it is not appropriate for Types 3 and 4 because ostension is available. Its use for Types 7 and 8 is doubtful. Pure forms or pure being may be conceived as "final causes" or as "the ground of finite being," but these would more naturally yield references in Mode E. Its use for Types 5 and 6 is doubtful also. To assign some extraordinary event to Nature as its cause is even less satisfactory as a *reference* (e.g., "What I mean by Nature is the cause of the earthquake") than to assign some series of regular events to Nature. Similar strictures apply to Humanity. No doubt we must leave room for causal agency to be construed in various ways, for example, as acting in, inspiring, and self-manifesting, as well as producing, begetting, creating, and the like. But the former set of expressions would take us nearer references in Mode E than the latter set.

Thus the principal use of this mode of reference is for proposals of Type 9. This does not mean that a transcendent active being is always referred to in this way. The deists did not refer to God by adducing some extraordinary event. On the contrary, deists were extremely critical of references of this sort. This is one of the ways they subordinated the individual and the unique to the universal.

This is a good vantage point for noticing various ways religions can relate themselves to historical events. A religion might require that its basic suggestion be conveyed by means of narratives of a certain historical event. And, for an adequate concept of its object, it might also require references based on this event. Such a religion would be historically based [5] in a strong sense. Some Christian theologians go even farther than this and say that Christianity is based exclusively on history, that it does not permit suggestions and references of other sorts. But most Christian theologians, though they regard the historical basis of Christianity as essential to it, have used other sorts of references also in the development of doctrines.

An important contribution to comparative religion could be made by studying the characteristic ways in which basic suggestions are conveyed and references to the religious object are made in various religions. It might be asked whether a religion requires historical suggestions and references and excludes others, or requires them and countenances others, or requires both, or requires others and countenances historical suggestions and references, or requires others and excludes historical suggestions and references.[6] One religion would be more historically based than

[5] This does not mean historically conditioned. All religions are historically conditioned in their origins and development. We discover whether a religion is historically based by studying its doctrinal scheme, as expressed not only in its literature but also in its nonverbal symbols and in its practices, and seeing what suggestions and references it requires.

[6] For an example of a religious proposal which seems to exclude references from historical events see Sri Aurobindo Ghose, *Essays on the Gita*, 2nd. ed., 1, 19–21, Calcutta, Arya Publishing House, 1926. History is unimportant for religion, he says, and hence the controversy over the historical Jesus "would seem to a spiritually-minded Indian largely a waste of time" (19).

another if historical suggestions and references are more determinative of its doctrines and practices.

Also, some versions of a religion (for example, of Buddhism or of Christianity) may be more historically based than others. In a Mahayana sutra the Buddha says he arrived at enlightenment "many hundred thousand myriads of kotis of aeons ago." And the bodhisattvas to whom he is speaking confess, "This point lies beyond the sphere of our comprehension." [7] This removes the crucial event into an incomprehensibly distant past and thus detaches attention from a particular occurrence at a definite time under a particular bodhi tree. The effect is to weaken, or perhaps indeed to rule out, a reference from an event in public history.[8]

We must distinguish between (a) using facts in references to the logical subject of a proposal and (b) using facts to support predications. We are concerned only with the first of these now. For example, take the Kalimah, the brief confession of faith used by Moslems: "There is no God but Allah and Mohammed is the prophet of Allah." Here a unique and extraordinary public event is adduced, since Mohammed lived at a particular time and place and no other. But the unique event is not being mentioned to support belief in the existence of Allah, or to reinforce the assertion that he is the only God. It is rather conjoined with this assertion. One use of the conjunction is to make the event a starting point for a reference. "God is the being who inspired Mohammed."

As in Mode C, using a causal explanation to refer to an utterly transcendent being would be problematical. If this being causes events (which occur in space and time), and perhaps especially if he causes extraordinary events like

[7] As given in D. T. Suzuki, *Zen Buddhism*, 43, Garden City, Doubleday, 1956.

[8] Even Suzuki has some concern to connect Zen with the teachings of the historical founder of Buddhism. *Ibid.*, 33–38. But see 59–60.

Mohammed's prophesying, then he cannot be transcendent in *all* possible senses. But utter transcendence need not be meant in proposals of Type 9.

MODE E. INTERPRETATION

In making a reference we move from some fact, as our starting point, to the goal of the reference, to what is being talked about. We have been looking at various ways this move might be made and now we come to another way, which is different from ostension, giving examples, and causal references. References are made to a whole of which a fact is a part, or to a reality of which a fact is an appearance or manifestation, or to a substance of which a fact is an attribute or an accidental property, or to a pure form which particular things approximate, as in the Platonic references discussed above. These and others like them I shall call references by interpretation.

This mode of reference seems inapplicable or inappropriate for proposals of Types 1–4, though border-line cases might be found. Certainly its principal applications are in proposals of Types 5–9. For example:

What do you mean by Nature?
I mean the whole of which our lives are parts.

What is Brahman?
Brahman is that of which all things in space and time are manifestations.

These references might be distinguished from causal references in the following way: Speaking generally, causal references would be used to refer to something of the same ontological order as the factual starting point ("By 'Abraham' I mean the father of Isaac"). In references by interpretation the goal of the reference must be of another ontological order than the factual starting point. (For example, a part is of a different ontological order than a whole.)

It is not possible, however, to refer in this way to something of an absolutely different order from that of the factual starting point. This is one problem about negative theology. Referring by means of negative contrasts is not the same as explaining predicates negatively. It is one thing to explain, for example, God's self-existence by saying, "God is not contingent like this tree," and so on for each finite thing that might be mentioned. It is quite another thing to try to refer to something by using such negative contrasts. Negative predication (the construction of negative contrasts of the form, "*n* is *F* but *m* is not *F*") looks like genuine predication because it presupposes that we know what is being talked about in this negative way. But it is not clear, to say the least, how by purely negative contrasts we could *refer* to what is being talked about, though perhaps by a systematic ordering of such contrasts we might succeed in *suggesting* it.

Nonsystematic interpretations may be distinguished from systematic ones. A nonsystematic interpretation makes use of some relational category it finds at hand (like "being part of a whole" or "manifesting a reality" [9] or "being an attribute of a substance") and relies on the natural force of these expressions, without putting them in the context of some systematic categoreal scheme designed to interpret experience generally. A systematic interpretation, on the contrary, takes the categories it uses for references from a systematic categoreal scheme, like those of Aristotle, Aquinas, Spinoza, and Whitehead. [10]

For example, as a way of referring to Mankind someone might say, "Mankind is the whole human community

[9] "Being an (or, the) incarnation of" would be somewhat like "manifesting," but not entirely. See Ninian Smart, *Reasons and Faiths*, ch. IV.

[10] See "The Concept of God as a Derivative Notion," in William L. Reese and Eugene Freeman, eds.: *Process and Divinity—The Hartshorne Festschrift*. La Salle, Ill.: Open Court, 1964.

of which you and I are parts," relying on the ordinary use of "whole" and "part" and "community" to convey his meaning. Then he is moving from his factual starting point ("you and I") to the goal of the reference in a nonsystematic way. On the other hand, as a way of referring to the One, Plotinus might say, "The One is the source of Mind, Soul, and the world of Sense and Nature," where the terms he uses get their meaning from a categoreal scheme he has developed. To understand his reference we would need to understand such terms as "being," "nonbeing," "not-being," "emanation," "sensibles," "intelligibles," as well as the terms in the reference, and also his rules for combining and contrasting these terms, that is to say, his principles of categoreal explanation. This would be making a reference by means of a systematic interpretation.

References by systematic interpretation are less direct than nonsystematic ones. Instead of moving directly from some particular starting point to the goal of the reference by means of a category in ordinary use, they introduce a phase of theory construction. Therefore they are liable to the perennial objection that the abstractions of metaphysics cannot express a living experience. But a systematic reference might explicate a suggestion conveyed in a more direct and imaginative way.

It follows that to support a systematic reference one would have to support the categoreal scheme as a whole, showing it is reasonably clear, coherent, and adequate for the interpretation of all the features of experience.

By way of summary it may be useful to give a table of the types of proposals discussed above and the modes of reference most appropriate to them:

Type 1 (qualities) .... Mode B (examples)
Type 2 (relations) .... Mode B (examples)
Type 3 (natural objects) .. Mode A (ostension)
Type 4 (human objects) ... Mode A (ostension)

Type 5 (Nature)	Mode E (interpretation)
Type 6 (Mankind)	Mode E (interpretation)
Type 7 (pure forms)	Mode E (interpretation)
Type 8 (pure being)	Mode E (interpretation)

Type 9 (a transcendent active being) ......
$\begin{cases} \text{Mode C (regular effects)} \\ \text{Mode D (extraordinary} \\ \qquad\qquad\text{effects)} \\ \text{Mode E (interpretation)} \end{cases}$

I do not argue that these are the only modes of reference. These show some important varieties of references and, incidentally, the importance of references. Let us take an extreme case. Suppose someone seems to be making a basic proposal and that we are quite unclear what he means to refer to as the logical subject of the proposal. Then we might address him in somewhat the following way:

"As I try to see what it is you are talking about, I am not even clear what question I should ask. Would it be fair to ask you any of the following? 'Will you give me an example of it?' 'What does it do?' 'What are its effects?' 'Am I acquainted with any of its parts or members?' 'Is it related in some other way to anything in my experience?' 'If it is beyond my experience, *how* is it beyond my experience?' If none of these is well designed to bring out what you have in mind, will you do so in some other way?"

Now suppose the proposer makes no response to this appeal. And suppose we conclude not that he cannot think what to say at the moment but that there is nothing to be said in response to the appeal. Then we would conclude that no reference to the logical subject of his proposal is possible. Then we would have to conclude also that in his proposal he is not making a truth-claim.

2. *References and some nonreferring expressions*

In a reference some expression (form of words) is used to identify the logical subject of some statement. By considering some expressions which are not useful for this purpose we can see the function of references more clearly. Consider first some expressions used in ranking. Plainly comparatives like "better," "greater," "more real," and "more important" are not used to identify some particular logical subject. These comparatives are used as predicates but they are not suitable for referring.

It looks different when we come to superlatives of ranking like "best," "greatest," "most real," and "most important." "That which is most important," for example, sounds as though it might be used in a reference. But this is illusory. Superlatives like this are indeed uniquely applying predicates; they are designed to be applied to one and only one logical subject, selected from some multiplicity. But they do not tell us to what they apply and, what is more to the point, they do not even tell us where to start looking for some particular logical subject.[11]

A phrase like "the cause of *e*" does at least this. It tells us to start with some event *e*. And it tells us in what direction to look, so to speak, starting with *e*. Even with this beginning the reference may go wrong. But it is a beginning. This is true also of references by ostension, by example, and by interpretation. None of these is foolproof or invariably successful, though some may be more reliable than others. But they all bring up some fact or other with which a reference might begin. And they indicate some direction or other in which to move from this fact.

Superlatives of ranking do not do this. They are predicates, not referring expressions. "That which is most important" has a very different logic from "that of which *x*, *y*, and *z* are manifestations." This is the reason why expressions of the former sort are useful in general theories of religion and those of the latter sort are not. What is needed

---

[11] Comparatives and superlatives of ranking may of course be used in references when (*a*) they modify a referring term and (*b*) where there is a standard ranking, e.g., "The most important man in the room," when everyone knows who *that* is.

for that purpose (for a theory applying equally well to different forms of religion) is precisely an expression that does not refer to some particular logical subject, and hence is applicable to more than one. A religious proposal, on the contrary, assigns a predicate to a particular logical subject. To do so it must identify this subject. But for this purpose predicates, even uniquely applying predicates, will not do.

To illustrate this point, consider the following passage by a philosopher of religion whose writings are neither as widely known nor as carefully studied as they deserve to be:

"The clear perception of what is of greatest value in our total environment, and hence is God, can come only when we form those habits which will enable us to perceive it." [12]

If we take this sentence by itself, apart from its context, we might be puzzled by it in the following way: It seems that a nonreferring expression ("what is of greatest value in our total environment"—or GV, let us say) is being used as though it were a referring expression. (It is said that we can "perceive it." [13] We want to ask, "But what *is* it that is GV?" For while we might suppose, in the sense explained in Chapter V, that there is something of which GV is true, this does not tell us of what it is true. And, it appears, it would not do to say "God," because the implicit rule seems to be: we give the name "God" to whatever is GV ("and hence is God"). "God" is not being used as a referring expression here, so it cannot be the answer to our question. Yet there is no other answer in sight.

Now suppose (*a*) that elsewhere references have been made to something called "the process of progressive inte-

[12] H. N. Wieman, *The Wrestle of Religion with Truth*, 92, New York, Macmillan, 1927.

[13] To isolate our problem we might substitute "know" or "understand" for "perceive." It is not "perceive" that causes the particular trouble I am discussing here.

gration," and (*b*) that it has been argued that it is this process which is *GV*. Then we would be in a position to see that *GV* is a predicate expression and that its proper use is not to point out something but to be applied to something, namely, here to the process of progressive integration. And we could construe the sentence as saying that our ability to find out and know concretely the reality of which *GV* is true, *whatever* that may be, depends on our having certain habits.

For another illustration consider Anselm's expression, "that than which nothing greater can exist or be conceived." Is this a referring expression or not? When we conceive that than which nothing greater can exist, are we thinking of a logical subject, of which something might be predicated? Or are we thinking of a predicate, which might be true of some logical subject? Anselm, I suppose, was thinking of a logical subject, of which existence in the mind and in reality might be predicated. And I suppose he would have been prepared to give a reference by interpretation, in a manner appropriate to proposals of Types 7 and 8, to this logical subject.[14] But the expression is so similar in form to superlatives of ranking that we are inclined to take it as a predicate and not as a referring expression, which may be one reason why we are puzzled by the ontological argument.

As examples of other uniquely applying predicates which are not suitable for references we might take:

[14] Would the argument have been clearer if its first steps took the following form?

1. We conceive Perfection (or Perfect Being).

2. Perfect Being is that than which nothing greater can exist or be conceived.

3. To exist both in the mind and in reality is greater, et cetera. The advantage of this way of putting it is that we would know more clearly at what point a request for a reference would be in order, namely, at step 1.

A. "The being I am thinking of"

and

B. "The Object of religious experience."

Now if someone used either of these expressions in reply to a request for a reference we would be unsatisfied. The speaker's behavior might tell us of what he is thinking. But taken by itself the utterance gives no factual starting point for a reference. We only know the speaker is thinking of something or other; we have no way of knowing what this is. This means that no purely "mental" categories (thinking, experiencing, imagining, conceiving, feeling, understanding, et cetera) are suitable for use in references unless they are supplemented in some way.

B is somewhat different. To use it as a referring expression we would have to assume not only that every religious experience has the same object but also that if anyone is religious he will know what this Object is. So it would have to convey an implicit injunction: Be religious, and you will know to what I am referring. Then we would have to be told how to be religious; and this would require evoking a religious interest. Narratives of historical events and descriptions of typical human situations might be used in a suggestive way.

Now suppose some experience is evoked by these suggestions. Then how could we tell whether the object of this experience is the same as the logical subject to which the speaker is referring? Arguments about whether our experience is indeed a religious experience will not help. Or, we might say, if the speaker offers such arguments this shows that he knows more about the Object of religious experience than he has told us.

So B is not suitable for use as a reference, though it might be useful as a predicate in the phenomenology of religion. It could name a function logical subjects might have. We might say, for example, "For M, m functions as the Object of religious experience." But this would not give us a reference to *m*.

3. *What references tell us about proposals*

We have been considering how the logical subject of a proposal might be referred to. And we have noticed that a certain mode of reference might or might not be admissible or appropriate for proposals of a certain type. Now consider this relation between modes of reference and types of proposals from the opposite end. If a certain mode of reference is being used, does this tell us something about what is being proposed? And may this logical connection be of some help in untangling confusions and sharpening dull edges in religious discourse?

Let us take some proposals which refer to Mankind or Humanity and see what we might learn about them in this way. Just as we might reach the notion of Nature by moving from particular natural objects, so we might reach the notion of Mankind by moving from particular human individuals and groups. In both cases the reference is by interpretation. What categories of interpretation, then, are available for references to Mankind? By what paths might we move from some fact about human beings to the conception of Mankind?

The most likely category is the whole-part relation. We might think of Mankind as a more or less loosely structured whole, with stronger connections among some of its parts than among others. The life of a Tibetan is less influenced by school board elections in Texas than by political events in China. But it would not be plausible to think of Mankind as an absolutely all-inclusive whole, or even as a self-sufficient whole, since it has a natural environment on which it depends for its existence.

Hence "whole" would have a weaker meaning than it has in some other contexts. Saying Mankind is a whole could mean: (*a*) that it is a group, not a mere collection or multiplicity, since it has some structure and (*b*) that it includes a larger number of units than any other human group. We could not plausibly think of Mankind as a whole in the further senses in which the Stoics thought of Nature as a whole, namely, as being all-inclusive and self-sufficient.

Now if we mean to move by this whole-part path to the conception of Mankind, we may start from any particular human group just as well as from any other. A particular family, whether close-knit and harmonious or estranged and discordant; a political party, whatever its purpose and program; a savage tribe in the valley of the Amazon; the Fabian Society; the Christian church; the French Academy; a ladies' sewing circle; a brothel—any of these is just as much a "part" of Mankind, in the present sense, as is any other. So our reference to Mankind may start equally well from any one of them. Of any one of these we might equally well say, in reply to the question, "What do you mean by Mankind?" "Mankind is the whole of which this is a part."

Suppose now we find a proposal which appears to be of Type 6 but insists on being more selective in its starting point. Suppose it says, in effect, that if we want to know what Humanity is we should look at Schweitzer rather than Hitler, or at the Soviet army at Stalingrad [15] rather than Nazi youths beating Jews, or at Socrates and the Royal Society rather than ranting demagogues and superstitious savages. What conclusions about the object of the proposal follow from its being referred to in this way?

Certainly it seems that the object cannot be Humanity considered as a whole of which all human individuals and groups are parts. What might be meant is a set of qualities (generosity, courage, rationality), exemplified by some men and groups and not by others, or by some more than by others. In this case we have a proposal of Type 1, not of

[15] See Harold J. Laski, *Faith, Reason* and *Civilization*, 43, where Stalingrad has a paradigmatic function for Laski (New York, Viking, 1944).

Type 6. And the justification for calling this set of qualities Humanity would be that, though not all men exemplify them, *only* men do exemplify them.

Or we might conclude, from the way Humanity is being referred to, that it is a certain pattern of relations (solidarity, community, mutuality) exemplified by some human groups and not by others, or by some more than others. The justification for calling this pattern of relations Humanity would be less clear. Or, depending on the reference that is being made, we might conclude the proposal is really of some other type. Perhaps what is being proposed is a pure form rather than a quality. Perhaps even—as when Auguste Comte speaks of Humanity as "this undeniable Providence, the supreme dispenser of our destinies" [16]—Humanity is being thought of as a transcendent active being, though perhaps only for devotional purposes and in a mythical way.

Of course there are comparable ambiguities in proposals of other types. Proposals about God would furnish an equally fruitful field for this kind of study. But the latter have had the benefit of much more critical analysis than other proposals have had, and some of the characteristic ambiguities are more familiar. The point I have wished to make is a general one and applies to any religious proposal: it is fair to make an inference from the kind of reference a proposal uses to the nature of the logical subject of the proposal, that which is being proposed as the religious object.

The reason is that there are logical limitations on making references in religion. A particular mode of reference is not applicable to all types of proposals without restriction. So if a proposer seriously means to use a certain reference, then this can tell us something about the proposal he is, in effect, making. We can pose a dilemma: either his proposal

[16] *System of Positive Polity*, II (F. Harrison, tr.), 53, London, Longmans, Green, 1875. See Hugh Miller, *The Community of Man*, New York, Macmillan, 1949.

is of a type for which the mode of reference is admissible, or the reference fails.

So one important task for philosophers of religion is to study the references which are characteristically relied on in various religious traditions, with a view to understanding more clearly what is being proposed. In this enterprise the aid of historians of religion and theologians would be essential. It would be interesting, for example, to study the kinds of references made by mystics.

4. *References and suggestions*

One difference between conveying suggestions and making references is that a suggestion is conveyed by an image or some other nonpropositional symbol, for example, the image evoked by the phrase used in Buddhist meditation, "The Jewel in the Heart of the Lotus." An explicit reference is made by stating a proposition, for example, "Nirvana is the state in which all desires have been extinguished." Now we might be tempted to say a suggestion is only an oblique, vague way of saying what could be put in a straightforward and clearer manner. This would be a mistake. It would overlook a difference of function, treating suggestions as an inferior kind of references. A suggestion has its own work to do and needs to be appraised in a different way. Its function is to evoke a concrete religious response.

The requirements for understanding a reference are: (*a*) acquaintance with the fact used as the starting point for the reference and (*b*) understanding the categories (causality, whole, et cetera) used in moving from the starting point toward the goal of the reference. To understand a suggestion, on the other hand, we need: (*a*) an openness to religious suggestions and (*b*) imaginative penetration or, we might say, "divination" in the sense suggested by Rudolf Otto.

This leads to another important difference between references and suggestions. While a reference must start with a fact, the vehicle for a suggestion need not be a fact. A suggestion *may* be conveyed by a factual narrative, for example, the story of the enlightenment of the Buddha or the story of the death of Christ, or by some other factual reference. But it need not be so. A suggestion may be conveyed by a timeless tale, a parable or a myth like Plato's myth of the Cave, or by a deliberately constructed paradox, like a Zen Buddhist *koan* or the Neoplatonic metaphor of the circle whose center is everywhere and whose circumference is nowhere. Instead of beginning with a fact, a suggestion may make use of a possibility, or an impossibility. Such nonfactual vehicles may serve very well for certain religious suggestions, though not for others. But they would fail to afford starting points for references.

Sometimes it is recommended that religious proposals use only suggestive language, that religious discourse be all poetry and no prose, out of a conviction that the use of abstract categories will distort the truth. But suggestions cannot replace references. Without references no truth-claims are made,[17] and without truth-claims religious discourse would lack a certain seriousness which is essential to its intention.

Much less can references replace suggestions in religious discourse. For references are a way of explicating suggestions and they are guided by the suggestions they explicate. So in religious discourse as elsewhere in our experience there is room and need for both imagination and reason.

5. *How references might fail*

In conclusion I shall sum up briefly the ways a reference might fail. This will show what kinds of objections to references are possible and the kinds of support references need. In this way we can see the general form of arguments about religious references. The specimen arguments developed in

[17] But see chapter XII on images and truth.

the next chapter will include some arguments about references, though their main point is to illustrate arguments about predications.

The function of a reference is to introduce the logical subject of a proposal for belief into experience and discourse. A particular reference (i.e., a particular use of some expression for this purpose) might fail to do this in the following ways:

a. A reference may be baseless. It may fail to offer any factual starting point. This is the trouble with superlatives of ranking like "that which is of greatest value," allusions to inner experiences like "what I am thinking of," [18] and other predicates when they are misused as though they were referring expressions.

b. A reference may be misconstructed. The categories it uses may be inappropriate to its factual starting point or to its intended goal. We have noticed a variety of such incongruities. Sometimes we want to say a reference is inadmissible, for example, the use of the ordinary notion of causality to refer to a pure form. Sometimes we want to say a reference is misdirected, when we infer from a reference that its proper goal is not what the proposer has in mind. In general a reference is misconstructed when, though it offers a factual starting point, it results in some sort of logical absurdity when its consequences are examined.

c. A reference may be insufficient. This sort of failure is relative to a context. We may say, in response to an insufficient reference, "I *think* I know what you mean," but we ask for further light on the subject. References in one mode may need to be supplemented by references in another mode. The factual starting point may need to be established more firmly. The categoreal structure may need to be clearer and more coherent.

Making references, whether in religion or elsewhere in

---

[18] When these expressions are in no way supplemented, either verbally or by other clues.

our experience, requires cooperation. We must be ready and willing to look in the direction of the pointing, so to speak. We must try to see what is being referred to. We must be prepared to think of something we have not thought of. But sometimes when we try we still do not see, so we ask for further help. And sometimes experience leads us to think that a reference is not just insufficient, but misconstructed, or baseless. So objections of these three sorts are in order.

If the points made in objections are well taken, the proposer must meet them in some way. Above all, he must become clearer about what he means to say. What is it that is conveyed in the suggestion he has adopted? What does he mean to propose? He might then decide that he is not really making a truth-claim after all, because no reference seems possible. Or he might discover that what he wants to refer to is not what he had thought. Then he might redirect and reconstruct his reference, finding or inventing categories appropriate for his purpose and using them in a clearer way.

CHAPTER XI

Predications

1. *Introduction*

The theory I have been developing is not a religious proposal. It explains how various types of religious utterances bear their meanings, paying special attention to the conditions of making and supporting religious truth-claims. Its point is not to attain religious truth but, instead, to understand how truth in religion is possible.

There are stronger and weaker senses in which a theory of meaning is "empirical," according as the factual conditions required for significant truth-claims are more or less stringent. A very stringent requirement would be that no sentence can be used to make a truth-claim unless it is publicly verifiable, meaning here what early positivists meant— that the truth of the sentence would necessarily follow from the truth of some finite set of sense-observation sentences. A theory of meaning which laid down this condition for truth-claims would be an empirical theory of meaning in a very strong sense. It would also run into a number of difficulties,[1] and it would be particularly unpromising as a theory of meaning in religion.

The theory I have been developing is an empirical theory of meaning in a much weaker sense, but it makes room for and requires factual[2] conditions of significance in two ways. In the last chapter we saw how both factual questions and categoreal questions are involved in arguments

---

[1] On such a theory could there be proposals for belief about toothaches? about decisions? about physical dispositions? about electrons? about beta particles? about Socrates?

[2] I have been using "fact" and "factual" in a nonsystematic but not, I hope, confusing way.

about references. Facts are required as starting points for references. The theory admits for this purpose both private facts (though not purely private facts) and public facts (though there may be no purely public facts), both events and states of things, both particular facts and general facts about the world.

In this chapter we move on from the references made in developed proposals to their predications. In a basic religious proposal a logical subject is not just said to *be*, in some neutral sense, but to be something or other. Something is said to be true of it. This introduces another way in which facts are relevant to religious proposals. Supposing something *m* has been referred to; then it may be asked, for example, "But is *m holy?*"

At this point also the theory is not empirical in a strong sense. I do not believe there are purely public facts which could be absolutely decisive in settling questions of this sort. Many travelers might have seen the old man, the leper, the corpse, and the monk that Gotama saw, without being enlightened as he was. Many people witnessed the outward events of the life of Jesus, as the disciples did, but were not, like them, moved to faith. But facts can be adduced in support of a claim that a basic predicate is true of some logical subject. Our next step is to look again at these predicates and see what is being done when they are applied.

2. *Some functions of basic religious predicates*

Consider predicates like "worshipful," "awe-inspiring," "holy," "most important," "supreme goal of life," "ultimate," and others as used in statements like "The Buddhanature is the ultimate reality." Along with the distinctive features of each, what functions do they have in common? This use of such a predicate has at least the following functions:

a. It marks off some logical subject from all else in a certain way.

b. It assigns to this entity a certain primacy.

The types of proposals set out in Chapter IX exhibit striking variations in the way something *m* is marked off from all else and in the sort of primacy assigned to it. Basic predicates have other functions also, but for the time being let us attend to these.

If the force of a predicate is to say, among other things, that something is in a class by itself, and that it ranks above all else, it follows that two sorts of challenging questions could be asked, namely: (*a*) Is *m* indeed in a class by itself, and (*b*) do all other things (e.g., *r*, *s*, and *t*) rank below it? Our main business in the rest of this chapter is to see how basic proposals might be supported in response to these challenging questions.

Questions of the first sort challenge the uniqueness of *m*. Their intention is to assimilate *m* to other things. Questions of the second sort challenge the primacy of *m*. Their intention is to downgrade it from the status proposed for it.

When we speak in this way of the uniqueness and the primacy of the religious object, we are not using these terms as basic religious predicates. They are not substitutes for terms like "holy," "ultimate," "awe-inspiring," "most important," et cetera. Speaking of the uniqueness of the religious object is only a way of referring to the fact that such predicates are used to mark off something from all else. Likewise, speaking of the primacy of the religious object is only a way of referring to the fact that religious predicates are used to rank something above all else. So we are not adding "uniqueness" and "primacy" to a list of basic predicates; we are calling attention to functions of these predicates.

Now if something *m* were shown to be unique, its primacy would still be open to question. Its primacy, on the other hand, would entail its uniqueness. So the main problem for arguments in support of religious predications is to support the claim to primacy. Before moving to this topic, however, we need to deal with some preliminary questions about uniqueness.

3. *The uniqueness of the religious object*

The marking off which is characteristic of basic religious predications is not identifying, calling attention to "this and no other," though it presupposes an identifying reference. It is a marking *off*. Traditionally, "sacred" and "holy" have had this function. A contrast is suggested between that which is sacred and all else, namely, the profane.[3] Similarly, when such terms as "supernatural" and "infinite" are religious predicates they are used to mark off something from all natural and finite things. This explains why capital letters are often used in writing English words for religious terms. For example, God is the Infinite, the Other, the Holy One. He is not infinite in the way an infinite series is infinite, nor other in the way other minds are other, nor holy in the way a holy place is holy. He is marked off from all else.

Negative theology, which exploits statements of the form, "*m* is not like *n*," is one way of developing and enforcing this function of basic predicates. Now in most religious traditions it is not supposed that negative contrasts ("*m* is not like *n*") rule out positive contrasts (analogies) altogether. Usually analogies are admitted in some way. But we can ask, "Is a *purely* negative theology possible?"

A purely negative theology would rule out analogies, permitting only purely negative contrasts between *m* and all other subjects of discourse. "For any *n*, *m* is not in the least like *n*." Taken strictly, this would mean that no categories which apply to anything else could be true of *m*. This would be an extreme way of marking off *m* from all else, and we might say that in this case *utter* uniqueness is being claimed for *m*. But then it would seem that no reference to *m* would be possible, since no mediating categories

---

[3] Which does not have to mean that the profane is unreal or unimportant or evil.

would be available for use in references, and it would follow from this that no truth-claims about *m* could be made.

The utterance of an extended series of purely negative contrasts might have a certain *effect* on the hearer. By saying something of the form, "*m* is not in the least like *r*, and not in the least like *s*, and not in the least like *t*, . . ." some peculiar state of mind (an objectless experience?) might be induced. Perhaps, indeed, this is what is intended. But an unordered series of purely negative contrasts (for example, "*m* is not in the least like a house, . . . a cloud of dust, . . . a nation, . . . a galaxy, . . . the color red, . . . a virtue, . . ."), however extended, cannot even convey a suggestion by itself. Such utterances could convey something about *m* only if the term used ("God," "Nirvana," "Brahman," e.g.) already has a referential connotation, as is usually the case. And if this is so, then something positive can be said also.

A suggestion can be conveyed by *ordering* a series of negative contrasts, if these are not purely negative contrasts; for example, "*m* is not like a stone; *m* is not like an animal; *m* is not like a man; *m* is not like an angel." But then it would be possible to construct some positive contrast which is latent in the ordered series. From the order of the series we might infer that *m* is more like an angel than a stone, though also unlike both. And this would be a sign that utter uniqueness is not being claimed.

Though a religious proposal need not, and usually does not, claim utter uniqueness for its logical subject *m*, it does claim that *m* is not just a member of some class. *m* may be like some other things, and more like some things than like others, but it is also different from everything else. This much is claimed in anything we should be likely to call a religious proposal.

Such claims can be challenged. For example:

A. Nirvana is just a state of insensibility, like being sound asleep.

B. God is just a projection of our wishes, like a fairy god-mother.

C. Jahweh is just a folk god, like the Philistine god Dagon.

The force of these objections is to deny the uniqueness of something m. After all, it is said, m is just one of a number of things. And therefore, the objection implies, m cannot be the supreme goal of life, or the ground of being, or holy.

Replies of two kinds can be made. A reply can concede the alleged likeness but preserve the claim to uniqueness by qualifying the likeness. Admitting the classification, at least provisionally, the reply would then contrast m with the rest of the class in question. Or a reply can deny the likeness, placing m outside the class and contrasting m with anything and everything in that class.

a. As an example of the first way of defending a claim of uniqueness, consider the following reply to objection C:

"Why, yes, Jahweh *is* a folk god, in a way. He singled out Israel to be his chosen people, and the Israelites looked to him for help against their enemies. He protected Israel from her enemies and brought destruction on them, for example, the Amalekites. And most of the Israelites in Old Testament times did not seriously expect (or even hope) that people of other nations would worship Jahweh, though this was not true of the great prophets, of course.

"But it seems reasonably clear that Jahweh is not *just* a folk god. He singled out and preserved Israel for the sake of some larger purpose. He judged Israel as severely as he did other nations, if not more so, and punished not only her unfaithfulness but also her unrighteousness. He means to use Israel as an instrument for blessing all mankind. So, while he may be thought of as a folk god in a sense, there are some very important ways in which he is not a folk god. Certainly he is very unlike Dagon."

Similarly, a reply to objection A might run as follows:

"I suppose you might think of Nirvana as a kind of insensibility. Certainly it might seem like that when we contrast it with our ordinary experience, in which our desires and our attachments to particular natural and human objects play such an important part. In Nirvana we have no desires. And we are no longer attached to any such objects. The monk who has renounced worldly ambitions has something in common with the child who does not yet have such ambitions. But there is also an important difference between them, which is plain enough when you come to think of it. Certainly Nirvana is very unlike being sound asleep, if that is what you mean by insensibility."

Replies of this sort concede that the category applies to the object, but only in a qualified way. So the object is still marked off from all else. This way of replying is in line with Ian T. Ramsey's remarks about "models and qualifiers." [4] God is the *heavenly* father. Nirvana is *complete* detachment.

b. Instead of conceding that *m* is like other things of some class (though also different from them), the likeness may be rejected. "No," the reply would run, "*m* is not really that sort of thing at all." Thus a reply to objection B might proceed as follows:

"No. God is not a projection of our wishes. He is not something we wish into existence. He exists whether we wish it or not. Showing there is a human need for God to exist would not settle the matter, any more than showing there is a human need for God not to exist would settle it. For that could be argued too. Some people do seem to want the nonexistence of God.

"God is the creative process which operates in every event, including the scientific inquiry in which you are engaged. We all participate in this process, more or less. And in participating in it we conform to it. God is what we conform to, in whatever we do, whenever we do things

[4] *Religious Language,* Chapter II, London, SCM Press, 1957.

right. God is something conformed to and participated in, not something projected. What I mean by God is not like a fairy godmother at all."

The issue is whether something m is just a member of some class of things (folk gods, states of insensibility, projections). The replies undertake to show how m differs from anything in this class. In replies of the first kind the strategy is to expand the category suggested in the objection (folk gods, states of insensibility) by a loosening-up process. Only if the category is stretched farther than the objector intends it to be, so the reply runs, can it apply to m. And even if this is done, we still do not have an adequate account of m. Something more needs to be said. In replies of the second kind the category (projections) is defined more sharply and narrowly. The front of the objection is contracted, so to speak. The reply is then a flank attack rather than, as in the first kind of reply, an infiltration.

4. The primacy of the religious object

Though these objections are directed against marking off something m from all else, their real intention might be different. The real intention might be to challenge the primacy of m. If we take, for example, objection B above, its real point could be expanded and argued as follows:

"God exists only in people's minds. He is not actual, and if they think he is actual they are having illusions. Of course such an illusion might have a certain value in some cases, as a stage in personal development or as a public neurosis that makes private neuroses unnecessary. So we can't say that God is meaningless to the believer. So it would not be true to say that God is nothing at all. That is why I said that God is a projection. For the believer, God has a place in his world. The issue is, What shall that place be?

"Though God may have not only a meaning but a value," the argument might continue, "this value needs to be weighed against other values. God is that to which the believer turns when he is frustrated in his deepest hopes and wishes. But this is not the right way to deal with frustrations. The thing to turn to is reality, not God. We ought to live by the reality principle, not by our hopes and wishes."

The interesting point is the comparative judgment that comes toward the end of this argument. Both God and reality are considered, one to be weighed against the other. The issue is, Which should be ranked above the other? This is remotely like voting for a candidate in an election. But there is a peculiar relation between the alternatives. One is "reality," and if something is chosen against reality, this means it is unreal. The implicit assumption in the argument is that the real has a priority over the unreal. (But of course just saying something is real or unreal is not so important as the way something is actually given some sort of precedence in experience.) So the force of this Freudian argument is not to challenge the uniqueness of something, but, instead, to challenge the primacy of something, by ranking it lower than something else. This is the real significance of calling God an illusion.

So we need to look more closely at arguments which use ontological terms, like "actual" and "real," to challenge or support the primacy of the logical subjects of religious proposals.

5. Ontological terms in religious arguments

What is the function of expressions like those italicized below when used in religious arguments?

A. But how can you reverence Harmony? It is only an *ideal*, not a *reality*.

B. But your conception of God doesn't correspond to anything that *exists*.

C. There is one thing that can be said for religious naturalism: it has to do with something *actual*.

D. The One is not something that *exists*; it is beyond *existence* and *nonexistence*.

E. But Nirvana is merely an *ideal* limit; it is not a *possible* state of experience.

F. But harmony is only a relation among *real things*.

G. But there is nothing *substantial* about the Way.

One function of these expressions, when they are used in religious arguments, is to upgrade or downgrade something. In C and in D something is being upgraded in support of a religious proposal. In the other examples, which are objections to religious proposals, something is being downgraded. This is one of the most natural and prevalent ways of arguing about religious proposals.

To explore this use of ontological terms let us construct a simple scale—a "scale of being," we might call it—which is generally accepted in ordinary life:

What exists (i.e., is actual)	/	What does not exist (i.e., is not actual)
What is (logically) possible	/	What is impossible (i.e., absurd)

According to this scale, the actual has priority over the possible. Also, the actual and the possible are preferred over their contraries, respectively.

In ordinary life this scale of being is so generally taken for granted as a norm of judgment that it is not thought of as a grading or valuation. But it may be challenged, and sometimes is challenged, in religious discourse in two ways. One way is by proposals which put forward an object describable only in paradoxical terms and thus logically absurd, as in some versions of Theravada Buddhism [5] and some existentialist versions of Christianity. Nirvana or God are said to be such that no logical concepts are applicable to them. The second way of challenging the common-sense

[5] See R. H. L. Slater, *Paradox and Nirvana*, Chicago, University of Chicago Press, 1951.

scale of being is by proposing something which, it is said, is not actual and yet is ranked above actual things, as in D above.

Such challenges show that these ontological terms are being used in a grading way. They are ways of saying that something *m* ranks over something *n*. Let us see how a religious predication might be supported against ontological objections.

Again, two strategies are possible, analogous to those against objections to uniqueness. One is to accept the scale of being that is implicit in the objection, and then adduce facts in support of a favorable position for something *m* in that scale. The other strategy is to reject the scale implicit in the objection as inadequate or irrelevant, and then adduce facts in aid of this rejection.

a. Take the common-sense objection B and suppose that both parties to the disagreement accept the common-sense scale of being as a norm of judgment. Suppose, further, that they understand "actuality" as equivalent to "having power to make some change in other things." Then facts must be adduced to show that *m* has power to affect other things of some sort, for example, events. The proponent needs to show how *m* has to be reckoned with, or taken account of, in perception or in thought or in practice. He must show that it has, or might have, some effects. Arguments for the actuality of *m* are called for.

Many arguments for the existence of God have this force. They begin with facts of various sorts: an instance of motion, some contingent natural entity like a particular stone, some constructed object like a bird's nest, a sense of moral obligation, the movement of thought from particular instances of qualities toward ideal forms, the occurrence of novel values in experience. Some of these facts are physical; some are psychological. Some are relatively public; some are relatively private. They are used in the arguments to show that God is actual and, in ways that still accord with the common-sense scale of being, has perfections other actual beings do not have. In attributing these perfections to God, the arguments refine the scale of being they assume. The problem is to interpret the perfections without implicitly rejecting the scale.

b. To illustrate the second strategy let us take objection E, which reflects a certain refinement of the common-sense scale of being. A proposal of Nirvana might be supported against it in somewhat the following way:

"Of course Nirvana is not a possible state of experience in the sense in which you mean that. It *is* beyond experience, meaning the experience we have as desiring, striving, suffering beings. But when you make this an objection you are assuming that we are indeed everlastingly bound to the wheel of life and can never be freed from it. Or, alternatively, you are assuming that, though we can be freed from it, we do not or should not choose to be freed from it.

"I cannot prove that *you* can be freed from the wheel of life. One crucial condition is whether you want to be freed. I can point out some other necessary conditions that would have to be satisfied. And I can point you to certain people like that monk there who, by conforming to these conditions, does seem to be on the way to being freed. And I can hope that you will find some intimations of this possibility in your own experience.

"But the whole point is that I am asking for a revolution in your conception of things. That is why we use paradoxical language sometimes to convey what is meant by Nirvana. We call it the Void, because compared with what we ordinarily call reality it seems completely empty of reality and meaning. Judged by your scale it seems nothing, or nearly that. But I suggest we look at things the other way around. This is what happened to Gotama when he saw the old man, the leper, the corpse, and the monk. Youth, health, and life itself are transient, and just to realize this fact itself detaches us to some extent from them. It makes us look at them and value them in quite a different way. Further, it makes us look at the processes that produce and destroy them in a different way. We can no longer make what you call actuality the primary value in our scale of being."

Notice certain features of this argument: (1) The objection has the effect of downgrading Nirvana along a scale of being which the objector is implicitly proposing as a norm of judgment. The argument against the objection begins by acknowledging that, along this scale of being, the downgrading is justified. (2) Unlike the argument in (a), which accepts the objector's scale of being, this argument rejects the objector's scale of being as a norm of judgment. (3) It adduces facts to support this rejection. (4) Since the argument has to attack the proposed scale of being, it must use its facts destructively. It is necessary to argue against the importance of things that are not *m*. It must downgrade the entities to which the rejected scale of being gives primacy. In this particular case it must be a world-denying argument. So arguments of this type must be negative in a way arguments of the first type do not need to be.

6. *Axiological terms in religious arguments*

Now look at another set of objections to the primacy of something *m*. They object not that *m* does not really exist, but, instead, that *m* is not really good. They use axiological terms. Here scales of value operate as norms of judgment. We want to see what objections of this sort amount to, how they might be met, and, incidentally, how facts may be adduced in meeting them.

A. If the gods command anything evil they are not gods.
B. If God is the sole ultimate cause of every event he is not good.
C. Calvin's God is a monster.
D. Nirvana is a negation of life.

E. If you give your devotion to Humanity your esthetic judgment will be underdeveloped.

F. If you revere anything but Humanity you weaken your sense of moral responsibility.

G. Believing in God keeps people from growing up.

H. If you devote yourself to anything that is strictly ineffable this will encourage you to ignore intellectual distinctions.

I. To worship something transcendental takes the joy out of life.

J. Nature is oblivious of moral distinctions.

K. We cannot worship anything so feeble and transient as Humanity.

L. ". . . greatness of soul is not fostered by those philosophies which assimilate the universe to Man." [6]

Some of these point to some quality the object has or lacks. In some way *m* is not really good. It has some defect it ought not to have, or it lacks some perfection it ought to have, to be rightly ranked above all else. Others point to the effect of revering (or worshipping or giving devotion to) *m* on the person who reveres it. Revering *m*, it is said, has some bad effect or other. Anyone who reveres *m* is thereby made worse in some way, or is kept from becoming better.

This is not a crucial distinction. For objections about effects on the believer can be reframed to make explicit points about the object proposed. The effect can be expressed as a predicate of *m*. Instead of G one might say, "God is such (i.e., a projection of a father image) that if you believe in it you won't grow up." For the point of G is that the effect is intrinsic to belief in *m*, not accidental. So I shall treat all these objections as challenges to the goodness of something *m*.

Just as with ontological objections, an axiological objection to the primacy of something m may look on its surface like a challenge to the uniqueness of m. For example, the superficial point of "Nirvana is just a state of insensibility" (section 3) is to classify Nirvana with certain other things (states of insensibility) and thus to challenge its uniqueness. But it might be used, instead, to challenge the primacy of Nirvana by urging against it the importance of sensibility.

How can these objections be met? Here again two strategies are available. The proponent may accept the principle behind the objection and show how his proposal conforms to it. Or he may reject the principle as a norm of judgment and bring forward considerations against it.

(a) A reply to G could show that the belief does not have the effect it is said to have. Granting it is good for people to grow up, this does not count against belief in God. Believing in God does not hinder people from growing up. Studies of human character, particularly studies of the effects of various beliefs on character in various cultures, would be relevant. Logical points as well as factual points are involved. What is to count as believing in God? What concept must be entertained, and how must it be assented to, if we are to say someone believes in God?

Or, again granting the principle underlying the objection, a reply to D could offer an analysis of "negation of life" and adduce the attitudes to life reflected in Buddhist teaching and practice. Here again both logical distinctions and questions of fact are relevant.

Again, in reply to objection J it might be asked whether "oblivious of moral distinctions" means "immoral," "productive of immorality," "not productive of morality," or something else. It might be granted, as by Spinoza, that Nature is not itself morally good in the sense that a man is morally good or evil. But this does not mean that it is morally evil. And it might be argued that a love of Nature is in fact productive of moral goodness.

In these cases the strategy is to refine the objection, and

to expand the proposal by explaining it further. The objector is forced to specify more closely the target of his objection, and the proponent, by explaining the proposal more fully, shows that this is not what he is proposing. He shows that the objection is aimed at the wrong target. In reply to C it might be asked, "Have you read Calvin with care?"

If this attempt to refine the objection is successful, the objector may continue to advance it, or he may not. He may find that the refinement has drawn its teeth. Or he may accept the refinement and still maintain his point. "Yes, I understand that Nirvana does not entail suicide, but it is still a negation of life." In this case the proponent would have (*b*) to reject the principle behind the objection and bring forward considerations against this principle. How can this be done?

(*bi*) One way is by dialectical argument. The proponent may ask whether the objector really wants to maintain this principle as a norm of judgment. In reply to objection J, when the objector loves his friends and relations, is he not somewhat oblivious of their morals? Does he love them in strict proportion to their moral worth? In view of his own practice, therefore, does he not want to reconsider the principle that lies behind the objection? For presumably his practice reveals what he believes. And presumably he wants to be consistent. The proponent is arguing that accepting the principle would commit us to certain lines of thought and action, and that some of these consequences conflict with other principles he assumes the objector holds. In doing so the proponent is adducing facts about the beliefs and attitudes of the objector.

(*bii*) More positively, the proponent can try to show how things look from the standpoint of the proposal. It would enable one to connect up facts r and s; it would put t in perspective; it would give a way of interpreting u. By representing the proposal at greater length and in more detail, the proponent hopes to weaken the logical force of the principle that conflicts with it. Here again facts are relevant. The argument is that the facts show a certain pattern, for example, that the facts of human experience (especially our hopes and fears) show that Nirvana is the supreme goal of life. Contrary views, it is argued, force us to distort the facts, to give less than full value to some facts (for example, old age, disease, and death) and an exaggerated value to others (for example, various temporal satisfactions).

Before going farther, notice a similarity between ontological and axiological objections to primacy. For an objection against the primacy of m to have force, it is not enough to charge that m does not exist or that it is not good, without some specification of the charge. Certainly m has to exist in some way or other, and be good in some way or other, to be a religious object (or, indeed, to be the object of any positive interest at all). To have point, the objection must specify some way in which m does not exist or is not good. "Exist" and "good" are colorless, like water; they are insufficiently specific to carry the point of an objection. The objection must be given some color.

This may be done implicitly, by relying on the context, so that the colorless term takes on the color of its environment. It may be well understood, in a given situation, that when it is said that m is not good this means that m is not morally good. Or it may be done explicitly, deliberately giving color to the objection by specifying the mode of being or goodness in which m is defective. "I mean m is not actual," the objector might say.

Similarly, in supporting a proposal it is not enough to say that m exists or that m is good, unless something more is understood. "m exists" does serve to call attention to m. And "m is good" does serve to express approval of m (though it does not *mean*, "I approve of m"). But "m exists" and "m is good" hardly need saying if m is being proposed. The proposer must explain how *m* exists and how it is good if he is to bring forward relevant facts to support his proposal.

7. Can religious predicates be reduced to ontological and axiological terms?

Though it is reasonable to challenge religious proposals by using ontological and axiological terms, it does not follow that basic predicates can be translated into those terms. It does not follow that, e.g., for "*m* is holy" we can now read one of the following expressions:

A. "*m* is actual."
B. "*m* is beyond existence."
C. "*m* is morally good."
D. "*m* is beyond moral good and evil."

Nor could we take a conjunction of A and C, or a conjunction of B and D, as an explicit statement of a basic proposal; something else must be said in an explicit religious predication. This has been made reasonably clear by Schleiermacher, Rudolf Otto, and other students of the phenomenology of religion.

More plausibly, it might be supposed that one of the following could be used to convey a basic religious proposal:

E. "*m* is perfect in being."
F. "*m* is perfectly good."
G. "*m* is perfect in being and goodness."

About this supposition three remarks are in order.

a. Interpretations of perfection would be needed. This might be done by: (1) specifying certain modes of being (e.g., actuality) and goodness (e.g., being the source of the moral law), and (2) ranking these modes above all other modes of being and goodness, and (3) showing how *m* not only satisfies the categoreal requirements for entities of the type in question, but satisfies them perfectly. It might be argued, for example, that m has all the generic features that mark off actual entities from ideal entities and that it expresses these features in a superlative way. And it might be argued further that the content of the moral law and the obligation to obey it become fully intelligible only in view of m.

b. An interpretation of perfection would not constitute a complete *argument* for the religious proposal that is being conveyed. It would not dispose of objections against the proposer's scales of being and goodness, for example, an objection that though m may be perfectly actual some other mode of being ranks above actuality, or an objection that though m is the source of the moral law some other mode of goodness ranks above this. Counterproposals giving other interpretations of perfection would be in order, and would have to be argued against.[7]

c. While E or F or G might be used to convey a basic religious proposal, it would do so implicitly. Their predicates are not explicit religious predicates. Though many philosophers in our Western tradition have assumed that "m is perfect in being and goodness" implies "m is worshipful," this is not strictly true. A religious predicate is not reducible to ontological or axiological predicates even if an interpretation of perfection is given. There are three ways in which the two predicates fail of saying the same thing:

(1) One function of a religious predicate like "worshipful" is to mark off something from all other things. For G to have this function, it would have to be added that *only m* is perfect in being and goodness. Thomas Aquinas argues for a proposition of this type in Part One of the *Summa Theologica* under Question IV (The Perfection of God) in the third article (Whether any Creature can be Like God) and under Question VI in the third article (Whether

[7] See Frederick Sontag, *Divine Perfection*, New York, Harper, 1962, and Charles Hartshorne, *The Logic of Perfection*, 31–44.

to be Essentially Good belongs to God Alone). And he supposes that arguments are needed.

(2) Another function of a religious predicate is to rank something above all other things whatsoever, whether or not these other things are ranked along some scale of being or goodness. So religious proposals are vulnerable to objections like those in sections 5 and 6. But suppose someone should argue that no scale of being could be significantly stated or reasonably defended. Or suppose it should be argued that some things cannot be fitted into any scale of being that is at hand. These considerations would not diminish the distinctive force of a religious predicate.

All that is necessary, to assign primacy to something m, is to say that, for anything n, m ranks above n. Scales of being or goodness, or any other systematic arrangements of the things with which m is being contrasted, are not essential to religious proposals. An interest in systematic schemes often accompanies a religious interest and affects the form of a proposal. But often this is not the case. Many people are unspeculatively religious.

So this is another way in which G and "m is worshipful" do not say the same thing. In one respect the latter says less than G. It does not commit the speaker to saying that things are systematically related along some scale of being or of goodness. In another respect it says more than G. It claims for m something that does not depend on G for its significance.

(3) Another function of a religious predicate is to convey the character of the interest it expresses. It needs to show that a response of a certain sort is being called for. Terms like "worshipful," "awe-inspiring," and "holy" serve in the context of our own tradition to convey this sort of meaning. They give some indication of the sort of response that is appropriate. But other terms might serve this purpose in other ways.

So this is a third way in which G and *"m is worshipful"* do not say the same thing. In some contexts it may be taken for granted that whatever is perfect in being and goodness is also worshipful or holy. Then G could be used so as to say, implicitly, *"m* is worshipful." My point is only that the two expressions do not explicitly say the same thing.

I have been arguing that basic predicates are not reducible to ontological predicates, to axiological predicates, or to conjunctions of these. Nevertheless these latter predicates are important in religious discourse. We must distinguish, as we have done before, between basic proposals and doctrines.

A basic proposal is of the form *Pm*, where *P* stands for some basic religious predicate. It answers a question of the form, "What (is that) is *P?*" A doctrine answers a further question. Taking *m* as *P* we ask, in effect, "What (further) is *m?*" A doctrinal question is of this form. So an answer to a doctrinal question is of the form *Rm*, where *R* stands for some predicate other than a basic predicate, as, for example, "a Trinity," "identical with Atman," "beyond the world," or "the soul of the world." Many doctrines in various religions take the forms of expressions A-G above. So terms like "being" and "goodness" [8] play an important part in religious discourse.

8. *Another sort of objection*

We have noticed two sorts of objections it is reasonable to bring forward against claims of primacy. Some ask challenging questions like "But does *m* really exist?" Others ask questions like "But is *m* really good?" In each case the "really" is a sign that some special mode of existence or goodness is meant.

There is another sort of objection it is reasonable to make against basic religious proposals. Someone may say that giv-

[8] The use of terms like "Being," "Perfection," "Beauty," "Goodness" as terms for logical subjects of religious assertions is another matter. See Types 7 and 8 in chapter IX.

ing *m* primacy leads to a partial view of things. It means leaving out, or failing to do justice to, some important elements in experience. If we accept this proposal, so these objections run, our view of the world will become too narrow to do justice to all the facts.

I am tempted to call these cosmological objections, in contrast with the ontological and axiological objections we have considered. There would be some point in giving them this name, for they proceed from a desire to see life whole, a sense of responsibility for taking account of all our experience, and a resolution to see how things have bearing on one another. This is the sort of interest that has led philosophers to construct speculative cosmologies.

The name we use for these objections is less important than what they reveal about religious predications. Let us take, for example,

A. But if you reverence Humanity, how can you do justice to (1) our dependence on nature and (2) nature's indifference to humanity?

We could not answer this by simply taking note of the facts it mentions. "Ah, yes, we *are* dependent on nature in various ways, and it *is* true that it doesn't matter to nature whether we exist or not." "Doing justice to" has a stronger force than "taking note of." Doing justice to a fact means taking adequate account of it, giving it due weight as we balance it with other facts in making decisions. A implies that if these facts are given due weight one cannot logically give Humanity a primacy over all else. Therefore, if we rank Humanity above all else we will either distort some facts or fail to give them due weight. The objector assumes that, instead of leading us to overlook or minimize or distort the facts, a religious proposal should enable us to put them in a clearer perspective.

Other examples of such objections would be:

B. Believing in God is likely to make us overlook our own freedom and responsibilities.

C. If you give your devotion to something beyond the world, how can you do justice to the claims of things and persons in the world?

D. If you make Nirvana the supreme goal of life you have no adequate way of interpreting our creative activity in art, engineering, and politics.

E. But making ideals supreme over all else fails to do justice to our embodied existence and to brute physical facts.

F. You say Nature is the source of our being, but what of the ideals that reach beyond nature?

Other objections might challenge the proponent to take adequate account of guilt feelings, the passage of time, the dignity of man as a datum of moral experience, the continuity of nature, or some other fact in experience.

All the major religious traditions have developed, in their doctrines, resources for replying to objections of this sort. We might glance at two sorts of replies to A. One would examine the alleged fact more closely. Is it quite true without qualification that nature is indifferent to human beings? Is it the case that what human beings do, and what happens to them, makes no difference to nature? Indeed, do not human beings, individually and collectively, transform nature in some respects and to some degree? Another sort of reply would specify more closely how Humanity has primacy over nature. Here the Humanist might borrow from Pascal. Granted that a man is a reed, "the most feeble thing in nature," still he is a thinking reed, so "if the universe were to crush him, man would still be more noble than that which killed him, because he knows that he dies and the advantage which the universe has over him; the universe knows nothing of this." [9]

Consider some replies to objection B of these two sorts, interpreting the fact, and specifying the proposal. Just how

[9] *Pensées*, 347, Trotter, tr., London, J. M. Dent, 1931.

are we free and responsible, and what are the limits of our freedom and responsibilities? Are we utterly free? responsible for everything? What makes us free, so far as we are free? Our creative powers, our powers of responding to situations productively and not compulsively? Then the proposal would be specified. Heteronomous belief in God is not meant, it might be said. On the contrary, God cannot take our place, as though he were a person, and exercise our powers. These powers are his gifts to us and only we can use them, though we use them best when we entrust our finite acts—and the whole living of a life is a finite act—to his providence and mercy.

These objections do not challenge the primacy claimed in the proposal as directly as ontological and axiological objections do, though they are similar to axiological objections. Like the latter they are concerned for a certain value, but this value is of a distinctive sort. They are concerned for comprehensiveness and wholeness in our understanding of life, and they question whether something is being left out. (Of course at best, with the aid of our most highly developed systems of philosophy and theology or without them, we are able only intermittently and obscurely to see any unity amid, or beyond, the multiplicity of human interests and their objects.)

If the relevance of these objections is granted, this tells us something about the proposal. A certain illuminative power is being claimed. It is being claimed that by taking something m as ultimate (or holy, or most important) we will be in position to illuminate the facts of life and do justice to them. If this is not claimed, these objections are not relevant.

This is not the same as the claim of a speculative system, and that is why I hesitate to call these objections cosmological. A speculative proposal claims to *have* thrown light on all the facts, by presenting an adequate categoreal scheme. A religious proposal might claim only to establish a standpoint from which illumination is possible.

This concern to do justice to all the facts of life might

be called an intellectual virtue, for it is closely related to virtues of other sorts and it is the remedy for fanaticism. William James attributed various religious excesses, including fanaticism, to "a relative deficiency of intellect." [10] The causes of fanaticism are not so simple as this, but we might say that the intellectual deficiency of fanaticism is a failure to do justice to important facts of life. The fanatic's vision is too narrow. He needs more breadth and balance in his view of things. His obsession makes him blind. So objections like those above have, indirectly, a moral value.

9. *Modes of primacy*

There are various ways in which something *m* might be given primacy over all else, and this is an important variable in religion. For some objections would apply to some modes of primacy but not to others. I shall confine myself to pointing out two ways of relating something *m* to other things which might, consistently with assigning it primacy, be avoided.

a. It is not necessary, in giving *m* a religious primacy, to say it is the only reality or the only good or the only end in life. There are world-denying religions, but there are also world-affirming religions.[11] A doctrinal scheme might find ways of saying that many things are real, that many things are good, or that there are many ends in life. So, instead of focusing attention exclusively on *m*, a doctrinal scheme might even enforce attention to other things as well. For example, it might be said that if we do not love other human beings we do not love God. And in the *Bhagavad-Gita* the upshot of Arjuna's colloquy with the divine charioteer is not that he withdraws from life but that he goes into the battle.

[10] *Varieties of Religious Experience*, 340.
[11] Generalizing and reading, for "world," "things other than *m*," Humanists need not deny things other than Humanity and Naturalists need not deny things other than Nature.

b. It is not necessary, in order to give religious primacy to *m*, to propose that all other things form an ordered system of which *m* is the controlling principle, whether as the apex of a hierarchy of being (as in Neoplatonism) or as the dynamic of a dialectical development (as in Hegel). Revolts against speculative philosophy have occurred in all the major religious traditions. One motive for these revolts, whether in primitive Buddhism, in Islam, in Judaism, or in Christianity, has been to mark off something *m* more clearly from all else, by detaching conceptions of it from systematic conceptions of the world.

10. *Conclusion*

We have been concerned with proposals which make use of predicates like the following: "holy"—"ultimate"— "most important"—"ground of being"—"that on which we are absolutely dependent"—"that than which nothing greater can be conceived"—"the source of meaning"—"the supreme goal of life." Many more such predicates could be constructed from passages in religious literature which explain or intimate the domain of religious experience. We have discussed two functions of such predicates, as follows:

A. A basic religious predicate is used to mark off its logical subject from all else.

B. A basic religious predicate is used to give its logical subject a primacy over all else.

To these we should add a third function we have noticed in passing:

C. A basic religious predicate conveys a subjective form of feeling (in Whitehead's phrase). It defines or suggests a pattern of response appropriate to the object proposed.

Further, we have noticed that some basic religious proposals claim to establish a standpoint from which illumination of all the facts of life is possible.

Our main question has been, How can the predications in basic proposals be supported? For, if no support is possible, no truth-claim is being made. The general requirement is that it be possible [12] to formulate, in the frame of the predicate in question, rules of relevance for appeals to facts, a procedure for judgment, and norms of judgment. I have explained in earlier chapters how this might be done for some of these predicates. And the specimen arguments in this chapter have shown how such rules, procedures, and norms can be used.

In these arguments, it is clear enough, we do not have mechanical decision procedures. These are matters for good judgment. The relevant facts have to be weighed and balanced. Where the weight of a particular fact is in dispute, we look more closely and clearly at the fact itself and at other facts connected with it. We do not consult some table of weightings for facts; nor do we throw up our hands when such disagreements appear.

What does some particular fact (for example, our anxious apprehension of death) amount to? We need to understand it more clearly and fully, in order to give it the right weight in our judgment. We look for its constituents (Of what is it compounded?), for its reasons (Why is it the case?), for wholes of which it is a part (Of what else are we apprehensive?), for contrasts (How does it differ from apprehension of moral failure?). In general we look for connections of the fact with other facts, to see what it amounts to.

The norms of judgment which can be offered as guiding principles for weighing facts are not themselves beyond dispute. In this respect religious arguments, like many other sorts of arguments, are unlike mathematical proofs. But this does not preclude genuine argument. For in any genuine

---

[12] I say "possible" because such rules, procedures, and norms are usually unformulated, though they regulate the course of our arguments.

disagreement there will be some norms which are not in fact disputed. What reasonableness in religion requires is that norms be put forward not as weapons in ideological warfare, nor as persuasive devices, but as steps toward truth which both parties to the disagreement might take together.

CHAPTER XII

Truth

1. *Truth and suggestions*

When we aim at truth in religious inquiry we aim at a certain satisfaction. We want to be more of one mind, less divided against ourselves. We want to clear up confusions and to stand on firmer ground. Then, we think, our purposes could be clearer and we might come nearer living up to our responsibilities and realizing our possibilities.

So we aim at settling the question we are asking. Sometimes we settle questions simply by ceasing to ask them. But if a question is both a good question and a real question we look for an answer. Some answers will not do. Some are inconsistent, intolerably inconsistent, with other things we believe to be true. Some have internal confusions which would only perplex us more. Some are only theories, we think, without grounding in reality.

For this reason the satisfaction at which we aim is not an emotional state, though emotions may attend it. We aim at a certain harmony of thought and reality. We want an answer which accords with the facts of life. In this sense our want is, as Bradley says, "a special one." It is a "theoretical want."

Also, the answer we look for cannot be a purely private answer. It must speak to our own condition, certainly. But it must speak to the conditions of others also. For the question we ask has its roots in common life, if it is a good question, and the experiences of others are relevant to our own. So we cannot be satisfied with an answer we could not propose to others. We look for an answer which can have a place in significant discourse.

We begin with a suggestion which occurs in some nonpropositional form, perhaps as a complex image. For wisdom speaks first in images, as Yeats says, though if we are wise we will not be content with images. Suggestions are promises of truth. May they also be "true"? This would mean that the adoption of a suggestion is something like a judgment, though not the same thing. Let us explore the analogy.

There are three questions to ask about a suggestion: *a*. Does it speak with one voice? Take an example. Mordecai Kaplan says that, in a period of his life when he was unsettled, the Zionist movement and in particular Ahad Ha-am's conception of the Jewish people as "a living organism animated by an irresistible will to live" enabled him to find "spiritual anchorage." [1] Here is a complex image which spoke with power. But images are not exempt from criticism. Is there disharmony within the image itself, analogous to inconsistency or incoherence among propositions? Is a people an organism? Do organisms have wills? One test of the "truth" of a suggestion is the internal harmony and unity of the image by which it is conveyed.

b. Another question about a religious suggestion is: Does it give us better understanding of ourselves? Does some suggestion about what is holy, for example, tell us what we do in fact take as holy? Often we have standpoints without knowing them, but sometimes we are enlightened about them. Does the suggestion give us clearer and deeper understanding of what we live by? Does it speak with power, as Kaplan's suggestion did? Does it give us self-knowledge? Does it in this way give us "truth"?

We can connect this sense of "true" with "truth is subjectivity" (Kierkegaard) and with "to thine own self be true." A suggestion may lead to more authentic existence; it may enable us to be more true to ourselves. We can con-

---

[1] I. Eisenstein and E. Kohn, ed., *Mordecai Kaplan, an Evaluation*, 23, New York, Jewish Reconstructionist Foundation, 1952, from "A Heart of Wisdom," in *The Reconstructionist*, xvii, No. 6.

nect this also with "Christ is the truth" and with the "Four
Noble Truths" of Buddhism, and more generally with the
notion of "saving truth," which is the primary force of
"truth" in religious literature. Truth is a way of being, not
just a way of thinking. "The moment of truth" in the
bull ring has affinities with these uses. In all these cases
truth is a quality of things or states, not a quality of
propositions.

At this point one option is to say that this is the *only*
sense of truth in religion. The possibility of authentic existence can be conveyed by images. But at most we can only
suggest what we mean. We cannot express religious truth in
propositions. "Those who say do not know; those who
know do not say."

c. But a third question about a suggestion is possible.
Will it yield propositions which will turn out to be true?
By explicating its suggestive meaning, can we derive from
it a set of propositions? And will these propositions bear
affirmative judgments?

One might ask, "How can anyone adopt a suggestion before exploring it?" But one may also ask, "How can one
explore a suggestion without adopting it?" On many occasions we choose before fully exploring what we choose,
not only in practical matters but also in various types of
inquiry including scientific inquiry. It is irresponsible to
choose without warrant; it is also irresponsible sometimes
not to choose.

So a suggestion might be "true" in the sense that it gives
good promise of yielding propositions which will turn out
to be true. We adopt it because we think it will guide us to
an explicit answer to our question.

This aspect of the "promise" of a suggestion is not independent of the others. For if an image lacks integrity it
will lack revelatory power, and if it fails to give self-
knowledge the propositions we derive from it will fail to
answer our questions. But this would connect these other

senses of "truth" with the truth of propositions. So, we could say, a suggestion "keeps" its promise of truth by (1) having integrity, (2) giving self-knowledge, and (3) yielding true propositions.

Before dealing with some objections to the possibility of propositional truth let us notice another sense of "true." A proposition might, or might not, be *true to* a suggestion. Suppose an utterance purports to explicate a basic religious suggestion, for example, some doctrinal proposal put forward in a religious community. Consider some disputed doctrine, like the doctrine of double predestination in Christian theology. Is it permissible? Is it essential? Such questions cannot always be decided by reference to previously established doctrines. Sometimes theologians ask whether some doctrine is congruent with the basic motif of the Christian faith.[2] Thus, Does not Origen's doctrine of the preexistence and fall of the soul follow from Orphism rather than from the Christian gospel? In such cases the claim of the doctrine to be true to the suggestion is an integral part of its claim to truth.

This sort of claim is related to the requirement of coherence for doctrinal schemes. For a growing doctrinal scheme can maintain its coherence only if there is some principle of unity, such as fidelity to the suggestion which generates the scheme. To recall an example offered in Chapter VI, Lippmann offers the doctrine, "A mature desire is innocent." [3] Then the problem is whether this doctrine is true to what is suggested by "the progress of the individual from helpless infancy to self-governing maturity." (*Is* this

[2] See A. Nygren, *Agape and Eros*, New York, Macmillan, 1932, and Nels F. S. Ferré, *Swedish Contributions to Modern Theology*, New York, Harper, 1939, on "motif research."

[3] *A Preface to Morals*, 192. He says: "The function of high religion is to reveal to men the quality of mature experience. . . . It announces the discovery that men can enter into the realm of the spirit when they have outgrown all childishness" (193).

progress a progress toward innocence?) Otherwise the scheme will be incoherent.

2. *Are there true religious propositions?*

Let us look in a critical way at some reasons which might be given for asserting:

A. There are no true religious propositions.

So we shall be discussing some objections to the possibility of true religious propositions.

First let us distingush A from the following two assertions:

B. All religious propositions are untrue.
C. There are no religious propositions.

C says no truth-claims are made in religious discourse. No religious proposals satisfy the conditions of truth-claims. So judgments, decisions about truth-claims, are not in order. B admits some truth-claims in religious discourse; in these cases judgments are in order. But all these truth-claims deserve to be judged negatively. In every case there is sufficient reason for saying that the proposition is untrue. A does not say that any religious propositions are untrue. This would presuppose that some truth-claims are made. But A does not presuppose this. It says only that *if* any truth-claim is made, then *either* this claim is too weak to warrant acceptance or rejection (hence judgment should be suspended) *or* there is sufficient reason to warrant rejection (a negative judgment).

The main force of A falls against basic religious proposals. It could be granted by many who are sceptical of propositional truth in religion that doctrines may conform to special standards in a particular community, for instance, that a certain doctrine of the Trinity may conform to the Bible and tradition. Given certain standards, proposals may conform to these standards.

But if we let the matter rest there we fail to do justice to the way religious doctrines are meant. A Christian doctrine is proposed as an explication of what is revealed in the Bible. A humanist doctrine is proposed as an explication of what is revealed in, say, mature human experience. But in proposing these doctrines Christians and humanists also make universal claims. They implicitly propose that these doctrines tell us something about "that in which we live and move and have our being" or about "the realm of the spirit." That is to say, when proposals about doctrines are made with serious intent, basic religious proposals are made also.

Let us consider three arguments in support of A, three objections against asserting there are true religious propositions. These are: (*a*) that certainty is not possible in religion; (*b*) that religious questions are not decidable; and (*c*) that claiming truth in religion involves being exclusive in certain wrong ways (being insensitive or intolerant or obsessive or idolatrous).

Such objections do not have to proceed from irreligious (or nonreligious) points of view. They are made sometimes by people who are genuinely and deeply religious. For example, philosophical scepticism has often been allied with theological dogmatism or with mysticism in religion.

3. *Truth and certainty*

One reason which might be given for holding that no religious propositions are true is that absolute certainty in religion is not possible. I have argued that we cannot be absolutely certain that any basic religious proposal is true, in the very strong sense of "absolutely certain" explained in Chapter VII. But it might be objected that if we admit the kinds of openness and tentativeness this entails we cannot be justified in making affirmative religious judgments. The argument might be developed in the following way:

In religion, unlike (perhaps) science and common sense, we cannot really *know* what is true. Now if we do not know what is true in religion, we ought not to make any affirmative religious judgments. Belief, if it is only belief, is inappropriate in religion. We are justified in having beliefs (without absolute certainty) about various other matters, for example, scientific and political questions. But religion involves our own being in such a deep and intimate way that we must be wholehearted about it. There is something irresponsible about believing a religious proposition when we do not, and perhaps cannot, *know* whether or not it is true.

I agree that certainty is necessary in religion. The problem is to show what sort of certainty is necessary. First I shall restate the sort of certainty which I have argued is not possible.

There are two objections against the possibility of knowing with absolute (unqualified and unconditioned) certainty that some basic religious proposal is true. (In stating these objections I am also giving the sense of "absolute certainty" I have in mind.) One is an objection to the possibility of gaining absolute certainty in an a priori way; the other is an objection to the possibility of gaining absolute certainty from experience.

The first objection has two steps: (*a*) any basic religious proposal has positive logical alternatives, and (*b*) we cannot know what all the possible alternatives are. The argument for the first step is that no basic religious predicate specifies some one logical subject of which it is true. For any proposal like "God is the ground of being" or "Nirvana is the supreme goal of life," alternatives like "The Absolute is the ground of being" or "The vision of God is the supreme goal of life" are logically possible. The argument for the second step is that we have no a priori reason for limiting the range of logical subjects of basic religious proposals. To the contrary, the history of religion gives us positive reasons for supposing that previously unthought-of proposals do emerge in the course of history. In sum, to attain absolute certainty by an a priori route, we would have to show that all possible basic proposals but one are self-contradictory, and I have argued that this is not possible.

The objection to gaining absolute certainty from experience is that we cannot be sure that no future experience will be a good reason for reversing a religious judgment. Our experience is always incomplete; we are never in a position to say that we know all the facts. In the past, experiences have been good reasons for reversing some of our judgments. What reason could we have for thinking this could not occur in the future? We are not in a position to know what all our future experiences will be. So we cannot gain absolute certainty about a basic religious proposition from experience.

It follows that any certainty which is possible in religion must fall short of absolute certainty. (Even if I should judge that the Bible, or the church, is infallible, my judgment that this is so is not infallible.) But is there not an absurdity in supposing that human beings could have this kind of certainty? Is it not absurd to claim this kind of certainty, not only for religious judgments but for judgments of any sort whatever? For it requires knowledge of all possible logical alternatives to a particular proposal, and knowledge of all possible experiences that might be relevant to its truth. And is not this too much to expect of a human mind?

Now let us see what kind of certainty is possible in religion. Certainty in religion can be represented as a three-layered structure in the following way:

Basic propositions Doctrinal propositions	(Reasonable certainty)
Illuminating suggestions	(Wholehearted adoption)
Basic suppositions	(Unquestioned)

Since these features of religious inquiry have been explained already, I need only indicate how they are elements in the structure of religious certainty.

Let us begin with "suggestions." If anyone is religious he has some central focus of illumination which gives him a point of view on the whole of life. He thinks and acts in the light of some basic suggestion. And the measure of whole-heartedness in response to a suggestion is the measure of the strength of one structural element in religious certainty.

Now it is possible to adhere wholeheartedly to a suggestion without being absolutely certain about the truth of some proposition one derives from this suggestion. A Christian might be wholehearted in accepting Christ as the Way, the Truth, and the Life, without being absolutely certain (in the strict sense explained above) of the truth of such a proposition as "God is the ground of being." Likewise, a Buddhist might wholeheartedly take refuge in "the Buddha, the Dharma, the Sangha" without being absolutely certain (in the strict sense) of the truth of a proposition like "Nirvana is the supreme goal of life."

This is because Christ and the Buddha are apprehended as elements in experience more concrete than propositions. For our fundamental orientation and basic guidance in life we rely on experiences which cannot be funded into propositional meaning without remainder. That is why they can evoke whole-responses and be central foci of illumination.

Now let us move downward instead of upward on our diagram and consider the relation of "suggestions" to "basic suppositions." It is possible to be religious without explicitly asking a basic religious question. Someone may have and act on a central focus of illumination without having stated for himself the problem to which the suggestion is relevant. Nevertheless in adopting the suggestion he has made a basic religious supposition. This can be explained as follows:

If asked about the function of the suggestion he can say something like "It tells me what is ultimate" or "It is my clue to the meaning of life" or "It reveals to me the ground of my being." Now these expressions imply suppositions like "There is something that is ultimate," "Life has a meaning," and "There is a ground of being." This implication is significant because, even if he should come to reject the suggestion, it would still be possible to make the supposition.

In Chapter V we saw how basic suppositions are unquestioned. Someone ceases to make some supposition or other only when he ceases to be religious. Analogously, someone ceases to make some basic scientific supposition (for example, that there are some uniformities in nature) only when one ceases to be scientific. Without some such supposition no inquiry would have point. So an unquestioned supposition is the foundation of the structure of certainty.

Though basic suppositions are suggested by experience they are not conclusions or preconclusions. They are not even theories, though a supposition gives point to a theory. Instead, they make it possible to ask the real questions to which various theories are proposed as answers. For example, if we do not suppose there are some uniformities in nature (and surely this is not an empirical conclusion), or that there is something we ought to do (and this is surely not a deduction from given premises), then "What are the uniformities in nature?" and "What ought we to do?" are not real questions. Thus basic suppositions underlie (logically) the process of thinking by which conclusions are reached.

We begin with an unquestioned supposition of the form, "There is something that is P," where P can be interpreted by some basic religious predicate. Then it is possible to formulate a question of the form "What is it that is P?" We may wholeheartedly adopt some suggestion which promises an answer to this question; we may state part of its meaning in a proposition; and we may judge that this proposition is true.

How certain, then, can we be about these propositions?

In general, reasonably certain. How certain we can reasonably be depends on two nonlogical variables—the availability of relevant facts and the urgency of decision. How strong the "evidence" is (how successful a reference to the logical subject is possible, and how much support can be given to the predication) and how urgent a decision is—these must be matters of judgment in any particular case. There is no general reason against someone's being reasonably certain that something m has a better claim to be P than anything non-m he can think of.

So our certainty about the truth of religious propositions is only one stratum in the structure of religious certainty. If this is understood the risks of inquiry need not be taken in an irresponsible way. For when we judge a religious proposition to be true we have other strata of certainty which are relatively independent of its truth. That is, if for some good reason the judgment has to be reversed or suspended, alternative explications of the illuminating suggestion may be possible. Further, if the suggestion should cease to illuminate, alternative suggestions are possible.

4. Truth and decidability

A judgment that some proposition is true or untrue cannot be an arbitrary decision. If a decision is arbitrary, then in that decision we are not deciding that something is true or untrue. Judgments must be made in accord with principles of judgment. So "decidable" means "decidable in accord with principles of judgment."

It follows that, whenever a genuine truth-claim is made, principles of judgment can be found. So one reason which might be offered for holding that no religious propositions are true is that principles of judgment are not possible in religion. This is the next objection we must consider. I shall rely on earlier discussions of religious judgments and principles of judgment, and on the specimen arguments in the last four chapters as illustrations, and come to the main point at issue.

Let us distinguish four sorts of cases:

a. Pure calculations. Suppose it is asked, "What is the product of 9 and 17?" In this case there are rules of calculation which are sufficient to determine the answer to the question. These rules are well known and they leave no room for dispute as to the correct answer. We might say that questions of this type are decidable but not arguable. All that is needed is a procedure for judgment.

b. Decisions when there are crucial facts without norms of judgment. Suppose it is asked, "At what time was Echo I visible from East Rock last night?" A number of principles of judgment could be elaborated so as to rule out, for example, the visual experiences of nearsighted people, of people who happened to be under a shelter on East Rock, and others. There would be rules for identifying Echo I and for correlating time zones. In this case, rules of relevance are important, as they were not in *a*. Here we need both rules of relevance and a procedure for judgment. This means that the question as it stands is arguable. But it is also decidable, within certain limits of error, by reference to some crucial fact. No norms of judgment are needed.

c. Decisions when norms of judgment are needed. Suppose it is asked, "Is Jones honest?" Here rules of relevance and a procedure for judgment are needed, but norms of judgment are also needed. We would need to know what quality we are looking for, and how to discover whether Jones has it. (Should we trust M's impression of Jones?) But we also need some standards in accord with which we decide. Do we call him honest if he cheats only rarely? So questions like this are arguable not only in the way questions like *b* are arguable but in another way as well. We must argue from the norms of judgment which guide us in making a decision, and we may have to argue *for* these norms also. Now shall we say this question is decidable? Or shall we say that it is decidable only if we can transform it, by suitable rules of relevance, into a question like *b?*

Again, suppose that three climbers are on a dangerous mountain in winter. One is seriously injured. The question arises, "Should we take him down with us, or leave him here, or stay with him?" Then, in addition to relevant facts (such as "He will probably die in six hours if we leave him" and "No one knows we are here" and contraries of these), norms of judgment (such as "It is better to help others than not to" or "Look out for yourself first") will be appealed to or tacitly assumed. It is not plausible to suppose that this case can be transformed into a case like *b,* so that some one crucial fact (without norms of judgment) could be decisive. But its question is arguable and in principle decidable— though the climbers may not agree in their decisions—even though the norms of judgment which are adopted are themselves arguable.

d. Pure confessions and injunctions. Suppose someone says, "I bow to the will of Allah." There might be circumstances in which we would construe this as a pure confession, conveying no implicit proposal. Then no issue would be posed for decision. Or someone might say, "Put a pinch of incense on the altar," and we might construe this as a pure injunction. Then this would pose no issue for religious judgment, for though there would be an issue for decision it would be posed by a proposal for action, not by a proposal for belief. In such cases there is no issue to argue in the way there are issues to argue in *b* and in *c,* and there is nothing to judge in the way there is something to judge in *a* or in *b* or in *c.* Neither arguments nor judgments are in order.

Now with these cases in mind let us say a decision is arbitrary to the extent that it is not made in accord with the principles of judgment required by the question at issue. Thus, to avoid being arbitrary, we would not expect a judgment about *a* to be in accord with rules of relevance, for the question does not require such rules. All we require is a procedure of judgment. And, to avoid being arbitrary, we would not require a judgment about *b* to be in accord with norms of judgment, for these are not required by the question. But we would expect judgments about the cases in *c* to be in accord with rules of relevance and norms of judgment. For principles of both these sorts are required by the questions.

No one would say that basic religious questions are matters for pure calculation. Further, it could not be maintained that basic religious questions are like *b*, or could be transformed into questions like *b*, so that no norms of judgment are required. There are always norms of judgment [4] in religious arguments. This does not mean there are no crucial facts in religious arguments but only that, when some fact becomes crucial, this is a sign of agreement on some norm of judgment.

Now it might be objected that, though religious judgments may be in accord with norms of judgment and thus not immediately arbitrary, still, decisions about norms of judgment must themselves be arbitrary. So we have not avoided the necessity for arbitrary decisions in religion. Decisions about religious proposals are infected with the arbitrariness of the norms of judgment which guide them.

The answer to this objection may be given in two stages. First, even if decisions about norms of judgment could be said to be arbitrary, basic religious judgments which appeal to such norms would not be arbitrary in the same way as decisions which make no such appeals. Appealing to a norm in an argument means offering a principle to which, it is supposed, both parties to the argument might be equally sub-

---

[4] Like, e.g., "Nothing is holy which includes envy and strife," and "Nothing can be the supreme goal of life if it involves unhappiness," and "An actuality is more important than a possibility," and contraries of these.

ject. In this way the use of norms in arguments is different
from the use of persuasive devices.

In the second place, we should ask whether decisions
about norms of judgment must be arbitrary and what this
would mean. We often discover that we have been guided
by unquestioned norms of judgment. But we would not say
that all unquestioned norms of judgment are arbitrary. The
essential point is what we do when we discover this. We
may look for reasons for the norm and be ready and willing
to offer them. We may place the norm in the domain of
argument. Further, sometimes we abandon norms of judgment and discover new ones.

In this way unquestioned norms of judgment are unlike basic suppositions. A previously unquestioned norm of
judgment can be made arguable in a way in which a basic
supposition cannot. This is precisely why, given only a basic
question, we can formulate a basic supposition but not a
norm of judgment.

The main force of the objection derives from an assumption that, unless there is some master norm of judgment
which is absolutely inescapable, all other norms are infected
with arbitrariness. But the search for such a master norm
in any significant inquiry is based on an illusion. There may
well be more warrant for some norms than for others, but
none is inescapable.

So in any inquiry in which norms of judgment are required the best we can do is to offer arguable norms. But
this is quite different from saying that decisions about norms
must be arbitrary. On the contrary, it implies that they
need not be so. It is fallacious to conclude that if a norm is
not inescapable it is arbitrary. The rule for avoiding arbitrariness would be: for any norm, be ready and willing to
give reasons for it. However norms have been generated
(and this is well worth understanding as a matter of historical and psychological fact), they may now be put forward to stand on their own feet and to be argued for if
challenged.

Finally, it is not necessary to argue that all basic questions are equally decidable. Some basic predicates might yield principles of judgment more readily than others do.

5. *Truth and exclusiveness*

Another objection is that religious truth-claims involve a certain exclusiveness, with unhappy consequences. The objection may be developed in various ways, as a phenomenological objection, as a moral objection, as an objection from normative psychology, or as a religious objection, as follows: In a basic religious proposal some logical subject is marked off from all else and ranked above all else. But (*a*) this leads to insensitivity to the varieties of religious belief. Or (*b*) it leads to intolerance (lack of respect and charity) toward those who fail to accept the proposal. Or (*c*) it is a symptom of obsession. Or (*d*) it is a demonic (Tillich) or idolatrous tendency, since it leads us to think of God (or Nirvana, or the One, or Brahman, or the Buddha-nature, or the Way, et cetera) as one object among many. Let us consider these in order:

a. The phenomenological objection might arise from a study of comparative religion. Many different religions have existed in the course of human history, and most of them have some commendable features. How could some one religious belief be true and all the others untrue?

I offer only some logical considerations on this point. If some basic proposition is true it would not immediately follow that all other basic propositions are untrue. Consider the following:

A. It is God that is holy.
B. Nirvana is the supreme goal of life.
C. Man's chief end is to glorify God, and to enjoy him forever.[5]
D. Nature is the ground of our being.
E. God is the ground of our being.

[5] It is worth noticing that the Shorter Catechism does not say "man's *sole* end."

Now D and E do appear to contradict one another. If both make genuine truth-claims, and if one is true, the other must be untrue. But A and B do not obviously contradict one another. From A it would not immediately follow that Nirvana is not the supreme goal of life. What would immediately follow is that it is not Nirvana that is holy.

Certainly we are inclined to think A and B conflict in some way. And if we can derive C from A we come closer to stating a contradictory of B. But in all these cases the proposals would have to be developed and elaborated before we could tell whether real contradictions occur and if so how.

Further, there is a place in religious inquiry for constructing new formulations of belief, to do justice to the truths which opposing views express.[6] Sometimes we do find room in a larger view for both of two opposed proposals. But we must not underestimate the conflicts, either. If true propositions are possible, genuine disagreements are possible.

More generally, in asserting some proposition p we are not asserting that only p is true. There may be, and indeed must be, many other true propositions as well. It is only *not-p* that we are denying. Therefore holding that some religious proposition is true requires neither a simple rejection of all other religious views nor insensitivity to their individuality and variety.

b. The moral objection is that admission of religious truth-claims leads to intolerance. This is a very different

[6] This does not need to involve an artificial syncretism. The real problem is how a religious system can react to external criticism in a creative way instead of a defensive way. See H. R. Niebuhr, *The Meaning of Revelation*, chs. i-ii, New York, Macmillan, 1941. For some contrasting views on this see W. E. Hocking, *Living Religions and a World Faith*, New York, Macmillan, 1940, and H. Kraemer, *The Christian Message in a Non-Christian World*, New York, Harper, 1938, and *Why Christianity of All Religions?* Philadelphia, Westminster, 1962.

point. Here we are directly concerned not with propositions but with persons. Insofar as tolerance is an attitude of respect and charity toward other persons, tolerance does not require scepticism. On the contrary, if tolerance is a moral virtue and therefore relevant to real situations, then real conflicts must exist, conflicts which might include genuine disagreements. We do not need to be tolerant toward those with whom we do not disagree. So making truth-claims, even if this leads to disagreements, cannot require intolerance.

Certainly if religious beliefs are compulsively held we will be tempted to be hostile to people who deny them. These people will be felt as threats to our security. But I have tried to show how religious beliefs do not have to be held in a compulsive way. And this bears on the next form of the objection as well.

c. The objection from normative psychology is as follows: To mark out and rank something above all else, as basic religious propositions do, would lead to a distortion of the field of experience. Something is magnified out of proportion, so that it takes on an unhealthy importance. The objects of other interests are affected by this distortion. They are displaced from their normal functions and tend to be excluded.

Certainly there are religious obsessions, where some of the objects of nonreligious interests are compulsively excluded by a religious interest. But by ordinary standards of normality many religious people are normal. Whether in a particular culture at a particular time, like our own, it happens that religious people are more likely to be obsessed in this way than not to be, or more likely to be obsessed than nonreligious people are, these are empirical questions. Again I have only a logical point to make.

It is not possible to deduce obsessiveness from an adequately general theory of religion. In ascribing a basic religious predicate to something *m* it is not logically necessary to exclude any non-*m* things from one's universe of experience, any more than it is necessary to exclude the Id from concern when Freud proposes to strengthen the Ego. It is possible to conceive varieties of religious experience in which the values of all non-*m* things are given due weight and positively accepted. Various patterns of connection between *m* and things non-*m* are possible, so that the uniqueness and primacy of something *m* need not involve any psychological rejection of any non-*m* thing.[7] Religion does not have to involve this kind of exclusiveness.

d. Finally, let us consider a religious form of the objection. This, I think, is the strongest form of the objection and requires more attention. Though its motive seems quite different from that of the psychological objection, some of the points I shall make bear on both. We might put this form of the objection as follows:

There cannot be any true religious propositions. For if we are concerned with something which can be the logical subject of a proposition, then either we are not religious or we are idolatrous. All religious propositions are untrue. Certainly we can try to express religious experiences verbally as well as nonverbally, but all such utterances are symbolic. They can only suggest religious truth. We should never try to convey religious truth in propositional form.

The construction of a proposition requires a singling out of its logical subject, and it is this singling out which is systematically misleading. For if we are religious we are not concerned with anything which is, so to speak, "singleable." Even though we *say* that what we single out is not a finite object, still, by virtue of the very fact of our singling it out

[7] For example, "We owe to the sense of Deity the obviousness of the many actualities of the world . . ." (A. N. Whitehead, *Modes of Thought*, 140, New York, Macmillan, 1938). Whitehead gives a systematic interpretation of this in his cosmology. See my discussions of patterns of subordination in chapter IV, section 3; types of proposals in chapter IX; and modes of primacy in chapter XI, section 9.

to say these things about it, we are treating it as a finite object.

So all statements purporting to convey religious propositions either are nonsensical, conveying no proposition at all, or they convey false propositions. We can suggest religious truth but we cannot say it, even in part.

Views like this bring relief from the anxiety of doubt. They remove the fear that truth may conflict with faith. There are no religious propositions to be defended against such threats. But, as we have seen, religious doubt might be dealt with in another way, and these views pay too great a price, in view of their consequences.

One consequence is that it becomes impossible to explain the context of religious discourse. Let us see how such explanations are useful. In religious discourse we ordinarily take for granted and rely on a certain experiential context. We presuppose religious interests. So ordinarily we do not confuse religious questions with scientific questions or moral questions or esthetic questions. But sometimes confusions occur. Utterances meant as religious remarks are taken as scientific or common-sense statements, or vice versa. The hearer misses the point. In these situations the context of discourse has to be indicated and established. How can this be done?

On the view we are discussing, it would have to be done by hints and suggestions. We would show the context by the way we speak, without explaining it. Why can we not explain it? Because on this view we could have no concept of the context. (But if we have some way of telling when our hints and suggestions are successful, must we not have a concept?) Now let us see why this view cannot admit such a concept.

If we had such a concept to guide our hints and suggestions we should be obliged to make it as explicit as we could if called on to do so. Now an explication of such a concept would include the formulation of some predicate like "infinite," "ultimate," "holy," "ground of being," "supreme goal of life," and others we have noticed. That is to say, a basic religious predicate is implicit in any concept of the domain of religious discourse. But to formulate such a predicate is to invite a basic religious question, asking of what it is true. And this is to admit the possibility of true basic religious propositions. So this view, which denies this possibility, cannot admit concepts of the domain of religious discourse.

In some cultures this consequence might not be serious. There might be little need for explanation of religious discourse. But in a culture where contrasting types of discourse are well marked, which is especially true of scientific discourse in our culture, we need not only to know intuitively what we are doing but also to be able to say what we are doing.

This view of religious discourse has a further consequence; it gives little or no basis for theology. If there are no true religious propositions, how could there be any systematic explication of doctrinal schemes? For this there must be a logic of some sort. But without concepts and the possibility of true propositions, what sort of logic might there be?

This consequence like the previous one might be accepted. It happens to be the case, it might be said, that religion is incompatible with theology. And we find a number of cases in the history of religion where this consequence is explicitly asserted. Again, this consequence might be less serious in other cultures than in our own.

A certain confusion might encourage this view of religious discourse. The importance of ordinary physical objects and individual persons in our experience tempts us to take these as paradigms of logical subjects of propositions. So we might be led to suppose that if we construct propositions about God or Brahman or Nirvana we are thereby treating these as things or persons.

Certain stresses in religious experience cooperate, so to speak, with this confusion. To keep life straight we need to differentiate God, say, from things and persons. For we discover that many actions and feelings which are appropriate to them are not appropriate to God, and vice versa. And this may reinforce our aversion from formulating propositions with God as their logical subject.

But it is not a logical necessity that the logical subject of a proposition be a thing or a person. Both in daily life and in scientific discourse we construct many propositions whose logical subjects are neither physical objects nor persons. It may well be that propositions about spatio-temporal particulars are basic to the structure of our beliefs.[8] But it would not follow that no other propositions can be formulated. And in Chapter IX we saw a wide range of possible logical subjects of basic religious propositions. If this confusion is avoided the objection loses some of its force.

For example, it might (logically) be said that no one thing but many things are holy (that place, that man, that occasion, et cetera) and that we do not look behind all these things for some other thing we worship. We take life as it comes and whatever turns out to be holy *is* holy.[9] So, it might be said, we can be open to whatever experience brings and avoid the distortions of metaphysics. But a religious view like this might admit true propositions about the quality which all these things have in common, which some might have more than others, and which others might lack. Questions about this quality would be in order, and arguments to support such a proposal would be needed.

The motive behind this objection is to avoid idolatry.

[8] See P. F. Strawson, *Individuals, An Essay in Descriptive Metaphysics*, London, Methuen, 1959.

[9] Compare: "The holy is a 'quality in encounter," not an object among objects. . . ." Paul Tillich in Sidney Hook, ed., *Religious Experience and Truth*, 6, New York, New York University Press, 1961.

But there are ways of guarding against idolatry without renouncing references and true propositions. One safeguard would be having a complex doctrinal scheme which, by its very complexity, forces our minds away from thinking of God (or of the One, or Brahman) as a finite individual. Another safeguard would be having an open concept, as against no concept at all (some mystics) and as against a closed concept (some deists).

A closed concept is one which leaves no room for the shock of recognition. It is not open to revision and development in the light of further experience. The object is, so to speak, enclosed within the concept. An open concept is one held subject to revision and development. (We can know something about something without knowing everything about it.) For some mystics God is both unintelligible and incomprehensible. For some deists God is both intelligible and comprehensible. But God might be thought of as intelligible but not comprehensible. An open concept leaves room for mystery and wonder.

Something like this is achieved by speaking of both Ishvara and Brahman as Shankara does, of both God and the Godhead as Eckhart does, and of both God revealed and God hidden as Luther does. Similarly, to take a less traditional example, Wieman speaks of God as both the structure of the universe relative to a given purpose and the totality encountered beyond all purposes.[10] Many other examples may come to mind.

Finally, a remark on the uses of religious propositions is in order. Their primary uses are in inquiry and in communication, not in contemplation and devotion. Within certain religious experiences there may be no need for propositions. But they have good uses outside those experiences, in reflection on them and in speaking of them. Also, inquiry

[10] H. N. Wieman, *The Wrestle of Religion with Truth*, 171–172, New York, Macmillan, 1927.

and conversation themselves can take on a religious significance.[11]

My argument in this section has been that, while, if truth-claims are admitted, some truth-claims in religion would be incompatible with others, admission of true religious propositions does not entail the kinds of exclusiveness which characterize insensitivity, intolerance, obsessiveness, and idolatry.

6. *Conditions of truth*

I have not given a complete argument against the negative view I have been considering. My aim has been to expose some assumptions and consequences of the arguments used to support it and thus bring out further points which need to be argued. For it could not be shown that there are true religious propositions without producing at least one such proposition. And this brings us to one of the boundaries of this essay. At this point analytical philosophy of religion would have to be supplemented by an essay in religious philosophy or in theology. All I have done is, at most, to explain some conditions which a complete argument would need to satisfy. These may be summarized in the following way:

A. It would need to be shown that some basic religious proposal satisfies the conditions of making a significant truth-claim, namely, that it permits of self-consistent formulation, that it permits the formulation of a self-consistent negation so that disagreement is possible, that it permits some reference to its logical subject and that some support of its predication is possible.

B. It would have to be shown that in the circumstances we

[11] "Right speech" is part of the noble Eightfold Path in Buddhism, and Emerson speaks of the Over-Soul as "that common heart of which all sincere conversation is the worship."

have sufficient warrant for accepting the proposal (i.e., since it is a proposal for belief, for making an affirmative judgment). This would involve showing:

B1. That in the circumstances (including the general conditions of human life and the consequences of deciding or failing to decide between the proposal and its alternatives) the need for decision is sufficiently urgent; and

B2. That our warrant for its truth its sufficiently good, which would mean that:

(B2a) It is possible to make a reasonably successful and adequate reference to its logical subject, and

(B2b) The available principles of judgment are reasonably clear and complete, and

(B2c) The available facts give reasonably adequate support for ascribing the predicate to its logical subject. Thus B1 and B2 condition one another.

There is one way in which no religious argument could be complete. There is one sort of question no argument can resolve. Consider the question, "Why should I be religious?" And rule out cases where the questioner has a religious interest but is not conscious of having it. Then there is a sense in which this is an unanswerable question. Certainly a great deal of discourse can proceed around it, as this essay has done—and as the testimonies of prophets, saints, and sages have done in a far different way. But it is a limiting question. A religious argument could deal with it only indirectly. Sometimes an interest is awakened but, as every teacher knows, we are very short on general rules for awakening interests.

This sort of deficiency is not peculiar to religious arguments. For there are other limiting questions like: "Why should I be moral?" "Why should I be philosophical?" and "Why should I be scientific?" The best anyone can do, if such questions are asked, is to try to convey a certain quality of experience, to show what it means to be religious, or

moral, or philosophical, or scientific, by historical examples
or in some other way, and hope that this quality of experience will come to be shared. Then, though only then, there
can be an inquiry which aims at truth, for every serious
and sustained effort of thought proceeds from some interest.

Then, I have argued, the real question is not of the form,
"Is there something that is P?" (where P in interpretable
by some basic religious predicate) but of the form, "What
is it that is P?" And this requires a choice among alternative
logical subjects of which P might be said to be true. Does
something m have a better claim to be said to be P than its
alternatives do? These alternative claims are included among
the circumstances in which the sufficiency of warrants for
belief are determined. It is in concrete situations, which pose
choices between particular alternatives, that religious judgments would have to be made.

7. *Religious inquiry and other types of inquiry*

A good general theory of meaning and truth would apply to thought and speech in ordinary life, to the formal
sciences, the natural sciences, history, the social sciences,
moral theory, speculative philosophy, esthetic criticism,
religion, and other domains. Constructing such a theory
would be a large, important, and difficult enterprise, which
I have not attempted here. I have not aimed at stating truth-
conditions for all inquiries, though some rudiments of a
general theory underlie my argument.

Often such theories are constructed by generalizing from
those criteria of significance and truth which are required
in some one of these domains, for example, in ordinary discourse or in the natural sciences. But if the generalization
of these concepts is not adequate, the theory will not be
powerful enough to extend in an illuminating way beyond
the domain of its origin. Therefore we ought to take full
account of the various ways in which we do (and might)
think and speak in each of these domains. I have meant to

throw light on some of the ways in which we do (and might) think and speak when we are prompted by religious interests.

At a number of points I have mentioned analogies and differences between religious inquiry and discourse and other types of inquiry and discourse. Now I want to sum up in a schematic way some bases for developing such contrasts. I state them in the framework of a possible distinction between "practical" truth and "theoretical" truth. But I put quotation marks around these terms to make it clear that, for a reason I shall explain, I am not proposing this distinction. I use it only as a device for putting the outcome of this study in a certain perspective.

A. By saying that religious inquiry aims at "practical" truth we might want to call attention to the following features of religious inquiry:

A1. Religious inquiry proceeds from and is governed by a religious interest.

A1a. Therefore it involves basic suppositions and commitments.

A2. In religious discourse a certain subjective form of feeling is conveyed.

A3. One function of basic religious predicates is to rank something above all else.[12]

A4. Norms of judgment are required for judging basic religious proposals because:

A4a. Basic religious questions cannot be decided a priori, and

A4b. They cannot be decided by crucial facts.

A5. Absolute certainty (as defined) is not possible in religion.

A6. Religious beliefs have practical consequences. A serious assertion of a religious proposition commits the assertor to some policy in conduct.

---

[12] As explained in chapter xi, a function of a predicate is not something it says but something it does in saying what it says.

B. In this way we might bring out certain contrasts between religious inquiry and some inquiry or other which, we might want to say, aims at "theoretical" truth. We might have *some* of the following features in mind:

B1. Its basic predicates have no ranking function.

B2. Absolute certainty is possible because:

B2a. Basic questions can be decided a priori.

B3. Basic questions can be decided by crucial facts.

B4. No norms of judgment are needed, because of B2a *or* B3.

Whether a certain inquiry, for example, logic or history, has any of these features would have to be determined by analysis of that particular inquiry. For example, there might be basic questions in science like "What are the uniformities in nature?" Then answers to this question would be proposed laws of nature. Are these decided by crucial facts? Again, are there norms of judgment (simplicity, elegance) in formal sciences?

C. But if we say that religious inquiry aims at "practical" truth, meaning something distinct from "theoretical" truth, this might cause us to overlook the following features of religious inquiry:

C1. A religious interest does not in principle exclude either pure curiosity or general curiosity. Being religious is in principle compatible with a "disinterested" aim at harmony of thought and being. Religious inquiry aims at harmony of thought and being in a certain important domain.

C2. Basic religious questions can be formulated and theories can be constructed in answer to these questions.

C3. Rules of relevance and procedures of judgment are possible, so that facts can be relevant to religious judgments.

C4. Norms of judgment can be argued for.

C5. It is possible in principle to avoid dogmatism in religion. It is logically possible to reformulate or revise theories or to exchange one theory for another.

D. Also, this distinction between "practical" and "theoretical" truth might cause us to overlook the following features of other inquiries:

D1. Any inquiry (ruling out idle curiosity) proceeds from and is governed by some interest, so that while it may be an exercise of pure ("disinterested") curiosity it is prompted by something more specific than general curiosity.

D1a. Hence any inquiry involves basic suppositions and commitments.

D2. Discourse in the domain of any inquiry conveys an appropriate subjective form of feeling.

D3. In any inquiry, where pure calculation is not possible, suggestions must be adopted for the development of theories.

D4. A serious assertion of any significant (nontautologous) proposition has some practical consequences and commits the assertor to act in accord with the assertion. If he fails to act in accord with it, either the assertion or the action will be misleading.

My reason for not proposing a distinction between practical and theoretical truth is that (a) where there is no theory there is nothing to be true (in the sense of "true" I am taking as primary) and (b) all significantly true propositions have some practical consequences. It is not because we do not need distinctions among different types of inquiry. On the contrary, this particular distinction seems too simple to be an organizing principle of a general theory of meaning and truth. Other dimensions of similarity and contrast among types of inquiries need to be traced and plotted also, as this rough scheme may suggest.

8. *Conclusion*

Without arguing for a particular religious judgment I have meant to show how religious judgments, and especially judgments of basic proposals, are possible. To review the significance of the argument let us look at some of the alternatives which would remain if its main conclusion were denied. Suppose we should hold that no basic religious proposals can make genuine truth-claims. The following logical possibilities would remain open:

a. Not being religious. Whether this is a reasonable possibility as well as a logical possibility could be argued (with the limitation explained in Chapter V, section 3). For example, does the outcome of reflection on our moral decisions make it unreasonable not to be religious?

b. Making a basic supposition without adopting any illuminating suggestion. It might be supposed that something or other is ultimate, or the supreme good, for example, without adopting any suggestion about what *is* the ultimate or the supreme good. In this case a religious inquiry has not gone beyond its (logically) initial stage.

c. Adopting a religious suggestion without explicating it in propositions. Conceivably one might choose to avoid using language at all in expressing and conveying the suggestion, using, instead, nonverbal symbols like gestures, actions, icons, nonverbal sounds, and significant silences. Or one might use language in a "symbolic" way. Narratives, metaphors, and other verbal expressions might be used without explicating their meaning in propositions. No doctrines and no basic proposals would be formulated. Whether this is a reasonable possibility could be argued, but it might be counted a logical possibility.

d. Adopting a suggestion and explicating it in doctrines without admitting any basic religious questions and proposals. Here the suggestion would be conveyed by (among other means) a more or less complex doctrinal scheme. So there could be an important role for theology, in the construction and criticism and development of such a scheme. There could be rules for the formation of doctrines. For example, the principles of judgment for the scheme might rule out "Jesus is God" but admit or require "Jesus Christ is God incarnate." So some doctrines would be ὀρθός ("right," "correct," "true") and others would not. Some statements might be not only untrue but blasphemous, or even nonsensical, by these principles, for example, "Allah conferred with Orpheus."

Some theologians might hold that doctrinal schemes are logically isolated from one another in the sense that they share no important concepts and hence have no important principles of judgment in common. To understand Buddhist concepts *at all*, it might be said, one must be a Buddhist. Most theologians, however, are not willing to confine the truth-significance of doctrines to those within the faith. Certainly a religion which aims at universality cannot do this.

So a different version of this view would admit doctrinal concepts which overlap concepts in other schemes, as explained in Chapter II. (From the history of religions, which tells us of the emergence of some religions from others, common ancestries, conflicts, borrowings, and syntheses, it would be strange if there were not many cases of overlapping concepts.) Further, some concepts in doctrinal schemes overlap concepts used in common experience, for example, "freedom," "dharma," "law." So moral disagreements, for example, between a religious community and nonreligious people who use these terms are possible. Then a doctrinal scheme need not be logically isolated; the truth-claims of *some* of its doctrines might extend beyond the community which generates them. So while, for example, Christian doctrines might be primarily "for Christians," and some doctrines might be only for Christians, some might be significant for non-Christians also. Common principles of judgment for particular doctrinal claims could be derived from the overlapping concepts.

Even so, on this hypothetical view, there would be no significant question to which more than one doctrinal scheme as a whole is a relevant answer, and hence no basic predicates and hence no formulation of basic proposals. Hence, though particular doctrines might make limited truth-claims, we could not interpret a doctrinal scheme itself as making a truth-claim. So there could be no comparative judgments of two or more doctrinal schemes taken as wholes.

Is this a reasonable possibility as well as a logical possibility? I have argued that it is not, because doctrinal proposals presuppose basic proposals in the way I have explained. Further, basic proposals extend truth-claims into those situations, if any, where no doctrinal concepts overlap. So the pre-eminent way in which religious truth-claims are extended into the public domain is by way of basic proposals. This is the reason I have concentrated on their place in the structure of religious inquiry and discourse, and on the principles of judgment which apply to them.

INDEX

analogies, 213f
Anselm, *see* ontological argument
arguments, 147f; dialectical, 28, 156–63, 225
Augustine, 96
awe, 36f, 54f
axiological terms, 222–30

Bhagavad-Gita, 154, 234
Braithwaite, R. B., 136–42
Brandt, Richard B., 53n, 135n
Buddhism, 100, 116f, 118f, 194

certainty, 109–12, 145f, 161, 164f, 243–48
coherence, 151–53
commitments, basic, 88f
communities, religious, 61, 108
Comte, Auguste, 158, 177f, 205
concepts, central, 20f; overlapping, 17f, 74, 268; open and closed, 260
confessions, 11, 133–35, 138, 142f, 250; implicit, 144f
consistency, 24f, 148–51
contrasts, 154; negative, 196, 213f; positive, 213f
conversions, 9f
curiosity, pure, 78f; idle, 79, 85; general, 79

Darwin, 98
decidability, 248–53
decisions, 104; arbitrary and non-arbitrary, 248, 250–52
dependence, absolute, 45f; maximal, 50–54
Dewey, John, 42, 183f
disagreements, 15; doctrinal, 15–19; basic, 19–24
doctrinal schemes, 16, 20–23, 81, 108f, 241, 267–69
doctrines, *see* proposals, doctrinal
dogmatism, 89, 106

exclusiveness, 253–61

facts, appeals to, 161–64, 226; weighing, 236
factual conditions of significance, 210f
Findlay, J. N., 180f
Freud, 98f

Glasgow, Ellen, 94–96
God, concepts of, 38f, 44, 183f, 224, 233; arguments for existence of, 167, 190f, 220f, *see* ontological argument
Guignebert, Charles, 160

historical events, religions and, 128, 191–94
Holbach, 175f
holy, 31–33, 52n, 54–56, 64, 72, 171f, 213, 259
humanism, 93, 176–79, 231f

imaginary events, 30, 126–28
informative utterances, 12f, 114n, 133, 138
injunctions, 11, 116f, 121–33, 139–42, 250; to believe, 124–33; implicit, 144f
inquiry, 41f, 43, 78–81
interests, 43, 60–64, 78–80, 85–87, 130n, 144
intolerance, 254f

judgments, 113f, 121; stability of, 146

Kant, 41–45
Kaplan, Mordecai, 239
Kierkegaard, 105f

Lamprecht, Sterling P., 180
Lippmann, Walter, 93f, 108, 170, 241